Odyssey to Excellence

How to Build Effective Schools Through Leadership and Management Skills

James Slezak

Merritt Publishing Company

San Francisco, California

ISBN 0-9613933-0-0

Current edition last digit

9   8   7   6   5   4   3   2

BK
18 50

Additional Copies may be ordered from

Merritt Publishing Company
P.O. Box 561 — 501 Broadway
Millbrae, CA 94030

To all my family,
especially my mother
and my wife.

Table of Contents

Chapter 14   265
Superintendent-Principal Decision Making

Chapter 15   287
Elementary-Middle School Decision Making

Chapter 16   301
High School-Junior High Decision Making

Preface

Odyssey to Excellence can be used as a resource book for practicing school administrators and professors of school administration. The book contains numerous process instruments which have been used effectively in school districts to improve academic achievement and learning climate.

I wrote this book because I was encouraged by several school administrators and professors of school administration who needed the material. I have used the resource material in the book in the last two school districts where I served as superintendent, and in the numerous workshops I have given in almost every state in the Union as a presentor for the National Academy of School Executives of the Association of American School Administrators, as well as for the National School Boards Association, National Association of Secondary School Principals, National Association of Elementary School Principals, National School Public Relations Association, and the Association of Supervision and Curriculum Development. I have also used this material in university classes I have taught at Central Michigan University, New Mexico Highlands University, the Universtiy of California, and California State Universities. This material comes from the best academic theory and research and has been adapted and field tested in two school districts with much success.

My professional experience enabled me to write the book for both school administrators and university administration classes. I have been a teacher and administrator at elementary, secondary, and university levels. Being an alumnus of the doctoral program at Columbia University in New York and the Executive Program of the Graduate School of Business at Stanford University gave me the academic background to complement my practical school administrative experience.

The book is organized in three parts. Part I is "Excellence in Leadership" and has resources for you—the leader. Part I has chapters on leadership style, time management, and stress. Part II is "Excellence in Administration" and has six chapters on planning, organization, evaluation, staff development, and learning climate. This part also includes seven chapters on all levels of decision making. Part III is "Excellence in Programs" and has five chapters on marketing, advisory councils, community schools, finance, and instruction.

Every attempt in first drafts was made to avoid the use of male pronouns to represent the generic third person singular. However, in the final draft I decided to use male pronouns in this situation to make the text read more smoothly. I assure you the pronouns used are intended to be universal.

Odyssey to Excellence was chosen as the title because of the reference to the extended, adventurous journey of Odysseus, described in the second epic of Homer, after the fall of Troy and his eventual return home.

The journey to excellence in education is analogous to Odysseus's journey because we are on an extended, adventurous journey to improve education. We are doing a commendable job in our schools, but we must strive to constantly improve just to keep pace with the rapid changes in the technical and sociological areas of society.

Excellence is not just a destination; it is a journey. It is not only a series of goals; it is a series of processes toward those goals. Excellence is not just accomplishment, it is doing, participating, progressing, growing, and learning.

This book provides 151 adaptable, flexible processes to achieve and maintain excellence. I believe this happens through the power of people as they become involved in the educational program.

October 1984   James Slezak

Acknowledgments

I am indebted to many people who have contributed toward making this book possible. Much of the material comes from an accumulation of experience, university classes, workshops, books, and articles. I have made these sources such an intregal part of my work it is impossible to give due credit to everyone.

Columbia University, where I received a doctorate degree and Stanford University Graduate School of Business, where I graduated from the Stanford Executive Program, were academically influencial.

The American Management Association and the National Academy of School Executives of the American Association of School Administrators have influenced my continuing professional development.

Paul Briggs, former superintendent of Cleveland, Ohio; Ernest Britton, former superintendent of Midland, Michigan; and Pat Murphy, former superintendent of Santa Fe, New Mexico, were mentors early in my career.

Willie Nielsen, Elmer Cameron, Sid Hollins, Sharon Bowman, Don Moss, and the other administrators in Escondido were the successful pioneers of the participative management system we developed.

Don Russell, Lauren Fickett, Howard Moorman, Herb Cole, Pat Howlett, Ev Watt, Paul Allen, Harvey Wall, Al Zamola, Bill Hansen, Jack Marlowe, many other administrators, and especially Joan Thisius were the leaders in developing the ISMS—Individual School Management System—in the Mt. Diablo Unified School District.

The work of the following people was an important source for various chapters. Janice Smith's material was a source for Chapter I on leadership styles; Joan Thisius and Harvey Wall's material for Chapter 10 on decision techniques; Fred Wellington's material on decision charts in varous chapters; The Executive Educator Magazine for my article in Chapter 15 on elementary decision making; Pat Howlett's material for Chapter 17 on marketing; Stan Oswalt's material for Chapter 20 on finance; and Marilyn Hammond's material for Chapter 21 on instruction.

I would like to thank Executive Educator magazine for permission to reprint the article I wrote with Bob Boone, "When Unions Start Wooing Principal, You'd Best Have a Better Answer — Here It Is," and the School Research and Service Corp. of Anaheim, Calif., for permission to use various decision charts.

The books *Theory Z* by William Ouchi, *One Minute Manager* by Spencer Johnson and Ken Blanchard, *Search For Excellence* by Tom Peters and Bob Waterman, *Corporate Cultures* by Terry Deal and Alan Kennedy, *Megatrends* by John Naisbett, and *Future Shock* and *The Third Wave* by Alvin Toffler all influenced my thinking.

Ted Witt served an important technical role in producing this book.

And finally I want to thank my wife, Lynn, who served as editor and whose hard work and dedication made this book possible.

Part I
Excellence in Leadership

Chapter 1
Leadership Styles

You lead people; you manage things. The ideal leader brings out the best in a group, an organization, or country. A leader inspires cooperation within a team of winners rather than within only the few who tend to rise to the top. A leader energizes the system, generates the magic that makes everyone want to do something extra, and exhibits the optimism it takes for progress to occur. A leader imagines that every employee is wearing the sign: "Make me feel important." He does.

As leaders in an educational enterprise, we must be the very models of good leadership. The young people with whom we work will eventually go on to other areas of endeavor, and we hope that they will have witnessed effective leaders in action.

In this chapter, I will discuss some of the basic elements of leadership and key characteristics of effective leaders. Years of research show that many effective leadership styles are possible. I will describe some of those styles.

GENERAL CHARACTERISTICS
OF AN IDEAL LEADER

Two positive elements identify the ideal leader. First, he is concerned with self-development in the best sense: development of one's reasoning and talents, and development of responsibility for one's own health, well being, and life. Second, the ideal leader, who

is more tolerant and more flexible than leaders of the past, is willing
to share power with those he leads.

SELF-DEVELOPMENT

A leader who values self-development has the ability to build and
sustain an individual's confidence in himself and to move him toward
his goals. Such an ability is more than mere technique or method; it
embraces a fundamental attitude, the positive approach. When an
administrator uses positive methods—"you are," "you can," "you
will"—he influences the thinking of other people and creates conditions that motivate. Confidence starts from within. A leader nurtures
an individual's self-confidence through counseling, through high
expectations, and through a belief in that individual. He also uses
effective intrapersonal and interpersonal skills.

INTRAPERSONAL SKILLS
The ideal leader has the ability to:
- Live with ambiguities, change, conflict and consensus.
- Be patient.
- Be objective.
- Understand, appreciate, and respect all people.
- Trust others.
- Make difficult decisions.
- Perceive the personal values and the perspectives
  which shape actions and decisions.
- Listen.
- Assess one's performance realistically and to sustain
  oneself with less praise than is deserved.

INTERPERSONAL SKILLS
The ideal leader has the ability to:
- Develop an atmosphere conducive to growth, personal development, and goal achievement.
- Involve individuals in groups in the decision-making
  process.
- Develop positive, open relationships which encourage people to feel free to examine problems, personnel, and institutions, and to express opinions with
  reference to them.
- Accurately assess group perceptions, relationships,
  and attitudes which shape actions and decisions.

- Create satisfactory working relationships among groups with different functions, but with common purposes—students, faculty, administrators, and the school community.

SHARING POWER AND INVOLVING PEOPLE IN DECISIONS

The need to share power and to involve people in decision making is essential now because of six realities regarding employees of today:

- They think for themselves.
- They are pro-active. One study indicates that students seek the following characteristics in their future careers: interesting and high quality work, self-development, respect, and freedom on the job.
- They are self-interested. Employees are asking "What is in it for me?" Competent employees these days are opportunistic and mobile. They make more stringent demands for an improved quality of work life.
- They expect to be heard. Employees voice ideas and opinions with the expectation of a cooperative response. When the opportunity exists for employees to influence their managers, productivity and morale almost always improve.
- They are more expensive than ever. As a result, they are expected to be more efficient and more productive.
- They have potential. Experts have estimated that the average person actualizes only 10 percent of innate human potential. Not one study indicates that average employees are working at anything near their true capability. Here is a key challenge of leadership: unleash and channel the untapped talent that exists at every level in any organization. Leaders today now spend more time explaining things and involving people, but they need less time later clearing up misunderstandings and correcting errors.

EFFECTIVE LEADERS

TYPES OF LEADERSHIP BEHAVIOR

A distinction should be made among three different types of leadership behavior—attempted, successful, and effective. Attempted

leadership is any effort the leader makes to influence superiors, associates, or subordinates. Successful leadership is the ability to get
others to behave as the leader intends. The job gets done and the
leader's needs are met, but those of other people are ignored. Effective leadership is the ability to work in enthusiastic accord with others
toward mutually acceptable goals. The following chart from the book
Leadership by James Cribbin offers more examples of effective leadership behavior.

ENTREPRENEUR

Motto: "We do it my way. Only risk-taking achievers
need apply."

Characteristics: Extremely competent, forceful, individualistic, egocentric, dominant, self-confident. Extraord-
inary achievement drive. Innovative, firm-minded, and
strong-willed. Something of a loner. Not only listens to his
own drummer but composes his own music. Can be very
loyal, protective, and generous to team.

Typical Behavior: Unable to work well in a subordinate position for very long. Must be prime mover and
binds small team to him with great loyalty. Offers challenges, opportunities to succeed, and great returns on
risks taken. Does not develop subordinates. Is not open to
ideas that differ from his own. Gets involved in all aspects
of the organization. Exercises very tight control. Motivates
by example, rewards, and fear.

CORPORATEUR

Motto: "I call the shots, but we all work together on my
team."

Characteristics: Dominant but not domineering.
Quite directive but gives people considerable freedom.
Consultative but not really participative. Sizes up people
well but relates to them on a surface level. Cordial to
people but keeps them at arms length.

Typical Behavior: Concerned about the good of the
organization. Wins respect. High task orientation. Polished
and professional manager. Makes people feel needed.
Delegates and consults but keeps effective control. Supportive but not emotionally involved with subordinates.

DEVELOPER

Motto: "People are our most important resource."
Characteristics: Trustful of subordinates. Intent on helping them actualize their potential. Excellent human relations skills. Wins personal loyalty, builds a supportive and achieving climate. Fine coach and counselor.
Typical Behavior: Very high people orientation. Although productivity is superior, at times people considerations may take precedence. People feel needed. Delegates and consults but keeps effective control. Supportive and emotionally involved with subordinates.

CRAFTSMAN

Motto: "We do important work as perfectly as we can."
Characteristics: Amiable, conservative, extremely conscientious. Principled, very knowledgeable and skilled, self-reliant. Highly task-oriented. Proud of competence. Work and family oriented. Self-contented, honest, straightforward, perfectionistic, independent, analytical, mild-mannered.
Typical Behavior: Likes to innovate, build, and tinker with quality products. Not overly concerned with status or politics. Motivated by a desire for excellence. Self-demanding but supportive of subordinates. Competes with projects, not people. Restive with organizational red tape. Likes to solve problems alone or in a small group.

INTEGRATOR

Motto: "We build consensus and commitment."
Characteristics: Egalitarian, supportive, participative. Excellent interpersonal skills. Superior people insight. A team builder, catalyst, adept at unifying different inputs. A subtle leader, prefers group decision making.
Typical Behavior: Shares the leadership. Thinks in terms of associates rather than subordinates. Gives great freedom and authority. Welcomes the ideas of others. Geared to win-win interaction. Acts as a synergistic catalyst.

GAMESMAN

Motto: "We win together, but I must win more than you."

Characteristics: Fast-moving, flexible, upwardly mobile. Very knowledgeable and skilled. Autonomous, risk-taking, assertive, and intent on winning but not petty or vindictive. Innovative. Takes no great pleasure in another's loss or defeat. Opportunistic but not unethical, not depressed by defeat.

Typical Behavior: Wants to be respected as a strategist who builds a winning team. Enjoys the game of winning within the organization's rules. Enjoys competition, jockeying, and maneuvering. Sharp, skilled, unbiased, and tough manager who challenges and rewards contribution. Impersonally eliminates the weak and non-achievers.

As you can see from the descriptions no pure types of leadership exist. None of the leaders described is inflexibly consistent. Each leader, even the worst, engages in behavior that at times varies from his characteristic approach. Yet, a dominant behavior pattern remains.

PRINCIPLES OF HUMAN INTERACTION

Principles are guides to thought and action. Leaders who wish to interact effectively with others should keep the following principles of human interaction in mind.

All people exist at the center of their own world of experience. As Carl Rogers and others have said, they react to the reality that they perceive and experience.

People have a basic drive to maintain and to actualize themselves.

People change in order to gain increased satisfaction and to avoid decreased satisfaction.

The language of feelings and emotions can be far more compelling than that of the intellect.

Feelings and attitudes change slowly. They are not changed by exhortation; they change when people can convince themselves of the advantages of new attitudes.

People who live differently think and act differently because of their unique perceptions of reality.

All behavior, regardless of how illogical or bizarre it appears to the uninvolved observer, makes sense to the person and is perceived by him at the moment to be goal-directed and need-satisfying.

The only circumstances people can understand are those that they can relate to their experience; the only courses of action they can understand are those that they helped to formulate.

The best vantage point for understanding the perceptions, attitudes, and behavior of another is from the frame of reference of that person.

Empathy means thinking with people, not for them or above them; feeling with people, not becoming emotionally involved; moving with people, not rushing ahead or lagging behind; working with people, not doing things for them; accepting people, not judging or evaluating them, but seeing situations from their viewpoint.

True cooperation is possible only if a mutual system of influence prevails, and if a climate exists in which collaboration is appreciated.

The methods of attaining cooperation may be more important than the decision, course of action, or a solution itself.

THE LEADER'S SUPERIORS

Most leaders operate in ways that are similar to those of their superiors. They do this for two reasons: First, organizations are not likely to promote anyone who departs too far from the esteemed mode of managing. Second, potential leaders who find the accepted mode intolerable are likely to seek their futures in another organization. Although leaders are responsible for their own behavior, it is their superiors who are accountable for it, who provide the authorization and the support, and who have access to those higher in command.

How can you secure the continued backing of your superiors?

See their problems and pressures through their eyes.

Learn their real expectations—sometimes in spite of what they tell you.

Get to know their true priorities, in spite of what they say.

Anticipate their needs.

Complement their weaknesses with your strengths; become an essential subordinate.

Go out of your way to make them look better and to make their job easier.

Volunteer to take some of the burden off their shoulders.

Serve as a buffer for them, absorbing some of the shocks when you can prudently do so.

When you honestly can, speak well of them to others.

Grow in and through your own job; do not wait for superiors to urge you.

Reveal yourself to them; make certain they know your strengths, and your willingness to take on more responsibilities.   Keep them informed of your contributions, achievements, and plans.

Work with them, not for them.

Avoid crying on their shoulders, stepping on their toes, twisting their arms, or shocking them with unpleasant surprises.

MOTIVATION

Six major strategies are often used to improve the quality of work life in organizations and to encourage motivated, productive employees: job enlargement, job rotation, job enrichment, autonomous work groups, quality circles, and participative management. Remember that all behavior, even the most puzzling, is caused, goal-directed, need-satisfying and justifiable at the time to the person who so behaves. In motivating others one should keep the following points in mind.

The same approach may engender different responses: Praise may stimulate one person, but may prompt another to become complacent.

Different approaches may engender the same response: Autonomy may induce production with one individual, while close supervision may do the same with another.

An approach that is overused will lose its effect.

Different people may have different ways of satisfying the same need: One may get attention by constant complaining; another by becoming an achiever.

Motivating others is like playing a piano. First you read the music—you try to understand the person. Next you practice hitting the right keys—you experiment with various motivational techniques. Finally, you develop your own style—you learn what approaches are best for you, your situation and your subordinates.

Work has technical, economic, social, and psychological aspects to it. Each aspect has its own motivational potential upon which to draw in interacting with your employees.

Be the model you want others to emulate. People are motivated by example and behavior more than by words or techniques.

Use research findings to help people learn, achieve, and grow. Try to make jobs meaningful, to provide incentives for subordinates, and to make rewards equitable and fairly distributed. Enhance the person's self perception of his competence, his adequacy, and his worth. Give feedback that is positively reinforcing and make certain you are rewarding the right behavior. As circumstances permit, serve as a path that subordinates can use to obtain their objectives and satisfy their needs.

Be realistic. You will not be able to motivate everyone, the chemistry will sometimes be wrong, but do not give up too easily. Be as patiently persistent as reality allows.

A FURTHER LOOK AT EFFECTIVE LEADERS

Why do some people outperform others? According to Charles A. Garfield, president of the Peak Performance Center and a clinical professor at the medical school of the University of California at San Francisco, six underlying traits are common to all high achievers.

- They are able to transcend their previous levels of accomplishment.
- They avoid the so-called comfort zone—that no-man's land where an employee feels too much at home.
- They do what they do for the art of it and are guided by compelling internal goals.
- They solve problems rather than place blame.
- They confidently take risks after laying out the worst consequences beforehand.
- They are able to rehearse coming actions or events mentally.

Another study, conducted under the auspices of the Mid-West Administration Center in Chicago, sought to identify major areas and analyze certain personal variables related to effective behavior in the school principal's role. The study identified six areas for effective principals.

1. Activity Drive. The effective principal engages in strong and purposeful activity. While on the job, he is sensitive to the responsibilities of the principalship. He exhibits concern for the appropriate use of time. At retirement he looks forward to continuing the present high level of activity. During leisure hours he participates in the activities of a number of organizations and holds leadership positions within these groups.

The ineffective principal, on the other hand, is slow to act. At work he engages in numerous random behaviors—serving as an errand boy, a report maker, a substitute teacher, a babysitter with disciplinary cases. At retirement he looks forward to a reduction in activity; during leisure hours he participates in a limited number and range of activities; and he prefers viewing television to more active forms of recreation.

2. and 3. Achievement and Mobility Drives. Keen achievement and mobility drives are characteristic of the effective principal. He has specific goals for further study, stresses better job performance as a goal in life, and views the school superintendency as a desirable vocational objective.

In contrast, the ineffective principal exhibits little concern for undertaking a planned program of further study, holding positions of leadership, or attaining any position higher than the present job assignment.

4. Social Ability. The effective principal is high in social ability. He is able to work successfully with others in reaching solutions to problems. He feels he obtained his initial principalship because of his ability to relate well to others and that his present relationships with teachers, central office personnel, and parent groups are satisfactory. Helping teachers with problems in instruction is his greatest source of job satisfaction.

By contrast, the ineffective principal experiences frequent conflict with teachers, parents, and central office personnel. He is more secure in the presence of children and derives his greatest job satisfaction from helping them. If the ineffective principal were now 20 years of age he would be more likely to enter some field requiring contact with adults.

5. Security. The effective principal is secure in his home and work environments. He views family relationships with pride and satisfaction and views authority figures as friendly and as serving constructive purposes.

Characteristics of the ineffective principal include such home difficulties as domineering parents, and such job-related problems as feeling that groups of teachers and members of the central administration may be antipathetic toward him. He feels that his own mental, emotional, and physical weaknesses may prevent the attainment of his life's goal.

6. Emotional Control. In reacting to frustrating, confusing, and irritating situations, the effective principal possesses greater emotional control than does the ineffective principal.

The ineffective principal clashes frequently with others, feels that actions by other people are most likely to drive him to distraction, and engages in strong emotional reactions in conflict situations.

In an article written by J. Hall and published in Psychology Today, August of 1976, further insights come to light as to what makes a leader good, bad, or average. When Hall compared the good, bad, and indifferent leaders on motivational needs, he found that motives were a good predictor of effectiveness.

Good leaders were driven mainly by the need for self-actualization; average leaders were concerned with ego status; and poor leaders were caught in a double bind—equally preoccupied with safety and ego status needs, they wavered back and forth trying to satisfy both and failing to accomplish either.

When Hall surveyed the subordinates, he found that good leaders create or find subordinates who get the job done. Poor leaders are play-it-safe bosses who shape employees in their own image—timid souls who worry mainly about job security, put in their time, and get their satisfaction elsewhere. Good leaders challenge people; poor leaders comfort people. Good leaders encourage others to share in decisions which effect them and are deeply interested in both people and production—high-task, high-relationship orientation. They use an integrative style of leadership in which production goals and people's needs are equally important.

Average leaders were described by their subordinates as high task, low-relationship people, so preoccupied with getting the job done that they often forgot about the people who have to do it. Poor leaders have a low-task, low-relationship style. The personnel manual and standard operating procedures are their guides; self-preservation is their goal. The good leader finds meaning in his work and strives to give the same meaning to others. What he does flows from his view that work is both a challenge and an opportunity for self-expansion. He looks upon innovation as an opportunity rather than a threat, and, therefore, is willing to take risks. He believes that to be successful he must work with subordinates and create opportunities for them to succeed.

LEADERSHIP STYLES

LIKERT'S FOUR SYSTEMS

One of the best analyses of leadership styles was described by Rensis Likert of the University of Michigan. He suggested that leadership styles can be defined through four systems.

System 1: Exploitive Authoritarian. This leader can be found in uneducated societies in which a dictatorial style is often successful.

14   Odyssey to Excellence

System 2: Benevolent Authoritarian. This leader leaves no doubt as to who is the boss, but he is nice to people in a paternalistic manner.

System 3: Consultive Manager. The consultive leader involves people in decision making, but everybody knows that the final decision rests with the boss, and their input is purely advisory or consultive.

System 4: Participative Group Leader. This leader creates a team which makes decisions together.

Likert has examined data from several hundred published and unpublished studies in business, government, hospitals, universities, military, and voluntary organizations. He was impressed by a consistent pattern in the relevant organizational variables. He concluded that the closer the management system and leadership style to System 4—the participative style—the better the overall performance; the closer the management system and leadership behavior to System 1—the exploitive authoritarian type—the poorer the performance. If that is so, what are some of the advantages of the participative leadership style?

ADVANTAGES OF THE PARTICIPATIVE LEADERSHIP STYLE

People who participate in and help formulate a decision support it—instead of fighting or ignoring it. They work hard to make it work because it is their idea and now part of their life and their "ego."

The leader consistently receives the benefit of the best ideas, talent, and operating experience of the employees. The rich informational source they represent becomes the leader's and becomes a key input into the decision.

Group discussion, even though time consuming before a decision is made, can force critical information to the surface. Such information can improve decision making, and can avert disasters which might have occurred if key operating level information had not been made available.

This style of leadership permits and encourages people to develop and to rise in the organization in terms of both the responsibilities they can assume and the services they can contribute.

Most people work better, more enthusiastically, and at a higher level of motivation when they are given a reasonable degree of freedom to act and to contribute. Because of this, they enjoy a sense of personal value, importance, and achievement.

Most importantly, as already implied above, the participative leader establishes a work climate in which the potential power of people is unleashed. Employees are motivated by, and will strive hard for, goals which they helped to create and in the accomplishment of which they gain deep personal satisfaction. They feel a sense of recognition, accomplishment and importance. Thus, the participative leader has the critical factor—the employees' sense of personal motivation—working for him.

LIMITATIONS OF THE PARTICIPATIVE LEADERSHIP STYLE

The participative style can be time consuming, and can, when used inappropriately, be inefficient.

Some leaders "use" the participatory style as a way of avoiding responsibility.

Employees resent the invitation to make recommendations which are subsequently ignored or rejected. Any leader who must reject a recommendation should quickly explain why, or, if necessary, should set perimeters within which the recommendations will be made. He should not reject recommendations often or he will lose the respect of the group.

Use of the participative style can, if not handled well, degenerate into a complete loss of leadership control.

COMMENTS

Decades of research show conclusively that participative leadership, with competent implementation and under appropriate conditions, can assuredly benefit organizations in terms of the hard criteria of performance and productivity.

In spite of the possible limitations on the application of participative leadership, its methods have been and are being used in organizations all across the United States: in the giant corporations such as General Motors; in the merely large organizations such as Motorola; in moderate sized manufacturing firms such as R.G. Barry Company; and in small manufacturing firms, such as one that makes automobile mirrors in Boliver, Tennessee. I have used participative leadership successfully for the last 16 years in two different school districts and in a large professional association.

I had the privilege of serving as superintendent of two school districts in which I implemented participative leadership successfully, if you will accept results over five areas as indicators of success. The results were: significantly improved student learning achievement, significantly improved learning climate, reduction of vandalism, reduction in absenteeism of students, and reduction in absenteeism of staff.

This approach developed into an individual school management system. It placed educational decision making as close to the learner as possible through the involvement of teachers, students, and parents. This management system has six basic components:

- Planning
- Organization of a school, or district for effective day-to-day operations
- Accountability or evaluation to determine how well we were doing the things we said we would do in the planning component
- Staff development
- School learning climate which fosters a total learning environment in both the affective and the cognitive domains
- Decision making

A description of each of these six components and of how they were implemented is discussed in Part II, "Excellence in Administration."

Participative leadership has proven itself; it now remains for American leaders and managers to learn and to apply participative approaches to obtain the performance and productivity benefits these approaches can yield.

Chapter 2
Time Management

Why is it so difficult to learn to manage time well? I liken this problem to that of an obese person who desperately wants to lose weight but does not. Both the overweight and the time-wasters want to be given a secret trick or technique—a way that will melt off pounds or magically make more hours in the day—with no change in basic behavior.

Too many people are looking for an easy way out; one does not exist. Everyone works within the same 24-hour day whether he is the president of the United States or a school leader. Yet some people accomplish much while others continually search for more time, never finding enough.

We in school administration usually have jobs that are open-ended; job descriptions and job responsibilities are not precisely delineated. As a result, we have more flexibility and must provide more structure for ourselves. Time management offers a way of providing that structure and a means for deciding those responsibilities on which to act first. Managing time is not easy; there are no magic tricks. You must use basic principles of time management, and you must have discipline.

Almost all leaders can identify at least 25 percent of their time that is wasted. By redirecting the use of that time they can be noticably more productive, more effective, and more efficient. Consider the words "effectiveness" and "efficiency." Effectiveness is doing the right things—making progress toward your objectives. Efficiency is doing things right—completing every task regardless of its importance. We should focus on being effective first; then work on being efficient. From the plethora of publications on time management, I have identified four key steps.

1. Set goals and priorities.
2. Find out how you currently spend your time.
3. Manage your time-wasters and develop increased discretionary time.
4. Efficiently use discretionary time to accomplish the goals identified in the first step.

SETTING GOALS AND PRIORITIES

The first step in setting goals is to consider eight main life roles: professional, family, community, social, cultural, recreational, personal, and self-service (physical maintenance activities). Then rank them in importance to you. Next, write goal statements delineating specific activities and specific professional growth requirements needed to meet those goals. Include concrete descriptions of the accomplished tasks and assessment mechanisms for the final evaluation.

Goal statements must be put in written form—lists, charts, diagrams, or index cards. Writing your goals makes them real.

Next, set priorities based on your point of view right now. You should update your goals and priorities when your point of view changes. Select the three most important goals and list specific short-term activities that will lead to the accomplishment of those goals.

WHO AND WHAT GET MOST OF MY TIME

How are you going to find time in an already over-burdened work day to pursue your priority goals? Identify time-wasters with the use of a daily time log and learn to manage those that are within your control. The first question to ask is who controls my time now? To find out, use the following chart.

TIME LOG

TIME	PERSON	SUBJECT OR ACTIVITY	I	II
8:15 a.m.				
8:30				
8:45				
9:00				
.				
.				
.				
3:45				
4:00				
4:15				
4:30				

The first column marks time in 15-minute intervals. The second column identifies the person who has the appointment. The third column lists the activity. The fourth column—labeled with the Roman numeral I—designates who or what caused you to perform that activity. The fifth column—Roman numeral II—indicates whether the activity was planned or unplanned. To complete columns I and II in the time log, use the following procedure.

In column I of the chart, identify what caused you to perform the particular activity you listed in each 15 minute slot. Use the following designations as guidelines:

BOSS

This category identifies work that is assigned to you by your superior, but is beyond regular responsibilities. Include the non-routine assignments such as questions, requests for special information, problem solving, and other needs that arise.

SUBORDINATES

A large part of your job as a leader is working with your subordinates in every phase of supervision, from counseling to motivation. They look to you for assistance in solving problems, in answering questions, and in giving them support. Some subordinates require more of your time than others. They become adept at "upward delegation"—they ask you to do some part of their job. Your time log will help you identify not only how much time you are spending with subordinates, but also which ones demand more than others.

SYSTEM

Your organization functions as smoothly as it does because of the routines its employees are required to follow. These procedures and policies enable each section to accomplish its objectives through ensured cooperation with other departments. Included in this category are the forms you must fill out, the purchase orders you must submit, and the people who must be consulted before an action is taken. We usually understand why our subordinates must follow the procedures we have established, but cannot understand the "red tape" that our superiors have created. How much time are you spending to satisfy the various systems in your organization?

OUTSIDE

Activities in this category are usually items that are a part of your job, but that come as interruptions—dealing with visitors or vendors, handling requests to perform a service, speaking at a community gathering, or contributing to any actvity beyond your routine responsiliblies.

SELF

Your self-imposed activities are probably the most important, since how you handle them shows what type of manager you are. These are such self-imposed tasks as planning; allocating resources; defining current problems and anticipating future problems; thinking up ways to improve coordination with other parts of your organization; setting, clarifying, or revising objectives; developing future opportunities; setting priorities; and thinking about how to motivate your subordinates. These important tasks may too easily be left undone since you are the only one who knows you should be doing them.

Once you have filled in column I of your time log, you are ready to analyze who or what gets most of your time. On the form below, list the total number of hours you have devoted to each category for the duration of your study. After you have filled out that chart, ask yourself these questions: Where did my activities mainly arise? How many self-imposed activities could I list? Do I feel that I am basically in control of my time, or do other people control it for me? Do I want to make any change in this mix? Now reconsider each category and decide how much time you think you should be spending on each item.

SOURCE OF WORK	TOTAL HOURS	PERCENTAGE
Boss		
System		
Subordinates		
Outside		
Self		
Total		100%

In column II of your time log, identify whether the activity in each block was planned or unplanned. Many activities during the day are initiated by a telephone call, a person dropping by, an item appearing in your "in" box, or tasks initiated to avoid working on something you perceive to be unpleasant. The ideal breakdown in this category is 80 percent planned time and 20 percent unplanned time.

After completing column II, ask yourself these questions: Was too much of my activity unplanned? Do interruptions lower my efficiency significantly? Is my day divided into too many small segments? Once again, consider your results and decide on percentages. Most leaders who make a thorough analysis of their time discover that: they consistently waste time in the same ways because of inefficiencies in their day-to-day operations; they spend far too much time on unplanned and relatively unimportant activities because of a failure to focus on the important ones; they let others waste their time in a variety of ways; and they waste the time of others.

Your time log will also help you see whether you are a reactive or proactive leader. A proactive leader sets goals and then pursues them effectively and efficiently with the help of others. This type of person takes control of time and manages it well. The reactive leader simply responses to events as they occur with no attempt at all, or only minimally, to plan or to follow through. This person allows others to manage his time.

MANAGING TIME-WASTERS

The time-waster is a two headed dragon. External time-wasters wear the face of the other—visitors, telephone calls, meetings, paper work, and co-workers needs. Internal time-wasters wear the face of the self—the inability to say "no," the inability to schedule and to set priorities, the inability to delegate, and the inclination to procrastinate.

THE PARETO 80/20 PRINCIPLE

Decisions	Produces	Results
20%		
		80%

The following examples, based on the Pareto 80/20 principle and drawn from everyday life, should encourage you to concentrate on high-value tasks, even at the cost of ignoring many lower-value tasks:

- 80 percent of sales come from 20 percent of customers.
- 80 percent of production is in 20 percent of the product line.
- 80 percent of sick leave is taken by 20 percent of employees.
- 80 percent of file usage is in 20 percent of files.
- 80 percent of dinners repeat 20 percent of recipes.
- 80 percent of dirt is on 20 percent of floor areas that are highly used.
- 80 percent of dollars is spent on 20 percent of the expensive meat and grocery items.
- 80 percent of the washing is done on the 20 percent of the wardrobe that is well-used items.
- 80 percent of TV time is spent on 20 percent of programs most popular with the family.
- 80 percent of reading time is spent on 20 percent of the pages in the newspaper (front page, sports page, editorials, columnists, feature page).

- 80 percent of telephone calls come from 20 percent of all callers.
- 80 percent of eating out is done at 20 percent of favorite restaurants.

EXTERNAL TIME-WASTERS

The visitors and telephone calls which become external time-wasters are those that are unplanned. In education people receive high priority, however, a school leader can manage time more effectively by making himself available at high visibility times.

As a principal you can be seen before school, during recess, during the lunch hour, immediately after school has been dismissed, and in the staff room when the majority of the staff is present. You should have regular meetings so staff can take care of most of their business at that time. When visitors arrive unexpectedly, get on your feet, get out from behind your desk, greet them, and stay standing. This should minimize the amount of time it is going to take to discuss their problem. Once you sit down you are inviting at least 15 minutes of time.

Have a system for phone calls worked out with your secretary so that calls can either be delegated, or put through only if they are high priority such as long distance. The majority of calls should be returned at a later time when you are not in conference or concentrating on a task.

Paper work is another frustrating area that can be an external time-waster. All incoming mail can be categorized according to action items, information items, or throw-away items. Your mail can be given to you in five folders that correspond to these three areas. The first, second, and third folders hold action items—signature or immediate action, important items, and staff items. The fourth folder holds information items, and the fifth, throw-away items.   Action items should be handled only once. Eighty percent can be answered immediately by being promptly routed. A note of direction to the proper person can be written in the corner.

Those action items that are going to take more time can be retained in a folder for completion at a scheduled time when you can concentrate on the action required. Reading material can be put in a special folder to be read either at home or at some other relaxing time.

INTERNAL TIME-WASTERS

A major internal time-waster is a person's inability to delegate. The more important the job you have and the further you progress in administrative responsibilities, the more activities you should delegate. A vice-principal should delegate 25 percent of the activity items that come to his attention; a superintendent 90 percent. Delegation is an investment that accrues long term benefits. One of those benefits is invaluable on-the-job training for your staff whose expertise reflects directly on you, their leader. Also, your ability to rise to a more challenging position is directly related to the knowledge, the ability, and the effectiveness of those you have trained while in your current position.

Another internal time-waster that certainly deserves mention is procrastination. Procrastination is professionally dehabilitating; we delay precisely those difficult, challenging, or high priority activities with which we should be most integrally involved. Low priority tasks on the other hand are quickly accomplished, are instantly gratifying, and are completed with more regularity.

Leaders must recognize the consequences of delay and the advantages of action. A complex high priority challenge can be accomplished faster by being reduced to subtasks. Working at a task for five minutes a day to initiate involvement; gathering additional data; performing a high priority subtask that coincides with your current mood; setting deadlines and announcing your deadline to someone else; taking rest breaks; and rewarding yourself when subtasks are completed are excellent ways to avoid procrastination of difficult, challenging, high priority activities.

EFFICIENT USE OF TIME

WEEKLY PLANNING FORM

One way to make efficient use of your time is to complete and follow a weekly planning form.

NAME ——————————— Week of———————————

MONDAY	7:00-9:30	Office routine
	9:30-10:00	Mail
	10:00-10:45	Classroom observation
	10:45-11:00	Write up observation
	1:00-3:00	Final editing of report for Superintendent's Council
	3:00-4:00	Meeting with Math Department

TUES.	7:00-8:30	Tour school plant
	8:30-9:00	Meet with head custodian and maintenance staff
	9:00-10:00	Office routine
	11:15	Mr. Sanchez
	1:00-2:00	Three classroom observations
	2:00-2:30	Write up observations
	2:30-3:00	Write parent bulletin
	3:30	Office routine
WED.	7:00-8:30	Office routine and meet with staff
	9:00-11:00	Superintendent's Council—report on athletics
	11:30	Classroom observation
	2:00-3:00	Office routine
	3:00-4:00	Meet with non-teaching certificated staff
THURS.	7:00-8:30	Office routine
	8:30-11:00	Visit high school
		Lunch with department chairpersons
	1:00-2:00	Visit student center
	2:00-3:00	Confer with assistant superintendent
	3:00-5:00	Teacher evaluation conference
FRIDAY	7:00-8:30	Office routine
	8:30-9:00	Review week with secretary
	9:00-10:00	Meet with deans
	1:00-1:30	Mr. & Mrs. Smith
	2:00-3:00	Make out next week's planning form
	8:00-10:00	Football game

Major Tasks to be completed this week:
1. Two teacher evaluation conferences
2. Meeting with Math Department
3. Meeting with non-teaching certificated staff
4. Superintendent's Council—report on athletics
5. Completion of six classroom observations
6. Completion of parent bulletin
7.
8.

Usually this form is made out on Fridays with copies distributed as follows:
1. To your secretary for her information.
2. To be posted on the bulletin board for staff, if you are a site administrator, so they will know when you are accessible.
3. To you.
4. To your superior.

To begin your weekly planning, establish three to eight priorities to be accomplished during the week, and list those at the bottom of the form. Next, estimate the amount of time it will take to accomplish these tasks. With priorities and time estimates established, work around the meetings and appointments already scheduled. Occasionally, to fit in the blocks of time necessary to complete a task, you may have to rearrange some appointments. It is far better to do this on a proceeding Friday when you are preparing the form than on a day or so before the appointment.

As you schedule the time blocks, be sure to allow for completion of prior tasks. In the example, the principal has scheduled an evaluation conference with a teacher on Thursday at 3 p.m., but prior to that, he must complete a third observation Monday at 10 a.m. and record the results on a district form. After the form is completed the administrator should immediately write any necessary memorandum, prepare agendas, and make other arrangements. These are the preparations for a well planned week. In addition to planned time, uncommitted time should be left for unforeseen problems.

OTHER IDEAS

Carry an appointment book with you; have your secretary compare her book daily with the one you carry and keep both books updated. Get memoranda to your assistants or staff early in the morning; this helps them recognize your priorities, set their own, and get to work. Write yourself reminders—near the phone, in your briefcase, in a pocket diary; keep a list of things to do which you add to regularly.

A cluttered desk wastes time and is a sure sign of not being organized. Often 80 percent of the material on your desk either belongs in files or should be thrown away. Go through your mail one time; letting it pile up day after day only causes you to shuffle repeatedly through the same correspondence. Learn how to use a dictating machine; it not only saves you time—you can dictate six times faster than you can write, but it also saves your secretary time. She can type directly from the transcriber.

COMMENTS

Many people in education feel that lack of time is their greatest obstacle to adequate job performance. The primary challenge to them is to unblock the route to effective time management by recognizing and replacing any unproductive values with productive ones.

Time management is primarily a challenge to your values and attitudes, and only secondarily a challenge to your skills. Time is a scarce resource; unless it is managed, nothing else can be. To make the most of your time is to make the most of your life.

Chapter 3
Stress

Stress is an adaptive response in which the body prepares for or adjusts to a threatening situation. Such a response manifests itself in symptoms which are both physiological—increase in heart rate, blood pressure, respiration, and levels of adrenalin; and psychological—irritability, depression, anxiety, and withdrawal. Stress is integrally related to control; the greater one's sense of powerlessness over the stressor, the greater the stress.

HUMAN PERCEPTION OF STRESS

Because one's perception of a threatening situation is subjective, discounting obvious physical calamities, stress itself is a subjective phenomena—all in the mind. Consequently, intellectual awareness of and emotional attitudes toward stress are important.

Stress can be self-induced, either directly or indirectly, from a lack of planning and of goal-setting both in professional and personal life; from a lack of skills to deal with other people and to deal with the job; from personal value conflicts; and from changing conditions.

The following attitudes contribute to stress: authoritarianism, intolerance, indecisiveness, worry, and perfectionism. Stockpiling hurts, magnifying minor irritants, not communicating feelings, believing that you are a victim of fate and of your feelings, and needing and seeking love and approval from everyone also promote stress.

By using a learned set of skills based on the understanding and management of stress, it is possible to develop control. A leader, before seeking to understand others, must first understand himself and develop his own stress control. Many are eager to learn what motivates others yet they neglect the more challenging task of knowing themselves.

Individuals have three basic drives: to maintain equilibrium, to strive for self-enhancement, and to avoid diminution of their prize states. Any perceived threat creates tension. It is the perception of threat, not necessarily the reality, that is important. Intensity of the reaction is also significant. Mild tension is an incentive, stirring us to meet the challenge to overcome the obstacle. Absence of all tension is not a sign of happiness; rather it is an indication of apathy or of ignorance of the situation. Acute prolonged stress can be not only disorienting, but disabling.

An optimum level of stress exists for each individual in each situation. The same source of stress can be debilitating to one person yet stimulating to another. Levels of tolerance to stress can vary markedly from person to person and from situation to situation with respect to the same individual. Some people have developed strategies for coping with a high level of stress while others have difficulty handling even a moderate amount.

The main contributors of stress in the personal life of an individual in order of degree are:

- Death of a spouse
- Divorce
- Marital separation
- Jail term
- Death of a close family member
- Personal injury or illness
- Marriage
- Job dismissal
- Marital reconciliation
- Retirement
- Change in health of a family member
- Pregnancy
- Sex difficulties
- Gain of a new family member
- Occupation readjustment

In addition to personal stress factors we know that the education profession contributes its own specialized stressors.

Contributors to stress for teachers in order of degree are:
- Disruptive students
- Lack of time
- Student apathy
- Non-teaching duties
- Financial pressure
- Lack of support from parents and the community
- Demands of multiability students
- Lack of positive feedback from administrators
- Lack of input into curricular and administrative decisions
- Lack of recognition for teaching achievements
- Lack of collegial support

Contributors to stress for school site administrators in order of degree are:
- Forcing the resignation or dismissal of a teacher
- Dealing with unsatisfactory performance of professional staff
- Involuntary transfer to another principalship
- Preparing for a teachers' strike
- Refusal of teacher to follow policies
- Criticism in the press
- Last week of school year
- Forced staff reduction
- Legal action against the school
- Assault on a staff member
- Reorganization of educational program
- Disagreement with superiors
- Verbal abuse from students or parents
- Serious vandalism to the building
- The first week of school year

From all those factors, the following conclusions can be drawn.

Administrative events associated with conflict between administrators and teachers are perceived by administrators as most stressful.

Administrative events associated with a threat to job or physical security and status are also perceived as highly stressful.

Conflicts between administrators and teachers are perceived as more stressful as one moves from high schools to middle and elementary schools.

Conflicts among students and student problems are perceived as more stressful by high school administrators than by elementary administrators.

DECISION MAKING UNDER STRESS

Consider the following phenomena.

The greater the stress, the greater the conceptual rigidity of an individual.

The greater the conceptual rigidity, the more closed to new information the individual becomes.

The greater the conceptual rigidity, the greater the tendency to repeat prior responses to the exclusion of new alternatives.

The greater the stress, the less the ability of the individual to tolerate ambiguity in the environment.

Intolerance of ambiquity leads to an inappropriate response to a stimulus before adequate information is available for the correct response.

Under increasing stress, there is a decrease in productive thought and an increase in non-productive thought.

The greater the stress, the greater the distortion in perception of the environment.

The greater the stress, the greater the amount of risk perceived in the environment.

The greater the amount of time spent on a task, the lower the amount of risk perceived in the environment.

In a crisis situation, decision makers have difficulty distinguishing between threats to themselves and threats to the organization.

The greater the fear, frustration, and hostility aroused by a crisis, the greater the tendency for aggression and escape behaviors.

In a crisis situation, negative psychological factors are reinforced.

In a stressful situation, the only goals that will be considered are those related to the immediate present, at the sacrifice of longer range considerations.

The greater the stress, the greater the tendency to make a premature choice of alternatives before adequate information is available for a correct response.

The greater the stress, the greater the likelihood that a decision maker will choose a risky alternative.

The greater the time pressure, the poorer the choice of the alternative.

Groups experiencing substantive conflict more frequently employ creative alternatives than groups without conflict.

Groups experiencing conflict show more effective performance in decision-making tasks than groups experiencing little or no conflict.

The greater the group conflict aroused by a crisis, the greater the consensus once a decision is reached.

In a crisis, the number of communication channels available to handle incoming information decreases.

In a conflict, there is greater need for effective leadership.

The smaller the group, the greater the amount of consensus that will be achieved through group discussion.

The tendency to choose a risky alternative increases with continued participation in decision-making tasks.

The greater the reliance on group problem-solving processes, the greater the consideration of alternatives.

MANAGING AND REDUCING STRESS

TIME MANAGEMENT

In any discussion of stress management, the one strategy always highlighted is that of time management. Properly executed time management creates the balance and control in your life that is needed. Time management can be subsumed by an even larger and more generalized concept, that of pacing or of consciously regulating the ebb and flow of your life. Time management will help you to do that. You can pace yourself by regulating the naturally occurring cycles of activation and withdrawal. While it is normal to alternate between periods of reaching outward and periods of quiet renewal, you should avoid abrupt swings between either extreme.

Time and stress management are two strands of the same braid. Not only does mismanagement of one exacerbate mismanagement of the other, but also specific problem areas in the management of both are identical. For instance, paper work, telephone and visitor interruptions, excessive meetings, lack of planning, and procrastination are both time-wasters and stress producers.

Like time management, the management of stress requires a shift in attitudes and in level of awareness; self-analysis and identification of stressors through use of a stress log; and practical techniques for the management of those identified stressors. As always, awareness and attitude come first.

JOB AND ROLE CLARIFICATION

Job and role clarification also contribute significantly to the management of stress. A job can be inherently stressful if one's role is unclear or subject to conflicting expectations; if the job involves too much or too little work; if there is too little opportunity for achievement; or if there is inadequate performance evaluation.

PROBLEM SOLVING

Another strategy for managing stress is applying the skills of problem solving so that delays in confronting problems will not create further difficulties. Such procrastination would not only allow the problem situation to deteriorate, but would also engender a mental exaggeration disproportionate to the problem's actual severity.

COMMUNICATIONS

A fourth strategy in the management of stress is control of communications. The importance of skillful communications to stress management becomes clear as one recalls that authoritarianism — excessive directive communications, intolerance—excessively negative communications, and failure to express feelings—excessively repressive communications are three key promoters of stress. It is important to recognize that the words you use and choose not to use do not merely describe reality, they create it.

STRESS REDUCTION PROCEDURE

The following eight-step procedure is a suggested way to help control stress:

1. Identify your most bothersome stressors and select one to resolve.
2. Search for the causes of this stressful event.
3. Generate a set of possible solutions to remedy the causes.
4. Specify a plan of action you will take to alleviate one cause.
5. Develop a time table to implement your plan of action.
6. Set a date and method for when how you will follow up and evaluate the effectiveness of your plan.
7. Investigate the potential problems or intended consequences (additional stress) your action plan may have created.

8. Clarify your own values and make sure your life is in harmony with them.

When stressors are beyond your personal control, such as statewide budget cuts, or personality conflicts with your immediate supervisor or the board of directors, you must seek to reduce stress in the one area left to you—within yourself. This can be accomplished through a series of strategies that build up resistance to stress and increase your level of tolerance.

PHYSICAL HEALTH

General physical health and well-being are fundamental. The importance of regular exercise, good eating habits and periods of recreation are cliches that merit repeating. I can speak from personal experience, having been a jogger for 20 years, that jogging is a quick and effective way to get the necessary exercise you need to get your pulse rate up and to sustain it for at least 30 or 40 minutes. Also, good nutrition, a reasonable amount of sleep, and keeping the amount of alcohol consumed to a low level are excellent ways to achieve well-being, to develop a high energy level, to sustain a positive mental outlook, and provide an increased ability to deal with challenges without incurring increased stress.

LOVE

Love is a powerful force in human life. The human attributes of love—tenderness, caring, sensitivity, and warmth—have a soothing, healing effect on the wounds that distress may have caused. The emotional support found in sharing genuine love with another person can refresh and nourish the human spirit. The strength that stems from this unconditional regard and commitment to another can lessen stress accumulation.

INSULTS

Because we have such a highly developed nervous system, we are vulnerable to psychological insults from others. From research and from practical experience, I have identified eight ways to strenghten your tolerance to insults.

Do not waste your time trying to befriend those who do not want to be recipients of your love and friendship.

Do not be a perfectionist; strive to do something that is within your capabilities.

Do not underestimate the genuine pleasure that can come from the simple things in life.

Concentrate on the pleasant side of life and on the activities which
can improve your life. As the old German proverb says, "Imitate the
sundial's ways; count only the pleasant days."

When you do experience a setback or defeat, re-establish your
self-confidence by remembering all your past accomplishments.

Do not procrastinate in tackling unpleasant but necessary tasks; get
them over with quickly.

Realize that people are unequal in many ways at birth, that all
people should have access to equal opportunities, and that their progress should be evaluated on the basis of their performance. Leaders
are leaders only as long as they have the respect and loyalty of their
followers.

Work on improving yourself so you can contribute to society.

One additional suggestion is to be cautious of the crutches you are
inclined to use when tension becomes stressful—excessive pill-
taking, drinking, sleeping, eating, and working. More important,
realize that they are crutches.

RECEIVING CRITICISM

The following suggestions can be helpful in receiving criticism.

Listen closely to what the critic has to say and ask questions.

Your major goal should be mutual understanding not conversion to
your point of view.

Try to understand the motivation behind the criticism by getting to
know your critic.

Keep in mind that some people just feel a need to complain, not to
discuss the issue in depth.

Avoid defensiveness; defensiveness implies guilt. Maintain the
offensive, without being "offensive."

Be open and honest.

Invite the person back for a second visit in your office.

Indicate that you want to reach an understanding.

Make a follow-up call or visit at an appropriate time.

RESPONDING TO CRITICISM

Be aware of the cultural and intellectual background of your critic.
Do not over- or under-estimate his intellectual background.

Evaluate the emotional climate. Some hostile critics want more to
release tension than to obtain an answer.

Find out something about the person's interest and needs. Relate
your comments to ideas the person understands.

Include illustrations and examples in your answers. Speak in concrete terms.

Avoid side issues and exceptions. Give simple answers to questions posed.

Do not dwell on history or background of problems unless asked to do so.

Avoid long answers that can destroy interest and can create more hostility.

Avoid professional jargon.

If possible, deal with critics individually and not at public meetings.

People ask you for criticism, but they want only praise.

ADDITIONAL SUGGESTIONS

SELF-RENEWAL

Stress cannot only engender tension and immobility in action, but can also create emotional and intellectual rigidity and strain. An avenue for countering such stress precipatated problems can be through self-renewal.

One avenue of self-renewal might be mind stretching activities primarily involving self-study and individualized learning. These can broaden your horizons and give you the warm glow of personal growth and achievement. Mind stretching activities emphasize imagination and creativity. The possibilities are as limitless as the range of the unfamiliar to a given person. The body may be confined, but the mind is always free to roam and explore.

Other suggestions for self-renewal are the following.

Explore the world of arts and crafts.

Investigate some avocational activities with money-making potential which could include arts and crafts that you could market.

Collect things for fun; this opens a new world, provides an opportunity for socializing, and often offers financial gains.

Grow things that can beautify your environment for yourself and for sharing with others, that can offer healthy outdoor activity, and that can contribute to a more nutritious diet.

Engage in nature and outdoor activities which promote mental, physical, and spiritual wholeness, and an opportunity for creative learning.

Become involved in a social service which helps others and which fulfills your basic need for moral, spiritual, and ethical expression and development.

Become involved in sports, games, recreation, and travel.

ATTITUDES

The attitude most relevant to stress is tolerance. Tolerance demands serenity on your part to become aware and then to make decisions about your response to the environment, people, and philosophies in it. Tolerant living requires positive, thoughtful development of personal values—values that are oriented toward an enriched, contributing, and accepting lifestyle.

Part II
Excellence in Administration

Chapter 4
Planning

Why is it such a problem for people to plan? I've puzzled over this for years and concluded that there are two major reasons. The first is that while planning is important it is never urgent, one can put it off easily because of daily emergencies. Of course, planning is the very thing that keeps these emergencies to a minimum. The second reason is that the typical executive is a person of action, he is impatient to get the job done and because of this he has a constant tendency to get on with the job before he has adequately described and planned what he is trying to do.

Frank Goble
Excellence in Leadership
American Management Association

Effective executives concentrate on the few major areas where superior performance will produce outstanding results. They force themselves to set priorities and stay with their priority decisions. They know that they have no choice, but to do first things first, and second things, not at all. The alternative is to get nothing done.

Peter Drucker
The Effective Executive
Harper & Row, New York

The basic and first indication of the existence of professional leadership in an organization is formal, skilled, long-range strategic planning. This means that, instead of leaving the future to chance, the professional leader determines what he wants the

future to be and then leads the organization toward the attainment of such pre-established goals. The leader is continuously
envisioning the future and then making the future similar to the
way in which he has envisioned it. The leader is not, therefore,
afraid of it because he knows what to expect.

Lawrence A. Appley
American Management Association

One of the key components of a management system is strategic
planning. Strategic planning should be a shared process which
involves all facets of decision making at both the school and the
district level. I found over the years that planning is often done spo-
radically, rather than in a consistent manner; that administrators either
get too complicated or they fail to set priorities and attempt too many
things at once; that planning is often not in conformance with the
goals and needs identified in the school or in the school district; and
that many times the plan is given to staff by the top executive or the
board of education, and, therefore, lacks ownership by staff and subsequent motivation for implementation.

It is my premise that planning is important, but that it must be as
simple as possible; school districts have neither extra time nor separate planning departments. Planning has to be done and should be
done by the people on the job—this means all the people in the
district as much as possible. Such plans should emanate from needs
assessments which are conducted for staff development, learning climate, and student achievement.

All decisions at school level should reflect efforts to implement
board of education goals. These goals are usually general in nature,
however, they can serve as an umbrella under which priority goals
and objectives can be determined.

While the planning component of the management system is
guided by goals established by the board of education, these goals are
then systematically translated by district and site level personnel into
a manageable number of performance objectives. These objectives
are influenced by monitoring data derived from the other five component areas of the individual school management system.

BOARD OF EDUCATION PLANNING

An organization needs to consider four elements of planning.
- Linear planning
- Budgetary planning—control system
- Conceptual planning—development of purposes and goals
- Management/board relations

To make planning as simple and as meaningful as possible, I suggest a two-day study session, preferably removed from potential interruptions. Here is an example of a planning outline to be used at the session.

OUTLINE FOR A PLANNING STUDY SESSION
PRESENT STATUS OF THE ORGANIZATION
- Profile
- Past milestones
- Purpose
- Characteristics of the organization
- District or school services
- Needs of various groups

INTERNAL FUNCTIONING OF THE ORGANIZATION
- Financial analysis
- Organizational chart
- Responsibilities and accountabilities
- Basic organization beliefs

AREAS OF UNIQUE COMPETENCE
- Basic capabilities
- Strengths and opportunities
- Weaknesses and problems
- Actions suggested

UNCONTROLLABLES
- Outside influences
- Effects of governments
- Activities of competitors
- Internal influences
- Critical exposures

ASSUMPTIONS ABOUT THE FUTURE
- Economic
- Technological
- Social
- Political

GOALS
- General
- Personnel
- Students
- Parents and the community
- Program
- Finance
- Publications

PHILOSOPHIES AND STRATEGIES
- Of top management
- Of regular staff
- Of finance
- Subject to challenge

ACTION PLANS
- General goals
- Related, specific objectives
- Strategies or activities
- Related assumptions
- Projects or programs
- Schedules
- Responsibilities
- Resources

FOLLOW-UP
- Alternatives
- Priorities
- Projected staffing

PROCEDURE

Establishing goals in the planning process can be done many ways, including using consensus systems. Many of the widely used systems require group interactions. I advocate using the Delphi system that I developed over the years, which is described in detail in Chapter 11. The Delphi system protects the identity of the participants and their stated goals. Using the Delphi takes a minimum of time and allows the group to participate and, with equal influence on the outcome, to set priorities.

BRIEF OUTLINE OF THE DELPHI PROCESS

1. Participants write one goal on each 3x5 card completing as many cards as they wish.

2. The facilitator and a secretary list the goals in a rating format that allows each participant to indicate choices from strongly agree to strongly disagree, and from his top 10 to his top choice.

3. Participants rate each goal.

4. The facilitator and a secretary tally and weight the responses.

5. Goals are then assigned weightings and ranked in descending order of acceptance.

6. Participants decide which goals to retain. I recommend keeping the total number to approximately six.

7. Goals are translated into performance objectives with timelines and responsibilities for staff.

The Delphi formats are discussed in Chapter 11. I usually establish two sets of goals: a set of one-year short-term goals, and a set of three-to-five-year long-term goals. An example of one-year goals for the staff set by the board of education follows:

SAMPLE DISTRICT GOALS ESTABLISHED BY THE BOARD

ONE YEAR GOALS FOR SUPERINTENDENT AND STAFF
1981-82
SET BY BOARD OF EDUCATION

On April 22, 1981 the Board of Education adopted the following set of goals for the superintendent and staff for the 1981-82 school year.

A. CURRICULUM, STAFF DEVELOPMENT,
   STUDENT ACHIEVEMENT (Paul A)

   1. Improve student achievement through an articulated curriculum and supportive inservice activities.

   Objectives

   1.1 By May 30, 1982, a written district plan will be developed which will include the following: implementation of curriculum continua for grades K through 8 in reading and mathematics; field testing, revision, and augmentation of the K-12 Writ-

ten Expression Guide; inservice training
for teachers and administrators to focus
upon refinement of instructional skills;
and selection of coordinated mathematics materials for kindergarten through the
eighth grade. (Betty E)

1.2 By June 30, 1982, the schools in each high
school attendance area will develop a
plan to improve the articulation of instruction from school to school. (Betty E,
Ralph B)

1.3 By June 30, 1982, a plan will be prepared
for developing courses of study for grades
7-12 based upon learning objectives, and
for implementing activities which can be
translated into learning skills at each
grade level for each discipline. (Betty E,
Ralph B)

1.4 By June, 1982, each elementary school
will have a description of its instructional
program in the areas of reading and
mathematics. This description will include a planned sequence of instruction
and a list of the materials used. (Betty E)

2. Provide ongoing staff development opportunities for
all personnel. (Paul A)

Objective

2.1 By August 15, 1981, a written plan will be
developed to provide:
Clinical Supervision Implementation Sessions for elementary principals.
Clinical Supervision Maintenance Sessions for elementary vice principals.
Clinical Supervision Input Sessions for
secondary principals and vice principals.
Elements of Instruction Sessions for
teachers. (Al Z)

COMMUNITY INPUT IN PLANNING

To supplement board planning, I have found it advisable to involve the community in helping to establish the goals for the education program. The example I am using is from an elementary district which involved the entire community in the goal-setting process. Using the computer, we processed over 3,000 responses from a random sampling of citizens. We also surveyed service, business, and retired citizens groups.

The results were surprising; the top goals of the community reflected values other than for basic skills. The number one goal was: respects public and private property, shares, cooperates, and is respectful and courteous. The second highest goal was: competence in math operations-adds, subtracts, multiplies, and divides whole numbers. The third highest goal was: has a self-esteem—a healthy self-concept, self-confidence, and self-security. Of the top 10 goals, only two were identified as basic subject skills. The least important goals in this community for their K-8 children were music and foreign language.

Involving thousands of people from the community in establishing the program goals for that school district, gave them—the consumers of the service—ownership. Using computer capabilities and random sampling techniques made this process feasible. After establishing these goals, the board and staff identified performance objectives for implementing the top 10 goals. An annual progress report was given to the community. Community goal-setting procedures follow.

SAMPLE DATA-GATHERING INSTRUMENTS
SAMPLE LETTER TO COMMUNITY MEMBERS

Escondido Union School District
Ash and Lincoln Streets
Escondido, California, 92025
October, 1980

Dear Participant,

We would like to know what goals you think are important in the school. We will use your ideas in evaluating and determining our goals. At the conclusion of our study we will send you a summary report of our findings. Your comments and judgments will, of course, remain confidential. If you find that for any reason you cannot participate, please return all the materials to us.

I hope you can cooperate in this important study. If you have any questions after reviewing the information on the instruction sheet in the attached envelope call Orange Glen school 734-1234.

Thank you for your help and cooperation.

Sincerely yours,
Don M
Principal

SAMPLE INSTRUCTIONS
INSTRUCTIONS FOR COMMUNITY APPROACH TO GOAL SELECTION

Introduction

This envelope contains a pack of 63 printed cards. Each card describes a goal of elementary education. We want to know which ones you think are most important. The school will devote more time, effort, and resources to having the students achieve the more important goals. Information about the relative importance of these goals is necessary in helping us plan both our educational programs and our procedure for evaluating them.

In order to gather this information, we would like you to rate each goal in terms of how important it is for the school to help the student achieve that particular goal. Base your judgments solely on how important a goal is in terms of the characteristics students should have as a result of their schooling. Some goals are, of course, more appropriate for some grades than they are for others. Thus, do your ratings on the basis of WHAT GOALS SHOULD BE ATTAINED BY THE END OF THE SIXTH GRADE.

Rating Procedure

1. Please do not make any marks on the cards or envelopes.
2. Place the five envelopes in front of you from left to right as follows:
   a. Least Important
   b. Less Important
   c. Average Importance
   d. More Important
   e. Most Important
3. Look through the entire set of 63 cards briefly to get an idea of the range of importance of the various

goals. Now find one goal for each of the five categories of importance (The number in the corner of each
card should be ignored since it is used solely for
clerical purposes in recording your choices).

4. Sort the remaining cards into these same five piles:
however, be sure to put at least five cards in each pile.
It is important that every goal card be placed in a pile.

If you are not sure into which pile a goal should be
placed put it into the one in which you feel it comes
closest. Do not spend a long time deciding into
which pile a particular goal card belongs. If you have
difficulty in evaluating a goal, put it at the back of the
pack and sort it last.

There are no "right" or "wrong" answers in this task.
Just rate the goals in terms of how important YOU
think they are.

5. When you have sorted all the cards, make certain that
you have put at least five cards in each pile. Then, put
the cards into their envelopes. Do not seal the
envelopes.

Additional Goals

If you feel there are some important goals that were not
included in the set of cards, list additional goals on a separate
piece of paper.

Please rate the added goal(s) as you did the original set. Place
each added goal in the appropriate envelope.

Returning Materials

1. Before returning materials, please check that you
have done the following:

Put each card into one of the five
envelopes.
Put at least five cards in each envelope
(not counting the cards you may have
written yourself).

2. Please tuck in the flap on the envelope, but do not
seal it.

3. Place all the materials in the large manila envelope
and return it to your school either with your child or
in person.

SAMPLE INFORMATION CARD

The following information was requested of the person completing the card sorting.

Male_____ Female_____ Over 35_____ Under 35_____
Non-parent_____ Parent_____ School Employee_____ Student_____
H.S. Graduate or less_____ College_____ College Graduate_____
White_____ Spanish Last Name_____ Black_____ Oriental_____ Other_____

Please place this card in the large brown envelope when completed.

SAMPLE LIST OF OBJECTIVES

ESCONDIDO UNION SCHOOL DISTRICT
GOALS & OBJECTIVES

1A ADJUSTMENT: Faces reality. Is well adjusted. Is generally happy.

1B GENERAL ACTIVITY: Is a healthy person with normal need for activity and for play.

2A INDEPENDENCE: Is self-sufficient and self-responsible.

2B FRIENDLINESS: Is friendly, generous, helpful, good-natured, and interested in people.

2C SOCIALIZATION: Has a healthy balance between conformity, acceptance, obedience, and independence. Is open-minded and tolerant to new ideas, nonconformity in others.

2D SOCIALIZATION: Respects public and private property, shares, cooperates, is respectful and courteous.

3A SCHOOL ORIENTATION: Has favorable attitude toward school, teachers, and studying.

3B SELF ESTEEM: Has a healthy self-concept, self-confidence, self-security, and self-esteem.

4A NEED ACHIEVEMENT: Desires to learn. Does his best. Pursues goals in spite of frustrations.

4B INTEREST AREAS: Has a wide variety of interests in recreational activities, hobbies, and school subjects.

6 EXPRESSIVE SKILL IN ARTS AND CRAFTS: Freely expresses himself in painting and other art work. Shows creativity in works produced.

8A CLASSIFICATORY REASONING: Organizes information, ideas, and things into classes or groups.

8B RELATIONAL OR IMPLICATIONAL REASONING: Solves problems and finds logical answers.

9A CREATIVE FLEXIBILITY: Finds many different ways to solve a problem and switches to another way when one doesn't work.

9B CREATIVE FLUENCY: Calls to mind much relevant information and many ideas when needed. Elaborates on ideas. Creates original information, art, invention, and ideas.

10A SPAN AND SERIAL MEMORY: Memorizes series, sequences, and lists by rote.

10B MEANINGFUL MEMORY: Remembers meaningful ideas and information; non-rote.

11 ORAL COMPREHENSION OF A FOREIGN LANGUAGE: Understands and speaks a foreign language as spoken by a fluent speaker.

13A SPELLING: Applies correct spelling to written work. Applies spelling rules and phonetic skills.

13B PUNCTUATION: Correctly punctuates written work.

13C CAPITALIZATION: Correctly capitalizes written work.

13D WRITTEN EXPRESSION: Shows originality in writing. Organizes written work well.

13E APPLICATION OF WRITING SKILLS: Appreciates the importance of good grammar to clear communication. Appreciates writing as a means of communication. Enjoys writing activities.

15 COMPREHENSION OF NUMBERS AND SETS IN MATHEMATICS: Understands numbers and number concepts.

16A MATHEMATIC OPERATIONS: Adds, subtracts, multiplies, and divides whole numbers.

16B FRACTIONS: Adds, subtracts, multiplies, and divides fractions.

16C OPERATIONS WITH DECIMALS AND PERCENTS: Reads and writes decimals and percents. Adds, subtracts, multiplies, and divides decimals and percents.

17 MATHEMATICAL PROBLEM SOLVING: Uses mathematical knowledge and skills (arithmetic, measurement, and geometry) to solve common practical problems.

18 GEOMETRIC VOCABULARY: Identifies points, lines, angles, plane figures and solid figures.

19A MATHEMATICS—MEASUREMENT: Understands the concepts of length, weight, time, area, volume, speed, money, etc.

19B MATHEMATICS—STATISTICS: Understands, interprets, and uses graphs and tables.

20 MUSIC INTEREST AND ENJOYMENT: Enjoys musical activities. Finds music and dance satisfying means of self-expression.

21A SINGING: Sings his part, stays on key, and keeps a tune. Has a good voice and clear diction.

21B MUSICAL INSTRUMENT PLAYING: Plays the simple classroom instruments effectively. Plays his part. Plays solo.

21C DANCE: Expresses himself freely through movement. Learns popular and folk dances.

22 MUSIC KNOWLEDGE: Understands major historical and national developments. Understands common terminology (e.g., chords, scale, key).

23A PRACTICING HEALTH AND SAFETY PRINCIPLES: Applies health and safety principles to daily life. Develops good habits of personal hygiene. Gets adequate rest, sleep, and physical exercise.

23B UNDERSTANDING HEALTH AND SAFETY PRINCIPLES: Knows about and understands health and safety: personal hygiene and physical fitness.

23C SEX EDUCATION: Understands growth in adolescence and maturity. Has healthy attitudes to all aspects of sex and identifies with own sex.

24A PHYSICAL EDUCATION—MUSCLE CONTROL: Is well coordinated when performing basic sport skills such as: running, jumping, kicking and throwing.

24B PHYSICAL EDUCATION—PHYSICAL DEVELOPMENT AND WELL-BEING: Has a healthy body and physical well-being. Has efficient body movements.

25 GROUP ACTIVITY—SPORTSMANSHIP: Is a good winner and a good loser. Obeys the rules of the game.

26 UNDERSTANDING RULES OF SPORTS AND GAMES: Understands the rules and directions of games and sports. Understands his role as a team member.

27A LISTENING REACTION AND RESPONSE: Listens attentively to a speaker. Gains information through listening and remembers it.

27B SPEAKING: Participates in discussions. Relates stories,
experiences, and events effectively. Uses correct grammar when speaking.

28A READING PHONETIC RECOGNITION: Uses phonics
as a reading tool. Identifies sounds. Sounds unfamiliar words that are phonetic.

28B READING STRUCTURAL RECOGNITION: Recognizes
root words, prefixes, suffixes, and syllables.

29A ORAL READING: Reads aloud with clarity and fluency,
expression, and comprehension.

29B SILENT READING: Reads at a rate suitable for age and
grade level.

30A RECOGNITION OF WORD MEANINGS: Has a broad
vocabulary. Recognizes word meanings through context.

30B REMEMBERING INFORMATION READ: Recalls main
ideas, supporting details, and events in their proper
sequence.

31A INFERENCE MAKING FROM READING SELECTIONS:
Correctly interprets what is read. Sees implications,
makes inferences, arrives at generalizations and
conclusions.

31B CRITICAL READING: Analyzes and evaluates reading
selections. Recognizes authors' points of view. Dis-
tinguishes fact from fiction.

32A ATTITUDE TOWARD READING: Appreciates the
importance of reading as communication and as a
source of pleasure.

32B ATTITUDE AND BEHAVIOR MODIFICATION FROM
READING: Is selective in choice of reading materials.
Independently turns to printed materials for specific
information and as aids to study.

34 RELIGIOUS BELIEF: Applies his religious beliefs to
daily life. Participates in religious activities. Believes
in his religion.

35A OBSERVATION AND DESCRIPTION IN SCIENCE: Is
more observant of his environment. Describes accurately what is observed in writing, orally.

37 APPLICATION OF SCIENTIFIC METHODS TO EVERY-
   DAY LIFE: Applies scientific knowledge and skills to
   solve practical and personal problems independent
   of school requirements.
38 KNOWLEDGE OF GOVERNMENTS: Understands the
   United States government; its origins, development,
   structure, and functions. Knows the rights and free-
   doms granted by the Constitution. Understands political systems.
39 KNOWLEDGE OF PHYSICAL GEOGRAPHY: Knows
   the vocabulary of geography. Understands geographic
   concepts.
40 SOCIAL ORGANIZATION KNOWLEDGE: Understands
   how people and nations are interrelated and interdependent. Understands communication between communities, states, and nations.
41A RESEARCH SKILLS IN SOCIAL STUDIES: Uses refer-
    ence materials, maps, globes, and encyclopedias.
41B CITIZENSHIP: Is concerned for the dignity, welfare,
    rights, and freedoms of every individual. Accepts his
    role and responsibilities as a group member.

SAMPLE RESULTS

COMMUNITY GOAL-SETTING RESULTS

RANK	GOAL	"MOST IMPORTANT" PERCENTAGE SCORE
1.	2D - RESPECT	98%
2.	16A - MATH OPERATIONS	97
3.	3B - SELF ESTEEM	95
4.	4A - DESIRES TO LEARN	95
5.	41B - CITIZENSHIP	95
6.	1A - ADJUSTMENT	93
7.	3A - SCHOOL ORIENTATION	93
8.	29B - SILENT READING	93
9.	2B - FRIENDLINESS	91
10.	27A - LISTENING	91

GOALS RANKING LAST

54.	39	-	GEOGRAPHY	53
55.	18	-	GEOMETRIC VOCABULARY	52
56.	6	-	ARTS & CRAFTS	50
57.	20	-	MUSIC INTEREST	45
58.	10A	-	MEMORY	42
59.	11	-	FOREIGN LANGUAGE	39
60.	22	-	MUSIC KNOWLEDGE	35
61.	21C	-	DANCE	34
62.	21B	-	PLAYS MUSICAL INSTRUMENT	32
63.	21A	-	SINGING	30

. . .

SCHOOL SITE PLANNING

Each school needs to have plans to improve its educational program. The same types of planning procedures that are used with the board can also be used with the school site members. What follows are three examples of charts that are used in the school-site planning process. A valuable resource is the Association of California School Administrators Operations Notebook "Planning the Principal's Year."

THREE SAMPLE PLANNING CHARTS

SAMPLE INDIVIDUAL SCHOOL
MANAGEMENT SYSTEM PLANNING GUIDE

INDIVIDUAL SCHOOL MANAGEMENT SYSTEM
PLANNING GUIDE

NEEDS ASSESSMENT

| Teacher | Climate | Student |
| Survey | Surveys | Achievement |

.

.

STUDENT NEEDS

.

.

SITE COUNCIL

Teachers	Parents	Administrators
	Students	

.

SCHOOL IMPROVEMENT PLAN

Objectives	Activities	Evaluation

.

STUDENT GROWTH

.

EVALUATION

. . .

SAMPLE SCHOOL PLANNING SUMMARY CHART

School:_____

Component   *Date To Be Completed*
1. Local System for Decision Making   _____
Describe _____
_____
_____
_____
_____

2. Site Council Organized   _____
         Meetings Held   _____

3. Analysis of Academic Test Data   _____
         Improvement Plan   _____

4. Learning Climate Surveys   _____
         Parents   _____
         Staff   _____
         Students   _____
         Improvement Plan   _____

5. Staff Development Surveys   _____
         Staff   _____
         Management   _____

6. Proposal for Inservice Program _____
    *(based on Test Data, Climate
    Survey and Staff Development
    Survey)*

    . . .

SAMPLE GANTT CHART (refer to Chapter 10)
STUDENT INPUT IN PLANNING

At the classroom level, in addition to the regular lesson planning, the teacher should use the Delphi technique two months into the year to find out how students view classroom programs. The teacher can ask "What do you like about this class?" and "What do you wish done to improve the class?" He can then make plans to enhance what the students like and can consider what can be done to improve the class.

COMMENTS

By using uncomplicated planning procedures you can maximize performance levels of all personnel within the district and increase learning achievement.

Planning is an essential component for effective schools. Successful planning incorporates the following ideas.

1. Leaders do the right thing and do things right.
2. "Right things" must be based on present and future needs of the majority.
3. People want things they do not need and need things they do not want.
4. It takes sophisticated marketing research to know the difference.
5. Many leaders are efficient; not all are effective.
6. Effectiveness begins with clearly defined objectives.
7. Organizations must be designed to accomplish objectives.
8. The most effective evaluation is self-evaluation. The most effective control is self-control.
9. The organization must be what it wishes to appear to be.
10. *Anticipation accelerates change; the future belongs to the responsive.*

Without planning you dare not delegate; without delegating you cannot motivate.

Chapter 5
Organization

Organization can help a school, or a school district, promote measurable improvement in learning achievement even within existing resources. The method of organization which I advocate is a participative individual school management system. Such a system places educational decision making as close to the learner as possible through the involvement of teachers, students, and parents. With an awareness of the district's broad goals, they have the authority and responsibility to make decisions at the school level reflecting the needs of the local school community.

To implement the individual school management system and to ensure its success, several basic beliefs have to be accepted by the board of education and the district office administration: faith and trust in the staff; a tolerance and enthusiasm for a diversity of school programs; and an in-depth understanding of the differing leadership styles of the principals, of the varied instructional methods of the teachers, and of the unique learning needs of the students. As a result, individuals and groups become involved in the decision-making process under the guidance of the principal who becomes the key leader. Recognizing teachers as competent professionals, the focus is no longer on finding ways to improve them. Rather it is on reducing learning problems and enhancing the progress of the students by involvement of staff and parents through the leadership of the principal. The teacher's competence is enhanced as a natural consequence of the knowledge and skills gained in the problem solving process. As a director of learning rather than a dispenser of knowledge, the teacher's own growth is measured in terms of the relevant changes in the learner.

The school management system has six major components: planning, organization, evaluation, staff development, learning climate, and decision making. All six components are important and have to be implemented simultaneously.

The organization component of the management system places most decisions at the school level. This is accomplished by involving parents, attendance area citizens, students, and staff in the decision making under the leadership of the principal, and by eliciting advice from the school site council. Each school must have a school site council which has an advisory role with the principal. The existing parent, student, and staff organizations continue to function normally but send representatives to the school site council.

The school board and the superintendent use monitoring instruments, cooperatively determined with the school site principal, to keep each school accountable. In this way both the school and the district level personnel know exactly what is expected of each individual school's program; yet the daily process and operation is left to the school.

All personnel and financial resources are allocated to the schools according to board-adopted formulas. The plan allows the school the authority to reallocate resources on the basis of their priorities and needs in order to solve their problems and to improve their programs.

A major element of this organizational plan is the establishment of ways to encourage the local school to increase their financial resources. Such an increase can be accomplished in four ways. As the average daily attendance increases during the regular year, summer school, and in adult school, increased attendance money is returned directly to the school rather than being placed in the district general fund. As vandalism is reduced, the money that is saved is placed in an individual school vandalism account. Such an account is usually tied in with the student body fund. As the use of substitute teachers decreases, the money that is saved is also returned to the school. A fourth way of increasing financial resources at the local school level is to have a local business or industry adopt the school and help finance its activities.

To help determine the level of administrative staffing, especially for elementary schools, a system can be worked out following six criteria.

1. Rate of turnover of students
2. Aid for Dependent Children count
3. California achievement profile or state testing program results
4 Number of personnel to be supervised
5. Number of students transported to that school
6. Enrollment

Statistics are gathered on each of these six factors for the schools in the district; a statistical Z-score value is given to each factor. Additional administrative help is assigned to the schools that are affected the most by the six factors.

In this organizational approach, which emphasizes the individual school management system, the principal is the key leader. Most superintendents and principals prefer to reorganize staff or reassign staff in keeping with their leadership style. During the 17 years I served as superintendent in four different school districts, I usually reorganized the administrative staff at the district office to better serve the principal as the key leader at the local school. In two of the districts, I reorganized the district office administration in response to the admonition by principals that they had little influence in decision making with the district office staff and the board of education; and in recognition of the fact that district office administrators had not been in a site level position for the last decade or more.

In the smaller district—7,000 students, I reorganized by having an assistant superintendent for educational programs, and made the position a three-year rotating assignment, selected from the principals in the district. The principals nominated three of their colleagues from whom I picked the assistant superintendent to serve a three year term. The principals could decide to renew that term one time for one to three years, or to bring in a new principal to fill the position.

In the last district in which I served, a school district of 50,000 students, I asked the 35 elementary principals to nominate five of their colleagues; and the nine intermediate and the nine high school principals to nominate three colleagues from each group respectively. The assistant superintendents and I then selected two elementary, one intermediate, and one high school principal from each group to come to the district office full time as directors of elementary, intermediate, and high schools. These four principals served staggered three-year terms. They served full time at the district office at their same principal's salary—plus a per diem amount for the extra days worked. They became full members of the superintendent's cabinet and of the management negotiating team, and attended board of education meetings—both public and executive sessions.

We also made certain that classified management staff—maintenance, custodial, food services, data processing, accounting and fiscal offices, and transportation—was also represented on the superintendent's cabinet.

The superintendent's cabinet in the large district had 12 to 15 members. In the smaller district, the cabinet included the entire management team which sometimes numbered up to 25 members. To enhance two-way communication and decision making, the cabinet met on Tuesday mornings; the board of education on Tuesday nights; and the four directors, representing the principals, on Wednesday and Thursday with their colleagues, mostly on non-school time. The elementary principals met in two different groups because of their number. This organization provided a one-week, tightly structured, decision-making cycle, giving principals input and participation in all levels of decision making.

As decision charts which appear later in this book show, most decision making is placed as close to the learner as possible; this means placing the decision making at the classroom level with the teacher and at the school level with the principal. All the decisions of the district and the school must be within the limits of the law, board policy, and negotiated employee contracts. Both the employee and the board negotiators should allow individual schools wide latitude in decision making, and should include a local school decision-making process in the negotiated contract rather than specific formulas or details for operation.

Organizing the school district in the manner just described meaningfully involves employees in a shared decision-making process.

Chapter 6
Personnel Evaluation

In the past, an employee might have felt insecure not knowing how his supervisor viewed his performance, or have felt threatened by traditional evaluations. In this chapter I discuss evaluation methods and procedures that can not only be helpful to both the employee and the employer, but can also motivate and improve performance. I am a strong proponent of reciprocal systems of evaluation: the supervisor not only evaluates the employee, but students evaluate teachers, teachers evaluate principals, principals evaluate district office personnel and the superintendent, and administrators evaluate the board of education.

Such evaluation procedures, however, will not suffice for eventual dismissal of an employee. If at any time, such dismissal is indicated, legal advice should be obtained immediately, and a thorough system of evaluation, in addition to the evaluation discussed in this chapter, should be completed.

BOARD OF EDUCATION EVALUATION

Through the years I have worked with boards of education who were willing to be evaluated by the administrative staff. The most common method of evaluation was through the use of the Delphi system (Chapter 11). The basic question the board member asked of themselves and the administrative staff was, "How can we be a more effective board of education?" Not only did the individual board members fill out 3x5 cards focusing on that question, but the superintendent and the cabinet also wrote cards. All entries were confidential and anonymous; the board of education cards were one color and the administration staff cards were another color, so the responses could be separated by group. A modified example of this evaluation follows.

SAMPLE EVALUATION OF CURRENT BOARD MEMBERS

HV SCHOOL DISTRICT

Date _____

Delphi for Board of Education
and Supterintendent's Cabinet

Question: How Can We Be A More Effective Board of Education?

	Board of Education N = 5 Ranking	Cabinet N = 6 Ranking
1. Procedures and Utilization of Time		
1.1 Minor details that are the responsibility of staff should not be dwelt on at board meetings.	71	86
1.2 A better balance could be achieved through more participation by all board members.	79	76
1.3 The board should only be concerned with policy and limit in-depth discussion into management and other unrelated items during meetings.	76	93
1.4 The chairman should limit excessively verbose individuals.	60	66
1.5 If a new item is to be introduced and it is controversial, the chairperson should announce the time limit to be spent on discussion.	68	45
1.6 Place motion on floor prior to discussion.	58	66
1.7 If the board is undecided, the item should be tabled immediately to provide time for additional individual study.	64	59

	Board of Education N = 5 Ranking	Cabinet N = 6 Ranking
1.8 The president should call for the vote after a reasonable discussion period.	66	78
1.9 The president should exercise more parlimentary control of meetings i.e., not allow an unbalanced discussion where only one person dominates the meeting.	83	62
1.10 Reduce discussion on routine items.	59	70
1.11 Board members must be willing to accept limitation of discussion if the chairperson uses authority to close the discussion and call for the vote.	78	61
1.12 Use meeting time effectively. Major time discussion related to most important items. Minor time such as wording of policies receive less time.	92	71
1.13 Keep meeting to the time schedule—not over three hours. The chair must sometimes be more arbitrary, be in charge, be unafraid to interrupt speaker, summarize for him, or ask him to summarize.	75	48

2. Decision Making

	Board of Education N = 5 Ranking	Cabinet N = 6 Ranking
2.1 The function of the board is to make policy. It should avoid getting into details and areas better handled by the administration.	83	95
2.2 Board members should make policy statements or decisions. Then staff should recommend how (procedures) or what method is used to implement the policy statement.	78	93
2.3 Staff recommendation on major issues should list options in priority. (Give board more than one choice.)	77	71
2.4 Board members should ask staff specific questions whenever possible, so staff can be more effective in researching answers.	60	69

	Board of Education N = 5 Ranking	Cabinet N = 6 Ranking
2.5 Be receptive and encourage vigorous discussions on important issues.	69	63
2.6 Above all, the board should concern itself with major issues and problems concerning the district and relegate to a minor position matters which can be handled by staff.	85	87
2.7 All board members should participate in all discussions.	81	64
2.8 Be sure that when we speak as a board member, we have only one vote. One member does not speak for the whole board.	70	61
2.9 Once a decision is made, all board members uphold it, even if they voted no and opposed the issue under discussion. Do not torpedo decisions. Put them up for re-examination at the next or later meeting if you still feel strongly opposed.	84	81
2.10 Accept split-vote decisions as logical, reasonable and representative.	66	78
2.11 Be more decisive, i.e., there is a time to cut off participative exercises with staff.	70	52
2.12 The board needs to reach a consensus as to the timing involved in decision making—sometimes judgments must be made without all of the desired data—timeliness of decision making can be one of the most important elements.	82	58

3. Specific Suggestions

3.1 Routine items, such as purchase orders, could be reviewed by one board member who would report at the meeting that all was in order. Other members would get copies, however.	44	62

	Board of Education N = 5 Ranking	Cabinet N = 6 Ranking
3.2 Follow up on our expressed commitments to use citizen's committees.	54	60
3.3 Board members agreed to call the superintendent or chairperson if they had questions or strong feelings on an item or issue in advance of the meeting for clarification. We agreed to do this, but we do not do it.	93	96
3.4 Hold briefing sessions prior to board meetings so we can be better prepared to act on major items.	40	63
3.5 Crucial issues should always be near front of agenda which is occurring more and more now with our revised agenda.	74	77
3.6 Use the services of a consultant to review our organizational structure.	47	50
3.7 Submit rough drafts of issues to the board for study before putting it on a public board agenda.	55	75
3.8 Devote more time to specific curriculum materials, methods and results.	68	47
3.9 Obtain the attendance of a representative from each school advisory council at board meetings.	54	75
3.10 Involve local teacher organizations in periodic formal presentations to the board on educational matters.	53	61
3.11 The board should require two separate documents: (1) A board policy book (2) An administrative procedures book The administrators' book would change often as state law changes and as staff recommends.	55	89

	Board of Education N = 5 Ranking	Cabinet N = 6 Ranking
4. Human Relations and Morale		
4.1 Improved public relations regarding use of funds.	64	43
4.2 This board is outstanding—compared to others—it is excellent.	86	75
4.3 Avoid argumentation and present only opinions, facts, points of view.	90	83
4.4 Keep personalities out of discussion—argue to issues.	98	85
4.5 Board members should not get personal in their rebuttals to each other in public meetings.	88	81

. . .

I have also had the principals involved in the board evaluation. In the larger districts, because of the number of principals, we separated them into groups—high school, intermediate, and elementary—through color coding the cards.

The evalation question I advocate is individual response to the phrases "I like" and "I wish you would." I prefer this question because the things that are being done well can be identified and reinforced. It is important to have a balanced approach to the evaluation by identifying positive things that are occurring as well as things people wish would be improved.

GUIDELINES FOR EVALUATING BOARD CANDIDATES

What follows is a form for evaluating candidates for the board. Such a form can be used by political action groups, organized unions, and other groups that wish to endorse board members for office.

GUIDELINE QUESTIONS FOR EVALUATING CANDIDATES

Personal Characteristics

Does the candidate:

- Think independently and objectively about problems?
- Have the necessary time to give to this position if elected?
- Demonstrate respect for the opinions of others and for the dignity of each individual?
- Show motivation for more than a quest for personal prestige or political gain?

- Show a cooperative spirit toward other board members even when their opinions differ?
- Possess the leadership skill to influence public opinion on behalf of positive programs to improve the educational process?
- Have the courage and ability to explain and support an unpopular policy?
- Demonstrate the ability to acknowledge errors and to change his mind without fear of appearing weak or of losing stature?
- Have the ability to withhold judgment on critical issues until he has all the available information?
- Appear free of personal or economic interests which would conflict with his ability to serve the interests of the school district?
- Have a sense of humor?
- Project an image which will enable him to be an unifying force in controversial situations?

Record of Public and Community Service
Does the candidate:
- Show familiarity with the social, political, ethnic, and economic compostion and resources of the district?
- Have sufficient background and practical experience to relate the school curriculum to the educational needs, resources, and aspirations of the entire community?
- Have recognition as a leader in his profession, community groups, or organizations?
- Have a record in public statements and past voting which indicates support for equitable and sufficient school finance, school integration, and other positions which are generally compatible with the interests of public education?
- Have sufficient residence in the community to understand its complexities and problems?
- Have a record of leadership that suggests he could represent the district as a whole rather than a particular group, cause, or area?

Understanding of the Components of Quality Education
Does the candidate:

- Have a strong commitment to the need for public education in a democratic society?
- Understand the cross currents of thinking about basic concepts of public education?
- Value the knowledge and opinions of specialists in helping to form his judgments?
- Have knowledge of what constitutes standards of employment and working conditions necessary to promote the highest quality education?
- Have an interest in seeking, listening to, and responding to staff opinion on educational issues?
- Recognize the relationship of physical facilities to the effectiveness of the educative process?

. . .

SUPERINTENDENT EVALUATION

I preferred my evaluation by the board of education and the immediate administrative staff to be two dimensional. The first dimension was a Delphi evaluation addressing the phrases "I like" and "I wish you would." As part of the priority system of the Delphi process, the board or staff would identify five items from the "I like" and "I wish you would" evaluations. The top five "I wish you would" items were translated into performance objectives. I was then evaluated on the accomplishment of these objectives. Many times they were the same objectives that had been established for the school district.

The second dimension of the superintendent's evaluation was a traditional rating form which identified the areas that were part of my responsibilities. The board rated each area using a five point scale. Each board member did the rating separately; the results were compiled and shared with me by the board president.

I found through the years that the two-dimensional approach of the Delphi and the standard rating form was a thorough and helpful evaluation procedure. Use of this method assured the school board that I was serving the school system in an effective way, and assured me that I was performing in a manner that not only satisfied me, but the board as well.

DISTRICT OFFICE ADMINISTRATOR AND PRINCIPAL EVALUATION

For the evaluation of district office administrators I preferred to use the following format: "I commend you for the following things" and "I recommend you improve the following things." As part of the reciprocal system, the principals also evaluated the district office administrators; they used the Delphi method and the "I like," "I wish you would" phrases.

Because the directors of schools were on three-year rotating terms, the principals also determined whether the position and the person would continue and, if so, how long the new term would be. An example of that evaluation form for the director of secondary schools by the high school principals follows.

SAMPLE DISTRICT OFFICE ADMINISTRATOR EVALUATION

EVALUATION—DIRECTOR OF SECONDARY SCHOOLS
By High School Principals (N-9)

Date_____

SA - Strongly agree
A - Agree
N - No Opinion
D - Disagree
SD - Strongly Disagree

* Did not reach 80 percent significance level of agreement

1.0 I LIKE	SA	A	N	D	SD
1.1 The effectiveness and vigor with which the high schools are represented.	5	4			
1.2 Your aggressive persual of problems.	4	4	1		
1.3 Your assertiveness.	3	5			1
1.4 Your credibility.	1	6	3		
1.5 Your grasp of problems.	4	5			
1.6 Your follow-through.	4	3		2	

1.0 I LIKE	SA	A	N	D	SD
1.7 The support that is forthcoming when it is needed.	4	5			
1.8 The response I get from your office when I have a problem.	3	5		1	
1.9 The way things are now; don't change it.	*2	4	1	2	
1.10 The fact that you are a principal and understand our problems.	6	3			
1.11 The job you are doing and the work you do on behalf of the secondary level.	4	5			
1.12 Your efforts to reduce red tape, to make the system more responsive to the needs of the school; i.e., purchasing, maintenance.	4	5			
1.13 Experienced representation by a high school principal at the district office.	6	3			
1.14 The position of director of secondary education, and it should be continued because of direct communications.	4	5			
1.15 The fact that we as a group are better organized.	3	4	1	1	

2.0 I WISH YOU WOULD

	SA	A	N	D	SD
2.1 Have more authority in cabinet where recommendations to the board are finalized.	4	4		1	
2.2 Have more power in the superintendent's cabinet.	*3	3	1	2	
2.3 Be more available.	*3	2	3	1	
2.4 Respond to my contacts regarding decisions affecting my school.	*2	1	1	3	2
2.5 Stay on the agenda; we tend to stray too much.	*1	3	1	4	
2.6 Proceed at a slower rate—at our meetings and for your own welfare.	*1	2	3	3	
2.7 Rotate the principal/director every three years.	*1	4		4	
2.8 Have more authority with maintenance, gardening and business services.	3	4	1	1	
2.9 Show more progress in prompt budget reporting.	6	3			

1.0 I LIKE	SA A N D SD

2.10 Achieve some progress with problems in the
business department. I recognize that you
may be unable to.   5   2   1   1

	Yes	No
Shall the position be continued?	9	
Shall the person be continued in the position?	9	
For one more year	4	
For two more years	4	
For three more years	1	

. . .

On the basis of this evaluation, the person will continue as director
of secondary education for two more years, at which time the secondary principals will be asked once again to evaluate the future of the
position.

SAMPLE SCHOOL ADMINISTRATOR EVALUATION

One of the better formats I have used for the evaluation of administrators is called "Competencies of the School Administrator" which I
discovered in a Phi Delta Kappa publication some years ago. The
format lists six domains of competencies attributed to excellent
administrators.

COMPETENCIES OF THE SCHOOL ADMINISTRATOR

Domain 1. Initiating and Responding to Change: Developing one's
own framework for initiating and
receiving proposals for change.

1 Needs Improvement
2 Some Progess
3 Acceptable
4 Above Average
5 Outstanding

	1	2	3	4	5
1.1 Demonstrates personal commitment to the education of all students in the schools.				x	
1.2 Supports the individual's need for personal development, for positive self-identification, for pride in ethnic back-ground, and for respect of life-styles of other cultural groups.			x		
1.3 Respects the legitimacy of concern shown by parents and community regarding policies and operation of the schools.				x	
1.4 Recognizes that interaction with the informal organization within a school is essential to the functioning and administration of the school.					x
1.5 Recognizes the power of primary groups of the informal organization and interacts with them accordingly.				x	
1.6 Demonstrates a suitably "open mind," able to review new ideas and information without threat of discomfort and to deal with them with relative objectivity.					x
1.7 Designs strategies for initiating and managing proposals at an action level.			x		
1.8 Monitors and supports processes and outcomes.				x	

Domain 2. Decision Making

	1	2	3	4	5
2.1 Recognizes when a problem exists and is able to identify it correctly.				x	
2.2 Clarifies problems through acquisition of relevant information.					x
2.3 Determines what is fact and what is opinion.					x
2.4 Assigns priorities to completion of problem-solving tasks.					x
2.5 Seeks, identifies, and evaluates alternate solutions.				x	

	1	2	3	4	5
2.6 Understands types of decisions which can be made—terminal, interim, conditional—and the likely consequences of making each type of decision.			x		
2.7 Seeks more information when necessary to solve a problem.				x	
2.8 Understands legal, economic, socio-cultural,and policy limitations in the decision-making process.		x			
2.9 Distinguishes between decisions that are and those that are not one's direct responsibility in reference to both superior and subordinate personnel.			x		
2.10 Establishes procedures for decision making in which community representatives, faculty, and students are active participants.			x		
2.11 Involves those persons who will implement the results of a decision in the making of that decision.			x		
2.12 Clarifies the commitments resulting from a decision to those who will carry it out and to those it will affect.		x			

Domain 3. Support for Instruction and Learning

	1	2	3	4	5
3.1 Distinguishes between fundamental and school instructional problems and symptoms of instructional problems.		x			
3.2 Assures the continuing development of a curriculum design in each area of study.				x	
3.3 Establishes and maintains unbiased schoolwide commitment to the academic achievement of all students.				x	
3.4 Develops a student-centered program of instruction.				x	
3.5 Shares with staff learning theories which are pertinent to classroom instruction.		x			
3.6 Executes a plan for developing understandings in the community of the instructional program in the school.	x				

	1	2	3	4	5

3.7 Develops a uniform system of
evaluation of faculty performance which is
clearly understood by those evaluated and
those to whom evaluation reports are sent. — col 4: x

3.8 Assists teachers to gain insight into
the learning styles of students. — col 2: x

3.9 Develops methods of helping teachers
gain insights into their own teaching styles. — col 2: x

3.10 Executes a plan for examining classroom dynamics by teachers. — col 4: x

3.11 Assists teachers in encouraging
divergent and convergent thinking in the
classroom. — col 5: x

3.12 Utilizes faculty members with unique
competencies in a manner designed to
achieve "multiplier effects." — col 4: x

3.13 Utilizes neighborhood, citywide, and
statewide resources in the execution of the
instructional program. — col 5: x

3.14 Maintains a relationship between
current school programs for students and
later vocational achievement. — col 5: x

3.15 Promotes student growth in aesthetic
sensitivity and in constructive use of leisure
time. — col 5: x

Domain 4. Human Relations and Morale

4.1 Initiates structure—delineates the
relationship between oneself and the
members of one's work groups and
establishes well-defined patterns of
organization, channels of communication,
and methods of procedure. — col 4: x

4.2 Demonstrates consideration through
behavior indicative of friendship, mutual
trust, respect, and warmth in relationships
between oneself and members of one's staff. — col 5: x

	1	2	3	4	5
4.3 Demonstrates a range of techniques to involve the staff in the effective formation of policy decisions which the staff will have to implement.					x
4.4 Shows support for the abilities of staff to teach and of the students to learn.					x
4.5 Communicates to parents information concerning major changes in school policy, curriculum, or teaching practices.				x	

Domain 5. Evaluating School Processes and Products

	1	2	3	4	5
5.1 Constructs and implements an evaluation design which systematically relates intention, observations, standards, and judgments.			x		
5.2 Executes an evaluation plan which stimulates rather than inhibits the personal and professional growth of individuals in the school organization (students, faculty, parents, community members).				x	
5.3 Relates evaluation to ongoing decisions and actions of the organization and its environment.			x		

Domain 6. Responding to Problem Situations

	1	2	3	4	5
6.1 Demonstrates sensitivity to role-identifications of co-workers.					x
6.2 Acts to reduce problems resulting from role-conflict and role-ambiguity.				x	
6.3 Recognizes the varying roles of individuals within a working group and thereby facilitates group process.				x	
6.4 Understands the dimensions of organizational climate and the role and function in establishing or changing the climate in a school.				x	
6.5 Recognizes that conflict can lead to beneficial change and therefore "manages" conflict toward positive resolution.			x		

	1	2	3	4	5
6.6 Plans and introduces range of structures, techniques, and processes for effective conflict management, focusing on efforts to keep the energies of group members directed toward goals consonant with those of the organization.			x		
6.7 Makes use of change agents from outside the schools to create a temporary social system within the school for the express purpose of facilitating change.			x		
6.8 Delegates responsibility for problems to appropriate subordinate levels when problems can be treated effectively at those levels.			x		

Evaluator's Comments:

Signature_____Date_____
Evaluatee's Comments:

Signature_____Date_____

. . .

SAMPLE SCHOOL PRINCIPAL EVALUATION

In this same large school district, the district office administrators and the school principals spent a year developing an evaluation form for school site principals. We identified nine different areas of responsibility—including fiscal, legal, and contribution to the district beyond usual job related assignments—for evaluation. According to his area of responsibility, each of the three assistant superintendents evaluated every principal.

Items identified were the specific job responsibilities, and whether the principal met expectations, needed improvement, or did not meet minimum requirements. Room at the bottom of the sheet was available for commendations and recommendations. This format was well received by the principals and district office administrators alike. A sample of this evaluation follows.

SAMPLE DISTRICT OFFICE EVALUATION OF PRINCIPALS

EVALUATION RATINGS FOR SCHOOL SITE PRINCIPALS
*3 Meets Expectations   *2 Needs Improvement
*1 Does Not Meet Minimum Requirements

FINAL AUTHORITY

Educ. Serv.	Pers. Serv.	Bus. Serv.	SPECIFIC RESPONSIBILITY	*3	*2	*1
			1.0 Fiscal and Legal Management			
		x	1.1 Develop an annual budget for the school.	x		
		x	1.2 Maintain accurate fiscal school records of public and private funds.			x
x	x	x	1.3 Punctually compile and submit accurate reports as required by district, state, and federal.		x	
x	x		1.4 Maintain accurate pupil records and punctually submit records to the district for transferred pupils.			(etc.)
x	x	x	1.5 Administer the rules and regulations of the district administration, policies of the board of education,and provisions of the Education Code and related codes.			

Commendations:

Recommendations:

Educ. Serv.	Pers. Serv.	Bus. Serv.	SPECIFIC RESPONSIBILITY	*3	*2	*1
			2.0 Plant and Property Management			
x	x	x	2.1 Maintain a clean and safe physical plant and environment.			
x		x	2.2 Maintain a current and accurate inventory of equipment for the school.			
x			2.3 Maintain a current and accurate inventory of library books.			

FINAL AUTHORITY						
Educ. Serv.	Pers. Serv.	Bus. Serv.	SPECIFIC RESPONSIBILITY	*3	*2	*1
x	x	x	2.4 Allocate facilities in accordance with "Policies and Procedures for Planning the Long-Range Utilization of Facilities."			
x	x	x	2.5 Plan for emergency operations.			

Commendations:

Recommendations:

			3.0 Personnel Administration			
	x		3.1 Evaluate and monitor performance of personnel assigned to the school according to district guidelines.			
	x		3.2 Make recommendations regarding the selection, retention, and promotion of personnel assigned to the school.			
x	x	x	3.3 Make work assignments for available personnel based upon program needs and staff strengths.			
x	x	x	3.4 Assign staff members to appropriate (adjunct) duty responsibilities.			
	x		3.5 Administer all school-site related aspects of negotiated employee contracts.			
x	x		3.6 Develop and implement procedures for consistent management of the school program when absent from the site.			
x	x	x	3.7 Develop and implement procedures for responding to identified problems pertaining to staff relations.			

Commendations:

Recommendations:

4.0   Program Effectiveness Management

x		4.1 Assume leadership in developing and/or adopting changes in practices as needed to respond to special needs of the school.
x		4.2 Assume leadership in developing and periodically revising and publishing a clear statement of goals for the school through the cooperative efforts of community and site personnel.
x		4.3 Develop short- and long-term plans for program maintenance and improvement based upon a comprehensive needs assessment designed to respond to measured needs of students (standardized tests, proficiencies, etc.).
x	x	4.4 Develop and implement a plan for staff development for site personnel based upon a comprehensive needs assessment designed to assist specific and general staff.
x		4.5 Develop instructional programs which are consistent with district guidelines and which are consistent with other instructional levels.
x	x	4.6 Organize and administer district and state mandated student testing and assessment programs in a manner consistent with district policies and test security.

Commendations:

Recommendations:

		5.0 Community and Parent Relations Management
x		5.1 Develop and implement procedures for frequent, positive interactions between staff members and parents.
x	x	5.2 Develop and implement procedures for ongoing, periodic contacts with appropriate agencies and organizations in the community.
x		5.3 Routinely and systematically inform community and parents of school goals, programs and activities.
x	x	5.4 Routinely assess community school climate perceptions and develop appropriate responses to the findings.

Commendations:

Recommendations:

		6.0 Student Management
x		6.1 Develop and sustain student activities, organizations and programs in keeping with assessed needs and interests of student population.
x		6.2 Develop and implement systems for routinely soliciting and considering student input into the conduct of the school.
x	x	6.3 Promote maximum pupil attendance and maintain accurate records as required by the district and the state.
x		6.4 Develop and implement procedures for supervision of student conduct on the campus, playground, in buses, and during activities before, during, and after school hours.

Commendations:

Recommendations:

7.0   Resource Management

---

x   x   x   7.1 Effectively use the services of
available district personnel in
curriculum and program development,
pupil services, special education
services, research, fiscal accountability,
facilities, utilization and maintenance,
public information, and allied
management functions for solving
identified problems in the school.

x   x   7.2 Explore and appropriately use
outside of district funding and service
resources to solve identified problems
in the school as needed.

Commendations:

Recommendations:

8.0   Professional Development

---

x   x   8.1 Annually show evidence of
participation in professional
development.

Commendations:

Recommendations:

9.0   Contribution to the District
Beyond Usual Job-related Assignments

---

x   x   x   9.1 Provide to the district services on
committees, staff development services,
and allied assistance beyond school site
management responsibilities.

Commendations:

Recommendations:

. . .

SAMPLE FACULTY EVALUATION OF PRINCIPAL

Through the years, I have strongly encouraged principals to have their staffs evaluate them. Therefore, I could not end this section on evaluation of principals without sharing a format for the faculty evaluation of principals.

MD UNIFIED SCHOOL DISTRICT

SURVEY FORM FOR FACULTY EVALUATION OF PRINCIPALS

The procedures for the evaluation of principals require that each faculty member have an opportunity to participate in the evaluation. You are, therefore, asked to complete the following form. You should bear in mind that, in accordance with the basic philosophy of the total evaluation procedure adopted by the board of education, your responses should reflect your evaluation within the context of the school program.

Please check the response which most closely reflects your point of view. Space is provided for any explanatory or modifying comments you may wish to make.

All survey forms are returned to principals. Principals are encouraged to share the outcomes at a faculty meeting subsequent to the evaluation.

1. Instructional Program and Related Areas.
    a. Is curriculum leadership in your school both adequate and effective?
        Yes_____ No_____ Usually_____
    b. Are you and other teachers involved in making curriculum decisions at your school?
        Yes_____ No_____ Usually_____
    c. Are curriculum innovations encouraged in your school?
        Yes_____ No_____ Usually_____
    d. Do you receive necessary help in evaluating and improving your individual program?
        Yes_____ No_____ Usually_____
    e. Are you aware of district policies as related to curriculum and instruction?
        Yes_____ No_____ Usually_____

2. Program Management
   a. In your school, is there a commitment to upgrading staff
      competency through providing for inservice education?
      Yes_____ No_____ Usually_____
   b. Are you reinforced in your responsibility for discipline?
      Yes_____ No_____ Usually_____
   c. Is staff involved in establishing budget priorities within the
      limits of available funds?
      Yes_____ No_____ Usually_____

3. In what ways do you feel the administration in your school has
   made contributions to the school, the community, and/or the
   profession?

                          Signature (optional)_____
                                · · ·

TEACHER EVALUATION

Accountability in education requires, not only the evaluation of
administrators, but also of teachers. In November 1981, Education
Week reported that an estimated 98 percent of the country's school
systems have policies requiring the evaluation of teachers and administrators, but are inadequate in implementing those policies. It was
reported that the litigation in the area of personnel evaluation is
rapidly growing.

When adverse employment decisions have to be made concerning
dismissal, demotion, salary, assignment, or tenure, school boards
have often had only inadequate evaluations; if the matter goes to
court the evidence presented to the judges is lacking.

A written district policy on employee evaluation concerning a
potential adverse employment decision for an administrator or
teacher should be adopted by the school board. The policy should
delineate specific standards of performance for the evaluation, and
should require multiple observations and observations by more than
one person.

I include such information at this point because I do not want the
reader to think that the personnel evaluation procedures which I am
suggesting are sufficient in the case of dismissal. I am not discussing
the standard evaluation formats for teachers; my approach uses the
evaluation procedure to motivate personnel.

SAMPLE PRE-OBSERVATION QUESTIONS

The following format has pre-observation questions for the observation of the teacher by the principal. The teacher is asked to complete information and return it to the principal a day before the date of observation, answering such questions as: Where are you in the course? What is the objective? How are you going to teach it? Are there particular areas of learning theory that you especially want monitored? How are you going to know if the students have learned?

PRE-OBSERVATION QUESTIONS FOR_____

CLASS_____PERIOD_____DATE_____

Please complete the following information and return to the observer one day before the scheduled date of the observation.

OBSERVER_____

1. Where are you in the course?
   (unit, lesson, page numbers in texts, etc.)
2. What is the objective?
3. How are you going to teach to it? (methods)
4. Are there particular areas of learning theory that you especially want monitored?
5. How are you going to know if the students have learned?
6. Are there special characteristics of the students that should be noted?
7. List teacher constraints that may be helpful to the observer.

. . .

SAMPLE PRINCIPAL EVALUATION OF TEACHER

The following guide, "The Classroom Observation Guide," is also helpful for the principal to use in observing classroom performance by the teacher.

Classroom Observation Guide

1. Did the teacher "set" the students for the lesson objective?
2. Did the students appear to be correctly diagnosed?
3. Were students motivated before and/or during the lesson?
   - Concern
   - Interest
   - Success
   - Knowledge of results

- Intrinsic
- Extrinsic
4. Were directions clearly given?
5. Were students attending to the learning?
6. Was there active participation of the learner?
7. Was reinforcement appropriately used?
   - Positive
   - Negative
   - Extinguish behavior—withhold all reinforcement
   - Desired behavior stated
8. Were techniques for retention used?
   - Meaning for the learner
   - Degree of original learning
   - Feeling tone
   - Transfer
   - Practice
9. Were provisions made for evaluating the students in relation to objective?
   - Short term
   - Long term
10. Was the objective achieved?
11. Were provisions made for reteaching or extension?
12. Were students held accountable for their learning?

. . .

TWO SAMPLE STUDENT EVALUATIONS OF TEACHERS

As a part of the reciprocal evaluation system, I suggest the following two teacher evaluation formats which students complete.

VALLEY HIGH SCHOOL

TEACHER EVALUATION QUESTIONNAIRE

1. I attend school because:
   a. I have to.
   b. I enjoy the social life.
   c. There is nothing else to do.
   d. I value an education.
2. After high school I plan to:
   a. Go to a university.
   b. To to a junior college.
   c. Go into an occupation.
   d. Undecided.

Mark yes or no

3. I took this class because it was easy.
4. I have tried to do whatever I could to help make this class a success.
5. I am filling out this questionnaire honestly and seriously.
6. Do you feel you are being taught things that will help you when you are out of school?
7. Is this class being taken only because it is required to graduate?
8. I am taking this class only to fulfill college requirements.
9. The objectives of this class were stated clearly.
10. The objectives of this class were reached.
11. I am taking this class because it was the only class available this period.
12. I think the outline of this course is interesting.
13. The information studied in this course is worth my time.
14. I feel that the course has taught me what I want and need to know in this subject area.
15. I think most of what we did was important, and not busy work.
16. I think the right amount of homework was given.
17. Because many teaching methods were used, the class was more interesting.
18. I value the homework that applies to this class.
19. This teacher knows the subject well.
20. I feel that the teacher likes the subject he teaches.
21. The teacher creates an atmosphere in which you can learn.
22. I think the teacher is lazy and does not like to work.
23. This teacher has a command of the class.
24. I feel that the teacher cares whether or not we learn what is being taught.
25. I respect this teacher.
26. I feel that the teacher treats each of us fairly, and does not play favorites.
27. I could get a good grade from this teacher by kissing up to him.
28. The teacher communicates on a one-to-one level with students.

. . .

SAMPLE EVALUATION FORM FOR STUDENT USE

Listed below are the most common areas in the evaluation of a teacher. It would be appreciated if you would evaluate this instructor on each of these areas by circling an appropriate letter and offering comments.

1. Knowledge of Subject   A B C D F
   (Knowledge of the subject, the degree of
   knowledge,etc.)
   Comments:

2. Method of Teaching   A B C D F
   (Clear and understandable instruction, organized and well-prepared lessons, student work
   evaluated and returned, etc.)
   Comments:

3. Classroom Control   A B C D F
   (Favorable atmosphere for learning, orderly
   class, etc.)
   Comments:

4. Personal Qualities   A B C D F
   (Neat, clean, well-groomed, pleasant, respect for
   students, considerate, speaks distinctly, etc.)
   Comments:

Overall Evaluation   A B C D F
   (Summary of 1 through 4 above)
   Comments:

To what extent do you feel you learned this semester:
          Very Little   Fair Amount   Much
   Comments:

What would you suggest to improve the course or the instructor's
performance?
   Comments:

. . .

I am closing this section on teacher evaluation with a poem by an
anonymous author.

NOTES ON A REMEMBERED TEACHER

SHE WAS A GOOD TEACHER BECAUSE:

On the first day of school she knew I was there—in that class of 40.

She did not replace anyone in my life; she found her own place.

What she did was not always as important as what she was.

She gave, and from the giving—grew.

She knew that she had not done it all—even when I told her otherwise.

She knew that if I moved ahead, she had to go first.

She sought with, found with, reconstructed with, confirmed for, and approved of—me!

She loved learning, and we both got excited about it.

She was hungry—not for food—watching, listening, doing, I got hungry too.

She convinced me that I could—in spite of myself—make it.

When a well-dressed gentleman from the county office visited us and stared at my bare feet, bib-overalls, and collar-length hair, she quickly pointed out to him that she was very proud of my work—and me.

When she said something, I could count on it.

She showed me a new world, pointed out the door, and gave me a key.

Though I had three teachers that year, she is the only one I remember.

Even now, so many years since I saw her, she is still making me think, and surely, that IS good teaching!

. . .

VARIABLES IN EVALUATION INSTRUMENTS AND PROCESSES

You can use the following checklist as a guideline to review the performance evaluation process you are currently using. This checklist will identify specific data to consider in deciding whether your present process is adequate.

- Information quantity: Does the process provide ample information?
- Information quality: Does the process provide information that is general in nature or highly specific?
- Format: Is the format of the process simple or complex?

- Information type: Is the information provided quantitative in nature or verbal?
- Applicability to job: Is the process directly or indirectly applicable to your job? Does it provide information on something you specifically do or only something that is inferred in what you do?
- Single or multiple measures: Does the process provide a single summary measure of overall performance or does it provide multiple measures?
- Information variety: Is all of the data provided by the process of a single type (e.g., checklist) or is information of several types provided (e.g., checklist, forced choice, quantitative scale, etc.)?
- Estimated cost of the process.
- Estimated time required for process.

. . .

Chapter 7
Program Evaluation

The consumers of an educational program—the parents and the students—have a right to know, and to help evaluate, the quality of the product they receive. I think educators should conduct market analysis and product testing to determine parent satisfaction. Throughout the years I have done just that by involving students and parents in program evaluation. A consumer will not pay for a television unless it works; a parent will not pay for an educational program unless his child achieves.

FIVE INDICATORS OF PROGRAM ACHIEVEMENT

LEARNING ACHIEVEMENT

The evaluation program I conducted in two school districts had five indicators of program success. The first indicator was learning achievement. California has a mandated testing program, and also requires proficiency testing by the local school district. In addition, we gave schools the option of supplementing evaluation of achievement with pre-post Comprehensive Test of Basic Skills and criterion reference tests.

The state testing results indicated program success. In our large district of 50,000 students, we raised percentile rankings in reading, writing, and math over a four year period.

		1975-76	1979-80
Grade 3	Reading	77	83
Grade 6	Reading	72	79
	Writing	74	77
	Math	76	80
Grade 12	Reading	76	80
	Writing	72	78
	Math	85	87

Five elementary schools were involved in an instructional improvement project. During the first two years of that project, they raised the reading scores in the state testing program as much as 43 percentile points. The following chart shows the project schools and comparable control schools.

STUDENT GROWTH

(Amount of percentile gain in two years in the
California Achievement Program in reading.)

PROJECT	SCHOOL	CONTROL	SCHOOL
A	37	A	3
B	43	B	5
C	10	C	5
D	20	D	4
E	24	E	2

LEARNING CLIMATE

The second indicator was learning climate as measured by a climate profile, an assessment instrument that is discussed in Chapter 9. We felt that a high satisfaction level among the students, staff, and parents was important because it results in high productivity. Therefore, we expended maximum effort to improve learning climate as well as achievement scores.

VANDALISM

The third indicator was vandalism. Most of the vandalism was done by off-campus people. However, we were providing community schools which made the school the center of the neighborhood community, and incidents of vandalism indicated attitudes toward the local school by people living in the area.

ABSENTEEISM OF STUDENTS AND OF STAFF

The fourth and fifth indicators were absenteeism of students and of staff. Absenteeism indicates attitude, satisfaction level, and stress among students and staff. Absenteeism was also evaluated from an economic point of view, because substitute teachers cost money, and absent students cause schools to lose money.

GENERAL GUIDELINES

The Individual School Management System that I used in two school districts over a 12-year period emphasized a thorough but simple evaluation program. Each school submitted a summary chart covering six items.

- Type of decision-making system present at each school.
- Effectiveness of the site council.
- Analysis of academic test data and development of a improvement plan.
- Analysis of learning climate surveys for parents, staff, and students, and development of an improvement plan.
- Input for inservice program—proposals for in-service programs were based on test data, climate, and staff development surveys.
- Communication plan for parents and staff.

SAMPLE PROGRAM EVALUATION FORMATS

PRE AND POST DATA FORM FOR STAFF DEVELOPMENT FUNDS

What follows is a form that we used to report pre and post data in several areas—academic achievement, learning climate, and staff participation in our development programs.

EVALUATION REPORT

K 1 2 3 4 5 6 7 8 9 10 11 12
Grade Levels Served

SCHOOL _____

PRINCIPAL _____

STUDENT ACHIEVEMENT DATA

Instruments Used	Grade	First Year	Current year
CAP	____	_____	_____
PROFICIENCY TEST	____	_____	_____
CTBS	____	_____	_____
_____	____	_____	_____

Other

SCHOOL/COMMUNITY CLIMATE

Climate Survey Instrument
Students (5-12 every 4th
student)   _____   _____
Parents (every 4th parent)   _____   _____
All Teachers   _____   _____
All Classified Personnel   _____   _____
All Management   _____   _____
All Site Council Members   _____   _____
_____   _____   _____

Other climate instruments

STAFF DEVELOPMENT

Name of Projects

Teachers   _____
Classified Personnel   _____
Management   _____

THREE FORMS FOR STUDENT EVALUATION OF PROGRAMS

The first example below is a student questionnaire that was used throughout the school district to get a general idea of how we were doing according to the students.

STUDENT QUESTIONNAIRE

School Name_____

Check the answer of your choice.
1. Do you enjoy attending school? Yes ___ Sometimes ___ No ___
2. Do you feel that the adults at
   your school are friendly?   Yes ___ Usually _____ No ___
3. Do you feel that the students at
   your school are friendly?   Yes ___ Most of
                                           them _____ No ___

4. Do you feel that the adults at
   your school have a personal
   interest in you?   Yes ___ Most of
                                           them _____ No ___

5. Do you feel that the staff
   members at your school trust
   the students?   Yes ___ Most of
                                           them _____ No ___

6. Do you think discipline
   problems are handled fairly?   Yes ___ Usually _____ No ___
7. Do you feel you have oppor-
   tunities to be of value to your
   school?   Yes ___ Sometimes ___ No ___
8. Do you feel that the needs and
   ideas of students are considered
   at your school?   Yes ___ Sometimes ___ No ___
9. Do you feel you have oppor-
   tunities to take part in extracurricular activities (clubs,
   athletics, drama, etc.)?   Yes ___ No _____
10. Does your program offer things
    that interest you and/or meet
    your needs?   Yes ___ Sometimes ___ No ___
11. Do you feel that the courses
    you are taking are worthwhile? Yes ___ Some of
                                           them _____ No ___

12. Do you feel that your school
    has helped you to discover the
    things which you are good at
    doing?   Yes __ No _____
13. Do you feel that you can get
    extra help when you ask for it?   Yes __ Usually _____ No __
14. Do you feel that you have been
    taught good study habits?   Yes __ No _____
15. Do you think that the students
    at your school are learning to
    be responsible for their own
    behavior and citizenship?   Yes __ No _____
16. Are students at your school
    given opportunities to make
    decisions and to help plan what
    they do in classes?   Yes __ Sometimes ____ No __
17. Do you think that the student
    government gets worthwhile
    things done?   Yes __ Sometimes ____ No __
18. Do you use the school library?   Yes __ Sometimes ____ No __

High School Students Only:

19. In general, do you feel that you are being adequately
    prepared for whatever you plan to do beyond high
    school?
                      Yes___ No___
20. Please comment on any things you particularly like
    about your school. Do not mention any specific
    names of people.

    _____
    _____
    _____

21. Please comment on any ways in which you think your
    school could be improved. Do not mention any spe-
    cific names of people.

    _____
    _____
    _____

22. Please make any additional comments you wish about your school. Do not mention any specific names of people.

_____

_____

_____

. . .

The second example was an attempt to find out how the Student Advisory Committee perceived good and bad classes.

At the last meeting of the Student Advisory Committee the members were asked to list on one 3x5 card the things they thought make a class a good one and on a second card those things that made a class a bad one. The results are recorded in the following two lists.

IN GOOD CLASSES

- You know what is expected of you.
- Teachers give you an outline or an idea of what you will learn.
- Students will work together to learn something.
- What you learn has something to do with real life.
- The teacher will be honestly interested in what he is teaching.
- The teacher uses a variety of techniques.
- There will be relevant speakers.
- Discussions will be open.
- The material will be challenging.
- There will be structure.
- The teacher will be in control and will respect the students.
- Assignments will be meaningful.
- The class will go fast.
- You feel comfortable.
- There is good interaction among students.
- There will be some individualization.
- You will accomplish a lot in class and not have an abundance of homework.
- The teacher will know the subject and know what's going on.
- The teacher will have a sense of humor.

IN BAD CLASSES

- Teachers don't follow their outlines.
- Immature students wise off and get away with it.
- Rowdy students get away with it.
- Students are allowed to laze around and no work gets done.
- There is too much busy work.
- A teacher will get off the subject, waste time, and then pile on the homework because "we didn't accomplish anything today."
- You will be told what to study for a test and then be asked questions in another area.
- Teachers (and students) don't come prepared.
- You stay on the same subject until it is driven into the ground.
- Things get monotonous with no variation in routine.
- You will see films that have nothing to do with what you are studying.
- The teacher may try to be one of the kids, but can't do it.
- The teacher lets you know he's not interested in what he's teaching.
- Teachers act like they're always right and put students down who disagree with them.
- The teacher will be too tight or too loose.
- There will be a lot of students who don't want to be there.
- There will be "nothing to do" periods.
- There will be surprise quizzes.

. . .

The third example was a follow-up survey of high school graduates to ascertain the level of satisfaction after graduation.

HIGH SCHOOL SENIOR SURVEY

As a former student of_____High School, will you please evaluate your experience while at _____High School — particularly in light of your present experiences and thinking so that we can use your opinions in developing better programs and experiences for our future students. Your response is important to us, and we certainly appreciate your cooperation in this matter.

2. SEX: F___ M___
3. Most of my courses were:
    (___) A. College prep. B. Comprehensive C. Vocational
4. How well did this high school prepare you for what you are now doing?
    (___) A. Very well B. Adequately C. About average D. Poorly

Departmental impact: In the first column please evaluate the impact each department had upon your plans for the future and upon your thinking about life in general.

In the second column please evaluate the effectiveness of each department in terms of teaching its particular subject. Use the coded letters below for the evaluation:
    A. Very positive
    B. Generally positive
    C. Did not make a significant impact upon me either way
    D. Negative experiences generally
    E. Does not apply—did not take any courses in that department

DEPARTMENT	IMPACT	EFFECTIVENESS
5. Art	(___)	17. (___)
6. Business Education	(___)	18. (___)
7. Drama	(___)	19. (___)
8. English	(___)	20. (___)
9. Foreigh Language	(___)	21. (___)
10. Home Economics	(___)	22. (___)
11. Industrial Arts	(___)	23. (___)
12. Mathematics	(___)	24. (___)
13. Music	(___)	25 (___)
14. Physical Education	(___)	26. (___)
15. Science	(___)	27. (___)
16. Social Studies	(___)	28. (___)

Counseling and Guidance Services: Please confine your evaluation of the following services to the guidance and counseling department when using the scale below:
    A. Very effective—very helpful
    B. Effective—some help
    C. No impact either way
    D. Negative experience for me
    E. Service was not provided

SERVICE   RATING
29. Interests—Understanding my own interests
    through testing and/or information.   (___)
30. Aptitudes and abilities—Understanding my own
    aptitudes and abilities through testing and/or
    information services.   (___)
31. Careers, professions, and vocations—
    Understanding career opportunities and their
    implications related to me.   (___)
32. Future education or training: Understanding
    schools or training programs which were most
    appropriate for me.   (___)
33. Increased self-confidence through counseling or
    guidance services.   (___)
34. Independence training—increased ability to make
    my own decisions through counseling and gui-
    dance services.   (___)
35. General assistance in getting what I needed in high
    school.   (___)

Additional comments—specifically about counseling, discipline, and
guidance services.

General School Environment: Listed below are selected influences
which the school may have had upon you. Please indicate the most
appropriate source of influence.
    A. Specific teachers
    B. Classroom related activities
    C. Counseling and guidance services
    D. Athletics, clubs or student government, etc.
    E. Did not occur—this influence was missing
36. I received leadership training.   (___)
37. Critical thinking—I learned processes by which to
    evaluate important issues—to think and to use
    reason.   (___)
38. I felt that somebody took a personal interest in me.   (___)
39. My self-confidence improved as a result of my
    experience at high school.   (___)
40. Talent, aptitudes, abilities—I was able to develop
    and/or use my special abilities at high school.   (___)
41. My parents received adequate information about
    my abilities, weaknesses, and my potential goals.   (___)

42. I was helped in appreciating art, music and other
    artistic work.   (___)
43. I was helped in improving my sense of responsi-
    bility.   (___)
44. I received help in understanding purposes in life
    for myself.   (___)
45. I received understanding of the ways I might serve
    others.   (___)
46. I increased my desire to learn.   (___)

Please offer any other comments about the school environment
(either positive or negative).

In your opinion did the school in general place excessive emphasis
upon a specific group of student abilities or characteristics? Please
specify (i.e. intellectual pursuits, athletics, discipline, etc.).

Did you participate in the programs for the gifted and talented?
47. (___) A. Frequently B. Moderately C. Rarely D. Never

Please check those programs (advanced) in which you participated.
___ 1. Field trips to musical events, dance, plays, museums.
___ 2. Foreign language field trips.
___ 3. Special presentations at school by musicians, poets, etc.
___ 4. Special mathematics projects and competitions.
___ 5. Individual projects.
___ 6. Advanced classes (foreign language, math, science).
___ 7. Guidance and counseling (College tours, special counseling).

. . .

PARENT SURVEY

Parent surveys were important to us though the years and took on
various forms. Two of those forms follow below.

UNIFIED SCHOOL DISTRICT
ADMINISTRATION BUILDING
1976 Carl Drive
Grape, California 94030
694-2111

February 6, 1983
Dear Parent:
Your school is one of several in our district participating in a project
involving the evaluation of the educational program. In order to

broaden the base of evaluation, selected parents of students within the school are being requested to complete the following questionnaire and return it in the self-addressed envelope.

Your responses along with those of the professional staff of the school will be used to assess the strengths and weaknesses of the school program. All questionnaires will be returned to the school after being tallied and summarized.

We would appreciate receiving your completed questionnaire by February 20, 1983.

Thank you,

George Lopez
Director of Secondary Education

PARENT EVALUATION OF

School Name_____

Your reactions to the questions below will assist us in the evaluation of your school. Please place an X on the scale below each question to indicate how you feel. Please return the form in the envelope provided. Thank you for your assistance.

1. Are you familiar with your student's program?   Comment:
   Yes___ For the most part___ No___
2. How well do you feel the school is preparing   Comment:
   your student for future education?
   Very well___ Satisfactory___ Fairly well___ Poorly___
3. How well do you feel the school communicates   Comment:
   to you what is happening at school?
   Very well___ Satisfactorily___ Fairly well ___ Poorly ___
4. Has the school provided opportunities for   Comment:
   parents to become involved?
   Yes___ For the most part___ No___
5. Do you feel your student's special   Comment:
   educational needs are being met?
   Yes___ For the most part___ No___
6. How would you rate your student's attitude   Comment:
   toward school?
   Likes school___ Tolerates school___ Dislikes school___

7. What kind of response do you feel you would   Comment:
   receive from the administration if you
   expressed a concern?
   Receptive, helpful___ Vague___ Unconcerned___

   Please respond to the following questions:
8. What do you consider to be the strongest aspects of your school?
9. What aspects of your school program do you consider need to be
   strengthened?
10. How many years have you resided in this attendance area?
11. Additional comments:

. . .

Another example of a survey to obtain parent opinion is given in
Chapter 17 in the discussion of local polls.

COMMUNITY GROUP EVALUATION OF PROGRAM

Occasionally, we involved other community groups in the evaluation of our schools. One particular study was conducted by the American Association of University Women. They used an individual rating
form which provided data for discussions within their association.
Either the superintendent, one of the administrators, or a teacher met
with the AAUW and joined in their school evaluation discussions.

INDIVIDUAL RATING OF THE LEVEL OF PERFORMANCE
OF CURRENT SCHOOL PROGRAMS

Listed below are the goals established for the school district at the
last meeting of AAUW members. The goals are not listed in a priority
order.

Your task is to read each of the goal statements and ask yourself:
   Community Member:
       "In my opinion how well are current programs meeting this
       goal?"
   Teachers/Students:
       "How well are my school's current programs meeting this
       goal?"
The answer to this question for each of the goals will provide the
board of trustees, administrators and teachers with the information
needed to revise existing programs and to develop new programs for
the students of the district. When the results are examined, the district
will interpret your statements in the following manner:

"Extremely Poor" means:

I believe students are not being taught the skills necessary to meet this goal. This goal is the school's responsibility but almost nothing is being done to meet this goal.

"Poor" means:

I believe programs designed to meet this goal are weak.

I believe that much more effort must be made by the school to meet this goal.

"Fair but more needs to be done" means:

I believe present programs are acceptable, but I would like to see more importance attached to this goal by the school.

I would rate the school's job in this area as only fair; more effort is needed as far as I am concerned.

"Leave as is" means:

I believe the school is doing a good job in meeting this goal.

I am satisfied with the present programs which are designed to meet this goal.

"Too much is being done" means:

I believe the school is already spending too much time in this area. I believe programs in this area are not the responsibility of the school.

For example:

If one believed that the goal "Learn How To Be A Good Citizen" is being met quite adequately, a 10, 11, or 12 would be placed in the score box.

Extremely Poor	Poor	Fair but more needs to be done	Leave as is	Too much is being done	Score
1 2 3	4 5 6	7 8 9	10 11 12	13 14 15	11

GOAL STATEMENTS:

1. Learn how to be a good citizen.
    A. Develop an awareness of civic rights and responsibilities.
    B. Develop attitudes for productive citizenship in a democracy.
    C. Develop an attitude of respect for personal and public property.
    D. Develop an understanding of the obligations and responsibilities of citizenship.

Extremely Poor			Poor			Fair but more needs to be done			Leave as is			Too much is being done			Score
1	2	3	4	5	6	7	8	9	10	11	12	13	14	15	_____

2. Learn how to respect and get along with people who think, dress, and act differently:

    A, Develop an appreciation for and an understanding of other people and other cultures.

    B. Develop an understanding of political, economic, and social patterns of the rest of the world.

    C. Develop awareness of the interdependence of races, creeds, nations, and cultures.

    D. Develop an awareness of the processes of group relationships.

Extremely Poor			Poor			Fair but more needs to be done			Leave as is			Too much is being done			Score
1	2	3	4	5	6	7	8	9	10	11	12	13	14	15	_____

3. Learn about and try to understand the changes that take place in the world.

    A. Develop ability to adjust to the changing demands of society.

    B. Develop an awareness and the ability to adjust to a changing world and its problems.

    C. Develop understanding of the past, identity with the present, and the ability to meet the future.

Extremely Poor			Poor			Fair but more needs to be done			Leave as is			Too much is being done			Score
1	2	3	4	5	6	7	8	9	10	11	12	13	14	15	_____

4. Develop skills in reading, writing, speaking, and listening.

    A. Develop ability to communicate ideas and feelings effectively.

    B. Develop skills in oral and written English.

Extremely Poor	Poor	Fair but more needs to be done	Leave as is	Too much is being done	Score
1 2 3 4 5 6		7 8 9	10 11 12	13 14 15	____

5. Understand and practice democratic ideas and ideals.
    A. Develop loyalty to American democratic ideals.
    B. Develop patriotism and loyalty to ideas of democracy.
    C. Develop knowledge and appreciation of the rights and privileges in our democracy.
    D. Develop an understanding of our American heritage.

Extremely Poor	Poor	Fair but more needs to be done	Leave as is	Too much is being done	Score
1 2 3 4 5 6		7 8 9	10 11 12	13 14 15	____

6. Learn how to examine and use information.
    A. Develop ability to examine constructively and creatively.
    B. Develop ability to use scientific methods.
    C. Develop reasoning abilities.
    D. Develop skills to think and proceed logically.

Extremely Poor	Poor	Fair but more needs to be done	Leave as is	Too much is being done	Score
1 2 3 4 5 6		7 8 9	10 11 12	13 14 15	____

7. Understand and practice the skills of family living.
    A. Develop understanding and appreciation of the principles of living in the family group.
    B. Develop attitudes leading to acceptance of responsibilities as family members.
    C. Develop an awareness of future family responsibilities and achievement of skills in preparing to accept them.

Extremely Poor		Poor	Fair but more needs to be done	Leave as is	Too much is being done	Score
1 2 3		4 5 6	7 8 9	10 11 12	13 14 15	_____

8. Learn to respect and get along with people with whom we work and live.
    A. Develop appreciation and respect for the worth and dignity of individuals.
    B. Develop respect for individual worth and understanding of minority opinions and acceptance of majority decisions.
    C. Develop a cooperative attitude toward living and working with others.

Extremely Poor	Poor	Fair but more needs to be done	Leave as is	Too much is being done	Score
1 2 3	4 5 6	7 8 9	10 11 12	13 14 15	_____

9. Develop skills to enter a specific field of work.
    A. Develop abilities and skills needed for immediate employment.
    B. Develop an awareness of opportunities and requirements related to a specific field of work.
    C. Develop an appreciation of good workmanship.

Extremely Poor	Poor	Fair but more needs to be done	Leave as is	Too much is being done	Score
1 2 3	4 5 6	7 8 9	10 11 12	13 14 15	_____

10. Learn how to be a good manager of money, property and resources.
    A. Develop an understanding of economic principles and responsibilities.
    B. Develop ability and understanding in personal buying, selling and investment.
    C. Develop skills in management of natural and human resources and man's environment.

Extremely Poor		Poor	Fair but more needs to be done		Leave as is	Too much is being done	Score
1 2 3		4 5 6	7 8 9		10 11 12	13 14 15	_____

11. Develop a desire for learning now and in the future.
    A. Develop intellectual curiosity and eagerness for life-
       long learning.
    B. Develop a positive attitude toward learning.
    C. Develop a positive attitude toward continuing inde-
       pendent education.

Extremely Poor		Poor	Fair but more needs to be done		Leave as is	Too much is being done	Score
1 2 3		4 5 6	7 8 9		10 11 12	13 14 15	_____

12. Learn how to use leisure time.
    A. Develop ability to use leisure time productively.
    B. Develop a positive attitude toward participation in a
       range of leisure time activities—physical, intellectual,
       and creative.
    C. Develop appreciation and interests which will lead to
       wise and enjoyable use of leisure time.

Extremely Poor		Poor	Fair but more needs to be done		Leave as is	Too much is being done	Score
1 2 3		4 5 6	7 8 9		10 11 12	13 14 15	_____

13. Practice and understand the ideas of health and safety.
    A. Establish an effective individual physical fitness
       program.
    B. Develop an understanding of good physical health
       and well being.
    C. Establish sound personal health habits and infor-
       mation.
    D. Develop a concern for public health and safety.

Extremely Poor			Poor			Fair but more needs to be done			Leave as is			Too much is being done			Score
1	2	3	4	5	6	7	8	9	10	11	12	13	14	15	_____

14. Appreciate culture and beauty in the world.
   A. Develop abilities for effective expression of ideas and cultural appreciation (fine arts).
   B. Cultivate appreciation for beauty in various forms.
   C. Develop creative self-expression through various media (art, music, writing, etc.).
   D. Develop special talents in music, art, literature, and foreign languages.

Extremely Poor			Poor			Fair but more needs to be done			Leave as is			Too much is being done			Score
1	2	3	4	5	6	7	8	9	10	11	12	13	14	15	_____

15. Gain information needed to make job selections.
   A. Promote self-understanding and self-direction in relation to student's occupational interests.
   B. Develop the ability to use information and counseling services related to the selection of a job.
   C. Develop a knowledge of specific information about a particular vocation.

Extremely Poor			Poor			Fair but more needs to be done			Leave as is			Too much is being done			Score
1	2	3	4	5	6	7	8	9	10	11	12	13	14	15	_____

16. Develop pride in work and a feeling of self-worth.
   A. Develop a feeling of student pride in his achievements and progress.
   B. Develop self-understanding and self-awareness.
   C. Develop the student's feeling of positive self-worth, security and self-assurance.

Extremely Poor				Poor		Fair but more needs to be done			Leave as is			Too much is being done			Score
1	2	3	4	5	6	7	8	9	10	11	12	13	14	15	_____

17. Develop good character and self-respect.
    A. Develop moral responsibility and sound ethical and
       moral behavior.
    B. Develop the student's capacity to discipline himself
       to work, study and play constructively.
    C. Develop a moral and ethical sense of values, goals
       and processes of free society.
    D. Develop standards of personal character and ideas.

Extremely Poor				Poor		Fair but more needs to be done			Leave as is			Too much is being done			Score
1	2	3	4	5	6	7	8	9	10	11	12	13	14	15	_____

18. Gain a general education.
    A. Develop background and skills in the use of numbers,
       natural sciences, mathematics, and social sciences.
    B. Develop a fund of information and concepts.
    C. Develop special interests and abilities.

. . .

ADMINISTRATOR EVALUATION OF PROGRAM STAFF

MD UNIFIED SCHOOL DISTRICT GUIDELINES
FOR EVALUATION OF CERTIFICATED PERSONNEL
IN RELATION TO PROGRAM

Education Goals

The purpose of the educational program in the MD Unified School
District is to help students to develop intellectually, socially, emotionally, and physically.

We believe that education has responsibility to the individual and
to society.

We believe that responsibility to the individual may best be
realized when the educational program provides for:

- Development of basic skills in communication and
  computation.
- Development of basic skills in good human relationships.

- Opportunities for the student to make choices, to think critically, to experience success, to deal with failure constructively, and to respect and respond to the principle of constituted authority.
- Development of a sense of personal worth coupled with self-discipline and governed by a code of moral and ethical values.
- Development of an understanding of the importance of physical and mental health.
- Opportunities in vocational education and on-the-job training.
- Development of interest and participation in recreational and leisure-time activities.
- Experiences that encourage the appreciation of and participation in the creative and fine arts.
- Preparation for continued education as well as an interest in life-long learning.

We believe that responsibility to society may best be realized when the educational program provides for:

- Knowledge, appreciation and understanding of the American heritage and development of a desire to participate in local, national, and world affairs.
- Knowledge, appreciation and understanding of the democratic form of government, the history of the United States, and the Constitution of the United States.
- Knowledge and understanding of various governments, societies, and ideologies along with their impact on human existence.
- An understanding of science in its relationship to human development and the impact of technology on man and his environment.
- Development of a wholesome attitude toward the family and a willingness to accept responsibilities in the family as a significant unit in our society.
- Development of respect for and understanding of the rights, privileges, and contributions of other individuals, groups, and peoples.
- Development of skills and attitudes which enable the individual to cope with change and conflict in our society.

We believe that these goals can best be achieved when the educational program:

- Is adjusted insofar as possible in degree and scope to the intellectual, emotional and physical capacities of the individual student.
- Is related to the student's past experience and future goals.
- Is provided in an atmosphere of kindness, sensitivity, and mutual respect.

. . .

COMMENTS

Showing a genuine interest in wanting to improve schools, working with groups in the community, and letting teachers know that it is important to improve the program can result in better feelings in the community, and better programs in the schools. It might be easier not to involve the consumers in program evaluation, however, the subtle pressure of involvement, observation, and desire for improvement can encourage significant results if properly orchestrated.

Consumer involvement can get out of hand, and can become a cacophonous array of dissident action. However, I can assure you that if you have a reasonable set of established goals translated into performance objectives for the school and for the district, such negative action is unlikely to occur.

Program evaluation can be thorough, yet remain so simple that it does not overburden the staff with paper work. These sample instruments will give you practical ideas for program evaluation of a school or school district.

Chapter 8
Staff Development

Why have staff development? Staff development is essential to every school program for two reasons: to improve student learning achievement and to improve school learning climate.

A principal or superintendent should encourage every one in the school or school district to become committed to staff development. Every one—superintendent, office administrators, site administrators, support personnel, teachers, and aides— should want to improve themselves and should want to become more competent each year. Every employee should commit himself to a minimum of 30 hours a year in staff development activities.

IDENTIFICATION OF STAFF DEVELOPMENT NEEDS

A staff development program should be highly flexible and should assess the needs of each individual member of a school. It should be based on needed improvement in student learning achievement and in school learning climate; and on a self-assessment of staff development needs from every employee.

Determination of the needed improvement in student learning achievement and in school learning climate is described in other chapters of this book.

The following are two examples of needs assessment instruments used with management personnel and with teachers.

TWO EXAMPLES OF A NEEDS ASSESSMENT INVENTORY

MANAGEMENT SELF-ASSESSMENT INVENTORY OF SKILLS AND INTERESTS

Please Respond To Each Item

NAME _____

	INTEREST		EXPERIENCE
	High	Minimal	Skilled and can share

STUDENTS

	High	Minimal	Skilled and can share
1. Planning and implementing effective and due-process student discipline practices.	X		X
2. Managing effective mainstreaming of disabled students.	X		
3. Developing and maintaining student leadership systems.		X	
4. Encouraging and maintaining positive student self-image.	X		
5. Other.			

STAFF RELATIONS

	High	Minimal	Skilled and can share
6. Organizing and conducting school site council responsibilities.	X		
7. Managing affirmative action practices and policies.		X	
8. Managing the district's contracts within Individual School Management System site council structures.		X	
9. Cooperatively planning budgets with staff and site council.		X	
10. Organizing accountability processes for administrative personnel.		X	
11. Organizing and maintaining accountability for district office personnel.		X	

| | INTEREST | | EXPERI-ENCE |
	High	Minimal	Skilled and can share
12. Managing personnel practices in marginally defined areas of contracts.		X	
13. Organizing and facilitating teacher staff development programs.	X		
14. Organizing and facilitating classified staff development programs.	X		
15. Defining staff performance standards.		X	
16. Refining shared decision-making processes.	X		X
17. Defining administrator rights and responsibilities.		X	
18. Other.			
COMMUNITY RELATIONS			
19. Creating and maintaining relations with parent club within site council structure.		X	
20. Organizing and facilitating community involvement in school programs.		X	
21. Using community resources in planning and programs.	X		
22. Developing and using effective communication systems with community and parents.		X	
23. Developing and using effective techniques in marketing.	X		
24. Other.			
CURRICULUM AND PROGRAM DEVELOPMENT			
25. Planning and using needs assessment procedures.		X	
26. Profitably using program evaluation processes.		X	
27. Developing competency-based course requirements.	X		

	INTEREST		EXPERI-ENCE
	High	Minimal	Skilled and can share
28. Improving guidance and counseling practices.		X	
29. Developing and using learning centers.		X	
30. Developing and using effective instructional goals.		X	
31. Developing and using diagnostic procedures for classroom purposes.		X	
32. Other.			
GENERAL MANAGEMENT			
33. Improving conflict resolution techniques.	X		
34. Improving plant and facilities management.		X	
35. Developing and managing differentiated staffing.	X		
36. Implementing data-based decision making.	X		X
37. Organizing and using effective classified staff evaluations.		X	
38. Organizing and using effective certificated staff evaluations.		X	
39. Organizing and using effective administrative staff evaluations.		X	
40. Finding and using procedures for improving school climate.	X		
41. Finding aɪɪd using procedures for improving personal well-being.	X		
42. Developing management by objectives processes.		X	
43. Improving time management procedures.	X		

	INTEREST		EXPERI-ENCE
	High	Minimal	Skilled and can share
44. Developing and using simulation games for improvement of management skills.			X
45. Improving techniques for analyzing forces working for and against solutions to problems.			X
46. Improving group process techniques.		X	
47. Other.			

. . .

TEACHER SELF-ASSESSMENT INVENTORY OF SKILLS AND INTEREST

NAME_____

GRADE LEVEL_____

SUBJECT AREA _____

SCHOOL_____

Please Respond to Each Item	INTEREST		EXPERI-ENCE
	High	Minimal	Skilled and can share
INTERPERSONAL COMMUNICATION			
1. Learning strategies for communicating to the community.		X	
2. Communicating and interacting with parents.	X		
3. Knowing when and where to refer student problems.	X		X
4. Developing strategies to successfully involve classroom assistants.		X	

| | INTEREST | | EXPERI-ENCE |
	High	Minimal	Skilled and can share
5. Initiating and building professional relationships with colleagues.	X		X
6. Resolving teacher/administrator differences in a positive and effective manner.		X	
7. Other.			
DEVELOPING PUPIL SELF-ESTEEM			
8. Facilitating pupil self-concept and worth.	X		X
9. Facilitating pupil social interaction.		X	
10. Instilling in the student the will to learn on his own initiative.	X		
11. Other.			
INDIVIDUALIZING INSTRUCTION			
12. Assessing and selecting appropriate materials and activities for individualized instruction.	X		
13. Creating and developing materials and learning options.	X		
14. Implementing and supervising individualized instruction.	X		
15. Other.			
ASSESSMENT			
16. Coping with the task of evaluating and communicating student progress.	X		
17. Selecting and specifying performance goals and objectives.		X	
18. Establishing appropriate performance standards.	X		
19. Constructing and using tests for evaluating academic progress.	X		
20. Involving students in self-evaluation.	X		

	INTEREST		EXPERIENCE
	High	Minimal	Skilled and can share
21. Diagnosing basic learning difficulties.	X		
22. Identifying students with disabilities who need referral or special remedial work.	X		X
23. Other.			
DISCIPLINE			
24. Using methods of classroom discipline at appropriate times.		X	
25. Maintaining classroom control without appearing as an ogre to students.		X	
26. Identifying student attitudes as an aid to solving problems in and out of the classroom.		X	
27. Other.			
DEVELOPING PERSONAL AND PROFESSIONAL SELF			
28. Evaluating your instructional methods and procedures.		X	
29. Developing or modifying instructional procedures to suit your own strengths.		X	
30. Developing a personal self-evaluation method.		X	
31. Developing a greater capacity for accepting others' feelings.	X		
32. Other.			
ORGANIZING FOR INSTRUCTION			
33. Using alternative methods in school organization—multiage grouping, continuous progress, open classroom, minicourses.	X		
34. Utilizing staff resources—team teaching, aides, flexible scheduling.	X		

	INTEREST		EXPERIENCE
	High	Minimal	Skilled and can share
35. Deciding on appropriate pupil grouping procedures for instruction within the classroom.		X	
36. Creating optimum physical environment for learning.		X	
37. Managing classrooms in order to get maximum learning.		X	
38. Presenting information and directions.		X	
39. Deciding which teaching technique is best suited for a specific purpose.		X	
40. Using questioning procedures that facilitate learning.	X		
41. Gearing instruction to problem solving.		X	
42. Using multimedia.		X	
43. Providing for reinforcement of basic skills.	X		
44. Other.			
FUTURE TRENDS AND ISSUES IN EDUCATION			
45. Keeping abreast of developments in your own subject matter area.		X	
46. Year-round schools.	X		X
47. Mainstreaming disabled children.		X	
48. Alternative education programs.	X		
49. Vocational and career education.		X	
50. Teacher centers.		X	
51. Professional retraining for future manpower needs.		X	
52. Legislation affecting teachers.		X	
53. Other.			

. . .

List every potential staff development need you can think of in the assessment instrument; leave ample room for additional items that the employee might identify. Include on the instrument a rating scale indicating little to high interest in each staff development item.

On the same assessment instrument, you should determine whether the employee is experienced in that particular staff development area. If the employee can share his knowledge with others, you have the opportunity of identifying a potential in-house consultant who can be used in your staff development training program. Not only do in-house consultants develop credibility with their colleagues, but they are available for necessary follow-up work during the year.

CONDUCTING STAFF DEVELOPMENT PROGRAMS

ESTABLISHING PRIORITIES

Now that you have determined potential areas for staff development, you must set priorities for these areas. Make certain that each employee's individual program is reviewed and approved by his supervisor or principal.

I suggest that you combine the needs assessment data, student achievement data, and the learning climate data, and that you identify 10 or 20 of the greatest needs. Have the employees, by school, rate the items on a five-point scale—strongly agree, agree, no opinion, disagree, or strongly disagree. In addition, have each employee rank the items. The employee picks the top 10 items, then the top five, the top two, and finally the top item. The compilation of the items will result in a list of priorites of staff development.

GROUPING

To keep your staff development program highly flexible, conduct programs for an individual, a small collegial team, a grade level or department level, a school, a number of schools, or a district. Staff development can be accomplished through reading, visiting other programs or schools, taking university classes, or participating in staff development seminars inside or outside the district. I find that working seminars are the most productive and rewarding for the staff. Each program should be evaluated no matter what type of staff development activity the individual undertakes.

LEVEL OF COMMITMENT

The principal of the school must participate in any sizeable staff development program. If the principal does not, significant improvement in the identified need area, whether it be student achievement or learning climate, is unlikely. In addition, it is important to work toward unanimity of participation in staff development activities. If complete unanimity cannot be achieved, at least there should be a general consensus that the staff development activity has the commitment and interest of all staff members. Do not conduct any staff development activity unless you have at least 80 percent support. The chances of overcoming the resistance by a sizeable number of staff toward the activity are slim and improvement or progress is unlikely.

LOCATION

A workshop needs comfortable room facilities. Participants should have comfortable seating arrangements, proper light and ventilation, and refreshments. They should be seated at tables in groups of six to eight. It is also desirable to have other areas available for small groups to work without interruption.

ARRANGEMENT OF TIME

The time spent on the staff development activity should be directly related to what needs to be accomplished. There are five basic levels of accomplishment in staff development.

- Awareness
- Knowledge
- Skill practice
- Skill application
- Validation

As participants progress through each of the levels, more time is needed. If you are only interested in making people aware of a particular staff development activity, a one- to three-hour workshop is sufficient. Participants might even reach the knowledge level in that span of time.

To achieve skill practice and skill application, as well as validation, I recommend that you arrange four to eight three-hour sessions, in order to provide the necessary staff development that will result in significant improvement of program.

BASIC ELEMENTS

Staff development has four basic elements.
- Needs assessment
- Planning
- Implementation
- Evaluation

Interspersed throughout this book are chapters that have an implication for each one of these four phases.

USE OF CONSULTANTS

Because you are going to invest your time and money, you want to be certain that the consultant is effective. At least one person who is knowledgeable about the consultant should make a recommendation concerning his effectiveness. I then suggest having a group, comprised of at least the principal and three or four teachers, participate in that consultant's workshop for final evaluation.

If it is not possible to obtain an individual report or to have a group participate in a consultant's workshop, then I recommend that you check with people you know concerning their opinion of the consultant. Though a consultant is listed by an association or group, he may not be effective. Few professional associations evaluate the effectiveness of consultants. They only list them by their field of knowledge and what they have to offer.

The fee for consultants varies; usually it consists of their expenses and an honorarium. You can negotiate the honorarium. If you are going to use the same consultant over a period of four to eight sessions, you can usually negotiate a much lower per-session honorarium.

Once you have arranged to use a consultant, make certain that you state exactly what you expect. Discuss the information that will be presented, and the method of presentation—lecture or small group participation. If you wish to achieve the skill application and the validation level of staff development, make certain the consultant understands this and will be using techniques with the group to achieve these higher levels. Talk with the consultant about travel and lodging arrangements, materials and equipment the consultant will need, the number of people in the group, the background of that group, what you hope will be accomplished, and how you will evaluate whether you achieved your goal for the staff development activity.

MOTIVATION OF STAFF PARTICIPATION

The principal should encourage the staff to commit themselves to self-improvement activities every year for a minimum of 30 hours. A second approach might be to trade time with the staff. To do this your site council must understand and agree that trading school time for staff development is essential to school program improvement. An example of trading time is to start school late and have your staff development activity in the morning before school. A third approach is to convince parents and staff to extend the school day four days of the week in return for one full day of staff development.

FINANCES

The most desirable approach for staff development funding is to convince the superintendent and board to provide money in the budget for staff development activities. If enough money is not provided you can use one of the following plans.

- Trade time.
- Use staff from within the district.
- Use special funds allocated to each school for reduction in absenteeism and in vandalism.
- Initiate money raising events.

You can refer to the Chapter 20 to get further ideas for staff development funding.

EVALUATION

How do you know whether you achieved what you wanted to do through staff development? Improvement in student achievement and learning climate could be an indication that your staff development program is successful.

In addition, each of the training sessions should be evaluated at the conclusion to determine whether or not that particular session was valuable to the participants. Suggestions for improvement should be part of the evaluation format.

The evaluation results should be shared with the parents, the superintendent, the board of education, and the community to show that the time, money, and effort resulted in improvement in the educational program. It is difficult to get legislatures and boards of education to provide money for staff development if they do not see the results.

COMMENTS

You should not have too many staff development activities being conducted for total group participation. It is better to have only one or two major activities for the entire group during the year. A variety of activities can be accomplished through individual or small group sessions in which you can provide flexibility to improve individual school programs.

Staff development is an essential component for the improvement of educational programs. It is one of the six basic components for managing schools along with planning, organization, evaluation, learning climate, and decision-making skills.

Chapter 9
Climate

Practitioners and researchers agree that school climate is important. Through numerous studies, researchers have demonstrated the impact of school climate on job satisfaction and productivity, and the relationship between organizational climate and leadership styles. Administrators and teachers also acknowledge the importance of school climate when they speak of boosting morale, increasing involvement, and, in general, maximizing job satisfaction and productivity. Despite this consensus little organized attention is being given in schools to the identification of factors which contribute to a favorable learning climate. Even if such factors are identified, how do we plan, implement, and initiate activities to improve the learning climate in the school?

This chapter addresses practical and successful ways to accomplish an improved learning climate. Ways that were successful even in schools within a district that faced such adverse circumstances as reduced budget, teacher strikes, school closures, transportation elimination, and personnel lay-offs due to declining enrollment.

SCHOOL CLIMATE

The booklet "School Climate Improvement," published by Phi Delta Kappa, offers an excellent approach to identifying, implementing, and evaluating the school learning climate. The school climate survey is a key element and should be administered every two or three years. Later in this chapter I provide examples of adaptations of the survey taken from the Phi Delta Kappa publication.

A positive school climate is both a means and an end. A good climate makes it possible to work productively toward important goals such as academic learning, social development, and curriculum improvement. Writings on the characteristics of a good school program usually describe only the nature of the curriculum and the instructional program. That is, they describe: 1) desirable classroom teaching/learning strategies and conditions; and 2) sets of courses and experiences to be offered to students within each area of the curricular and extra-curricular programs.

The approach I advocate, the individual school management system, to which I refer throughout this book, goes further than just these concerns. It describes in concrete terms facets of the school climate as they relate to the school climate goals; to the assessment of climate and of program; to desireable relationships among staff, students, parents, and others comprising the school community; and to the leadership responsibilities of the school principal serving as the climate leader.

A climate of faith and trust is the foundation of such a system. These elements must exist reciprocally among the board of education, district office, school staff, and parents for the system to be successful.

To establish such faith and trust, people must communicate; they must have the opportunity to participate and to feel that their ideas and thoughts are important. To facilitate a climate which emphasizes individual involvement, a diversified communication program should be available for all personnel at each school.

SCHOOL CLIMATE GOALS

The concept of school climate improvement does not de-emphasize skills, attitudes, and knowledge students gain through studies in academic areas such as language arts, social studies, mathematics, and science. It suggests that the most efficient learning programs occur in a wholesome and humane school climate.

Two goals of school climate are: to provide throughout the school a wholesome, stimulating, productive learning environment conducive to academic achievement and personal growth of youth at different levels of development; and to provide a pleasant and satisfying school situation within which young people can live and work.

These primary goals focus on the young people for whom schools exist. A corollary is the provision of a stimulating and productive environment for the adults of the school community, the staff, and parents. These goals can best be characterized as productivity and satisfaction. One without the other is insufficient.

What follows below are components of these two goals.

Productivity of students and educators
- In achieving basic skills.
- In developing constructive attitudes.
- In developing and expanding an adequate knowledge base.
- In clarifying values and purposes.
- In using inquiring and problem solving processes.

Satisfaction on the part of students and educators
- In gaining a sense of personal worth.
- In enjoying school as a pleasant place to live and work.
- In gaining rewards from participation in worthwhile activities.

The principal, as a climate leader, provides an accountability system consistent with the school's philosophy for school-based task forces of staff, administrators, parents, and students. Working with colleagues he also provides the basic leadership for:

- Assessing school climate improvement needs.
- Setting goals to provide needed improvements.
- Reducing goals to manageable projects with measurable objectives.
- Devising strategies for obtaining the objectives.
- Implementing these strategies.
- Evaluating progress by establishing check points and periodically monitoring the achievements through cooperatively determined systems and instruments.
- Improving each project in light of evaluative processes.

SCHOOL CLIMATE SURVEY

The school climate survey serves two purposes: 1) to provide a convenient means of assessing the school's climate factors so that initial decisions can be made concerning priority targets for improvement projects; and 2) to serve as a bench mark against which a school may measure climate change.

The survey includes sample indicators for each of the climate factors. Since it does not pretend to include an item for every indicator that might be important, the instrument is more valuable as an overall school climate assessment tool than as an exhaustive survey.

It can provide data to help decide what factors of the climate should be looked at more intensively. Data gained from this instrument would be more powerful if gathered from people who see the school from different perspectives. Therefore, plans should be made to gather data from teachers, students, support staff members, and parents. The data based on people's perceptions of how things are or how they feel about them are important; most behavior is motivated by the individual's perceptions of reality. Other kinds of information, such as obtained from observation or behavioral analysis, would also be useful as part of a more extensive diagnostic effort.

The data provided by this survey can be analyzed in several ways by asking the following questions.

• Which climate factors are lowest on the scale? Which are the highest? Perhaps the lowest ones should be considered as candidates for climate improvement projects.

• For which climate factors are the discrepancies between "what is" and "what should be" the largest? If a large discrepancy exists, perhaps the underlying reasons should be examined.

• Are there marked discrepancies between how one group ranks a climate factor and how it is ranked by another role group? If so, these discrepancies furnish a stimulus for further discussion and examination.

SAMPLE SURVEYS

The first step in the process of determining the climate in the school is to send a survey to parents, staff, and students—three different groups and perspectives.

PRINCIPAL'S LETTER
March 4, 1983

Dear Parents,

Some of you are aware of the ISMS (Individual School Management System) Hidden Valley has participated in during the last three years. The thrust of this project is to improve student performance through staff development and through improved school climate.

To put together such a plan, a School Site Council which includes parents, teachers, and administrators was formed and became the responsible body for gathering community information regarding climate—how parents feel about our school, monitoring our progress, updating information, and offering future recommendations.

This year, like three years ago, every fourth family received a climate survey to complete. The site council is requesting that this survey be returned to school as soon as possible. A special box has been placed in each learning center to ensure your privacy. You can also mail your completed survey to the school.

Our School Improvement Plan was written using the information we received from you. It has been worthwhile: Former surveys indicate that communication between the school and the community has improved; records show increased teacher participation in staff development; and CTBS scores show increased student learning achievement.

Sincerely,

Joan T.
Principal

The survey was simplified by being marksensed so that it could be read by the scanner in preparation for a computer analysis. The survey was reduced to 48 items from the original Phi Delta Kappa survey which had over a hundred items. By doing this we were able to expedite completion of the questionnaire and still receive sufficient information.

UNIFIED SCHOOL DISTRICT CLIMATE SURVEY

Response Group_____ School_____ Date_____

DIRECTIONS:

This survey measures your feelings about an individual school. Indicate how you feel about your school under "What Is," and how you would like to feel about your school under "What Should Be." Use the following scale for each statement:

1 = ALMOST NEVER
2 = OCCASIONALLY
3 = FREQUENTLY
4 = ALMOST ALWAYS

PART A: GENERAL CLIMATE FACTORS

	WHAT IS	WHAT SHOULD BE
RESPECT/TRUST		
1. Teachers treat students with respect.	1 2 3 4	1 2 3 4
2. Students can count on teachers to listen to their side of the story and to be fair.	1 2 3 4	1 2 3 4
MORALE		
3. Students feel enthusiastic about learning in this school and enjoy coming to school.	1 2 3 4	1 2 3 4
4. Staff enjoy working in this school.	1 2 3 4	1 2 3 4
INPUT		
5. I feel that my ideas will be listened to in this school.	1 2 3 4	1 2 3 4
6. Parents are considered by this school as important contributors.	1 2 3 4	1 2 3 4
CONTINUOUS ACADEMIC AND SOCIAL GROWTH		
7. Staff in this school are continually seeking ways to improve the educational program.	1 2 3 4	1 2 3 4
8. The school program is appropriate to students' present and future needs.	1 2 3 4	1 2 3 4

	WHAT IS	WHAT SHOULD BE

COHESIVENESS

9. All staff work together to make the school run effectively. — 1 2 3 4 · 1 2 3 4

10. Students would rather be at this school than transfer to another. — 1 2 3 4 · 1 2 3 4

11. Staff would rather be at this school than transfer to another. — 1 2 3 4 · 1 2 3 4

SCHOOL RENEWAL

12. Teachers and administrators participate in inservice programs to continue their professional growth. — 1 2 3 4 · 1 2 3 4

13. Changes in educational programs are based upon the particular needs of this community and school. — 1 2 3 4 · 1 2 3 4

CARING

14. There is someone in this school upon whom I can rely. — 1 2 3 4 · 1 2 3 4

15. The staff really cares about students. — 1 2 3 4 · 1 2 3 4

PART B: PROGRAM FACTORS

OPPORTUNITY FOR LEARNING

16. This school places enough emphasis upon the basic skills. — 1 2 3 4 · 1 2 3 4

17. Each student's special abilities (intellectual, artistic, social or physical) are challenged. — 1 2 3 4 · 1 2 3 4

INDIVIDUAL PERFORMANCE EXPECTATIONS

18. Students know the basis for the evaluation of their classroom work. — 1 2 3 4 · 1 2 3 4

19. Performance expectations are tailored to the individual student. — 1 2 3 4 · 1 2 3 4

	WHAT IS	WHAT SHOULD BE

VARIED LEARNING ENVIRONMENT

20. Teachers use a wide range of teaching materials and media.   1 2 3 4   1 2 3 4

21. Students have opportunity for learning in individual, small group, and classroom groups.   1 2 3 4   1 2 3 4

22. A student with special problems gets help.   1 2 3 4   1 2 3 4

FLEXIBLE CURRICULUM

23. Students have alternative ways for meeting academic requirements.   1 2 3 4   1 2 3 4

24. High school extracurricular activities and/or elementary enrichment activities appeal to all types of students.   1 2 3 4   1 2 3 4

SUPPORT TO LEARNER

25. The school encourages students to develop self-discipline and initiative.   1 2 3 4   1 2 3 4

26. Students can get close supervision without feeling "put down."   1 2 3 4   1 2 3 4

RULES COOPERATIVELY DETERMINED

27. There are enough rules to run a good school.   1 2 3 4   1 2 3 4

28. Staff enforces the rules fairly.   1 2 3 4   1 2 3 4

VARIED REWARD SYSTEMS

29. The staff lets students know when they have done something well.   1 2 3 4   1 2 3 4

30. Staff members are recognized when they do something well.   1 2 3 4   1 2 3 4

	WHAT IS	WHAT SHOULD BE

PART C: PROCESS FACTORS

PROBLEM-SOLVING ABILITY

31. People in this school solve problems; they do not just talk about them. 1 2 3 4   1 2 3 4
32. I know I can get help if I have a school-related problem. 1 2 3 4   1 2 3 4

IMPROVE GOALS

33. I can participate in the development of this schools' goals. 1 2 3 4   1 2 3 4
34. Each year this school sets goals and I know what they are. 1 2 3 4   1 2 3 4
35. Goals of this school are periodically reviewed and updated. 1 2 3 4   1 2 3 4

WORK WITH CONFLICTS

36. In this school people with varied ideas or values get a chance to be heard. 1 2 3 4   1 2 3 4
37. This school believes there may be alternative solutions to most problems. 1 2 3 4   1 2 3 4

EFFECTIVE COMMUNICATIONS

38. Teachers are available to students who want help. 1 2 3 4   1 2 3 4
39. Parents can get specific information about their student. 1 2 3 4   1 2 3 4
40. Parents freely discuss problems and ideas with school staff. 1 2 3 4   1 2 3 4

INVOLVEMENT IN DECISION-MAKING

41. I can influence school decisions which directly affect me. 1 2 3 4   1 2 3 4
42. Teachers are involved in deciding priorities for their programs. 1 2 3 4   1 2 3 4

	WHAT IS	WHAT SHOULD BE

PART D: MATERIAL FACTORS

ADEQUATE RESOURCES

43. There are sufficient staff in this school to meet the needs of its students.   1 2 3 4   1 2 3 4

44. The instructional materials are adequate for our school program.   1 2 3 4   1 2 3 4

SUPPORTIVE LOGISTICAL SYSTEM

45. Teachers and students are able to get instructional materials when needed.   1 2 3 4   1 2 3 4

46. Staff work together in selecting and using materials.   1 2 3 4   1 2 3 4

SCHOOL PLANT

47. It is pleasant to be on this campus; it is kept attractive and in good repair.   1 2 3 4   1 2 3 4

48. The school has adequate space and facilities for its program.   1 2 3 4   1 2 3 4

. . .

Once the survey is returned and compiled, the results are reported to each of the schools, the students, and the parents, so they know how each group scored the survey according to their perception of "what is" and "what should be." A sample of a report to the parents follows.

PRINCIPAL'S LETTER
May 3, 1983

Dear Parents,

Last March you were asked to complete a school climate survey. The purpose of that survey was to assess your feelings about our school. Items for which you indicated room for improvement were:

- A need for a more cohesive feeling with the school.
- A need for more information about our school goals.

After studying your replies and working with the School Site Council, we have:

- Tried to increase communication with the community via information sent in the school newsletter—Hooter, the Site Council Minutes and the Principal's Letter.
- Attempted to share our school goals at the recent parent-teacher conferences.
- Arranged parent participation in evening activities.
- Planned activities in the Parent Club to provide opportunities for community participation—cook book, book fair, and family field day, June 10.
- Sent several teachers to conferences and workshops.
- Had regular meetings of the Site Council and the teachers to plan a staff development program.
- Prepared and presented for approval bylaws for governing the Site Council at Hidden Valley.

We realize the March survey was long; we thank the parents who took time to return it.

Thank you,

Joan T.
Principal

What follows next is a survey for parents. It was reduced to 15 questions and given to every parent, not just to a random sample.

Dear Parent:

In order to understand the educational climate at your school, this brief survey asks all parents to give reactions to specific issues by using the letter code which best describes your reactions to each statement.

CODE
A = Strongly Agree
B = Agree
C = Disagree
D = Strongly Disagree
E = No Opinion

Response (A-E)

_____ 1. Parents are routinely informed about educational practices (i.e. grading, discipline, etc.) of our school.

_____ 2. Our school's program places the proper amount of emphasis upon basic skills subjects.

_____ 3. Parents have a good understanding of our school's learning objectives.

_____ 4. If given the chance, I would become more actively involved in our school's affairs.

_____ 5. Discipline is appropriate and fair for the students.

_____ 6. The principal treats all students the same way when they break a rule.

_____ 7. Our teachers are generally fair to students.

_____ 8. My student looks forward to going to school each day.

_____ 9. Students are recognized as having individual learning needs and the teaching reflects this recognition.

_____10. I find it easy to get specific school information about my student.

_____11. When a parent or student has a problem, the teacher and principal work together to try to solve the problem.

_____12. My student is treated with respect when he comes to the office.

_____13. My student is treated with respect by the teachers.

_____14. When my student has a problem, an adult at the school will listen to the student.

_____15. The principal is responsive to parent concerns.

Thank you for your assistance. Please use the enclosed pre-addressed envelope for the return of your responses by March 21, 1983.

Sincerely,

Harvey W., Director
Research and Development

What follows is a summary of the 15-question survey.

SUMMARY OF HIDDEN VALLEY CLIMATE SURVEY

In March 1983, Hidden Valley Elementary conducted a special survey to obtain parent's feelings about school climate. All parents were asked to indicate for each of the 15 questions the following: strongly agree, agree, disagree, strongly disagree, or no opinion.

Of the 458 families, 232, or 51 percent, responded. This survey was done in addition to the regular 48 item School Climate Survey which is completed by only one-fourth of the families and measures other areas.

The results indicate that parents believe that school climate is very good at Hidden Valley. For most items, 90 percent of the parents indicated they were satisfied or had no opinion. In general, less than 10 percent of the parents indicated they were not satisfied.

The only question with over 13 percent "disagree" or "strongly disagree" was #4: "If given the chance, I would become more actively involved in our school's affairs" (29 percent disagreed). These parents may have thought the school was doing fine and did not need their help.

In short, parents at Hidden Valley indicated on this survey a high degree of satisfaction with all areas measured: parent/school communication, basic skills emphasis, discipline, respect, student attitude, individualization, staff cooperation, and school attitude.

. . .

A non-computerized profile is listed for your information. This survey was reduced to 25 questions for use with a middle school.

MIDDLE SCHOOL SURVEY

	WHAT IS	WHAT SHOULD BE
RESPECT/TRUST		
1. Parents are considered by this school as important contributors.	1 2 3 4	1 2 3 4
2. Students can count on teachers to listen to their side of the story and to be fair.	1 2 3 4	1 2 3 4
3. This school makes students enthusiastic about learning.	1 2 3 4	1 2 3 4
4. Attendance is good; students stay away only for good and urgent reasons.	1 2 3 4	1 2 3 4

	WHAT IS	WHAT SHOULD BE
5. I like working in this school.	1 2 3 4	1 2 3 4
6. I feel that my ideas are listened to and used in this school.	1 2 3 4	1 2 3 4
7. The principal really cares about students.	1 2 3 4	1 2 3 4
8. This school places emphasis upon reading, writing and arithmetic.	1 2 3 4	1 2 3 4
9. Enough attention is given to the students with high ability.	1 2 3 4	1 2 3 4
10. Enough attention is given to those students with low ability.	1 2 3 4	1 2 3 4
11. Enough attention is given to the average student.	1 2 3 4	1 2 3 4
12. Teachers use a wide range of teaching materials and media.	1 2 3 4	1 2 3 4
13. Many opportunities are provided for learning in individual and small-group settings, as well as in classroom groups.	1 2 3 4	1 2 3 4
14. The school's program is appropriate for ethnic and minority groups.	1 2 3 4	1 2 3 4
15. Extracurricular activities appeal to each of the various subgroups of students.	1 2 3 4	1 2 3 4
16. The school's program encourages students develop self-discipline and initiative.	1 2 3 4	1 2 3 4
17. Those few students who need close supervision and high structure do not feel "put down."	1 2 3 4	1 2 3 4
18. Faculty and staff want to help every student learn.	1 2 3 4	1 2 3 4
19. Rules are few and simple, and violations of rules are treated fairly.	1 2 3 4	1 2 3 4

	WHAT IS	WHAT SHOULD BE
20. Students know the criteria used to evaluate their progress.	1 2 3 4	1 2 3 4
21. Problems in this school are recognized and worked upon openly; not allowed to slide.	1 2 3 4	1 2 3 4
22. Teachers are available to students who want help.	1 2 3 4	1 2 3 4
23. The student government makes important decisions.	1 2 3 4	1 2 3 4
24. Curriculum materials used in this school give appropriate emphasis and accurate facts regarding ethnic and minority groups, and sex roles.	1 2 3 4	1 2 3 4
25. It is pleasant to be on this campus; it is kept clean and in good repair.	1 2 3 4	1 2 3 4

COMMENTS:

. . .

THREE SAMPLE SURVEY ANALYSES

What follows are three sample survey analyses each with a different intent. The first analysis, School Climate Improvements, was given to each school to show its progress compared to other schools. The second analysis, Summary of School Climate Survey, completed by the students, was given to the school surveyed to show them responses of a specific group. Though in this example, the analysis was of student responses, an analysis was done for each of the groups. The third analysis, Summary of School Climate Survey, completed by all groups, was given to the school surveyed to show how the responses of the groups compared.

SCHOOL CLIMATE IMPROVEMENTS

(Percentage Reduction of Critical Climate Factors)

School	Percentage
A	5
B	5
C	10
D	35
E	35
F	50
G	50
H	70
I	70
J	80
K	100
L	100
M	100
N	100

. . .

SUMMARY OF SCHOOL CLIMATE PROFILE

SCHOOL_____

* WHAT IS

ROLE GROUP - STUDENTS

x WHAT SHOULD BE

FALL 1983

	Almost Never 1	Occasion- ally 2	Frequently 3	Almost Always 4	Difference In Perceived and Desired Ratings
A. GENERAL CLIMATE FACTORS					
1. RESPECT/TRUST		*		x	1.06
2. HIGH MORALE			* x		.36
3. OPPORTUNITIES FOR IMPUT			* x		.45
4. CONTINUOUS ACADEMIC & SOCIAL GROWTH			* x		.28
5. COHESIVENESS			x*		-.06
6. SCHOOL RENEWAL			* x		.25
7. CARING			*	x	.68

B. PROGRAM FACTORS
C. PROCESS FACTORS
D. MATERIAL FACTORS

SUMMARY OF SCHOOL CLIMATE PROFILE

DIFFERENCE IN PERCEIVED
AND DESIRED RATINGS
S = STUDENTS
P = PARENTS
T = TEACHERS
SC = SITE COUNCIL
C = CLASSIFIED

	S	P	T	SC	C
A. GENERAL CLIMATE FACTORS					
1. RESPECT/TRUST	1.06	.87	.73	.91	.94
2. HIGH MORALE					
3. OPPORTUNITIES FOR IMPUT	.45	.96	1.13	.73	.31
4. CONTINUOUS ACADEMIC & SOCIAL GROWTH					
5. COHESIVENESS	-.06	.87	.88	.80	.63
6. SCHOOL RENEWAL					
7. CARING					

B. PROGRAM FACTORS   (etc.)

.
.
.

C. PROCESS FACTORS

.
.
.

D. MATERIAL FACTORS

.
.
.

. . .

Regardless of the kind of survey you choose, use the same survey, administer it every two or three years, and plot the results for the school. By doing this over a period of time, you will have an excellent idea of school climate improvement.

Improving learning climate became one of the highest priorities in the school districts where I was superintendent; I think it was a major factor in improving academic achievement. As stated earlier, one of our elementary schools improved the academic achievement 43 percentile points on the state testing program in just two years after we had been in the Individual School Management System. I am convinced that improving school climate correlates strongly with improving academic results.

In *A Place Called School,* John Goodlad states that the factors making a difference between effective and ineffective schools were those concerning climate and the relationships among students, staff, and parents.

COMMUNICATION

As part of creating a positive learning climate, it is important to keep in mind characteristics of supportive communications. The following suggestions foster a productive and humane interaction in discussions.

- I would like to expand upon your idea by looking at it from another angle.
- I think I hear you saying (then summarize).
- I hear a need in what you are saying, would you please state that in the form of a positive question.
- Would you please clarify? I wonder if you could: a) give us an example of what you are saying, b) give us an analogy for what you are saying? What are you imagining as some possible solutions?
- What ways can you suggest for working together?
- May we hear from someone who has not had an opportunity to contribute. I would appreciate hearing your thoughts and feelings (specify person).
- Would anyone care to help by adding to, or refining this idea?
- Let us follow that idea all the way through before we pass final judgment. Let us build on it first.
- Will someone please summarize our areas of agreement?
- It sounds like you have a point which is worth exploring further. Would you make a note of it so we can come back to it (This would be a response for someone who interrupts or strays from the point).
- Let us consider the advantages of that idea.
- Let us see what other options are available before we take a final position.

- You are expressing concern about part of the idea. Please offer your specific comments in any areas of agreement to see how far apart we are.
- I understand and respect your point of view; now let us see how similar our views are.
- Although I am uncertain if I agree entirely, I generally share a similar point of view.
- I offer this idea for you just to think about.

PARTICIPATIVE MANAGEMENT

No chapter on climate would be complete without mentioning the participative management philosophy which has been exemplified in numerous articles and books, and the improvement of the quality of work life. The quality circle approach to increased participative management has created interest in greater productivity, improved quality control, less waste, and more profit. People in business cite specific instances of increasing productivity 40 to 50 percent, fine-tuning quality, reducing costly waste, and changing financial outcomes from loss to gain.

Given the many successes of participatory quality circle teams, it is no wonder that the number of companies implementing the concept has been soaring dramatically. Such companies as RCA, Hughes Aircraft, General Electric, Bethlehem Steel, Control Data, General Motors, Hewlett Packard, and Honeywell have programs encouraging employee teams to meet on company time for an hour or so every week in a structured attempt to identify, analyze and resolve work-related problems. "Quality circles are the right philosophy for managing people now and in the future," a mid-western corporate executive says. "The program brings decision making closer to those who actually do the job and know it best."

There is yet another significant dimension to the burgeoning use of quality circles; it cannot be graphed, marked on production charts, or placed in financial statements. It reaches beyond performance into the misty realm of individual human satisfaction. Contemporary American workers aspire not only to an improved work life, but also to jobs offering participation in the decisions that affect them. They care more than they generally admit. Working men and women of the 1980s and 1990s are better educated, more individualistic, and less responsive to traditional authority figures. Consequently, quality circles, which more and more companies are using primarily to step up lagging production, contribute another essential element—the satisfaction of participating in decision making—that does not appear on the familiar bottom line. Quality circles also increase the pride, self-confidence, and self-esteem of a company's most valuable resource—its employees.

In education, participative management and quality circles can be translated into a management system which emphasizes group planning, participative organization, reciprocal evaluation, staff development, learning climate focus, and effective decision making.

The "bottom line" in education should be to bring the student to his greatest potential. This can be accomplished through an optimum learning climate in which a high satisfaction level produces a high level of learning achievement.

If we truly believe that productivity can be accomplished in a humane and satisfying learning climate, it is imperative that we make a concerted attempt, in a systematic way, to identify whether a good climate exists and then to do something about it.

Chapter 10
Decision Techniques

All people have the right to be involved in decisions affecting their lives. I feel it is necessary to have confidence in the ability of others to make decisions; such confidence is an integral part of a good school management system. However, this belief brings with it the acknowledgment that there will be shared decision-making through total staff involvement. Shared decision-making will require more time and tolerance, but will ultimately encourage staff to recognize the opinions of individuals and of minority groups. The understanding, satisfaction, and commitment that result through shared decision-making should bring measurable and significant progress in educational programs at each school.

Schools may differ in their approaches to decision-making, but all schools need to involve staff, parents, and students in the process through the leadership of the principal. Schools need to implement their decision-making process by using such instruments as the decision charts for the superintendent and board, for the superintendent and principals, and for the school principals and teachers. These three instruments, which appear in later chapters, help clarify decisions to be made at the district and the school levels.

Most of the decision techniques in this chapter emphasize a consensus approach in which the entire group can feel strong support toward the decision. A simple majority vote having just slightly over half of the group in favor of a controversial issue creates a condition in which almost half are strongly opposed. I have found over the years that if you are making a decision of any significance that is going to effect many people, it is essential that you have a least 80 percent of the group in support of the decision if it is to survive and not be sabotaged.

ANALYSIS OF DECISION-MAKING STYLES

It is imperative for an administrator of the '80s and '90s to have adequate knowledge of many decision techniques which can be called upon in the varying situations he might face either as a leader of a school or of a school district.

To give you insight as to what type of a decision maker you resemble at this time, you can complete the next exercise "The Management of Differences."

MANAGEMENT-OF-DIFFERENCES EXERCISE

Name_____ Date_____

INSTRUCTIONS: Consider situations in which you find that your wishes differ from the wishes of another person. How do you usually respond to such situations? On the following pages are several pairs of statements describing possible behavioral responses. For each pair, circle the "A" or "B" statement that is most characteristic of your own behavior. In many cases, neither the "A" nor the "B" statement may be typical of your behavior; select the response that you would more likely use.

1. A. There are times when I let others take responsibility for solving the problems.
   B. Rather than negotiate the things on which we disagree, I try to stress those things upon which we both agree.
2. A. I try to find a compromise solution.
   B. I attempt to deal with all of his and my concerns.
3. A. I am usually firm in pursuing my goals.
   B. I might try to soothe the other's feelings to preserve our relationship.
4. A. I try to find a compromise solution.
   B. I sometimes sacrifice my own wishes for the wishes of the other person.
5. A. I consistently seek the other's help in working out a solution.

B. I try to do what is necessary to avoid useless tensions.
6. A. I try to avoid creating unpleasantness for myself.
   B. I try to win my position.
7. A. I try to postpone the issue until I have had some time to think it over.
   B. I give up some points in exchange for others.
8. A. I am usually firm in pursuing my goals.
   B. I attempt to get all concerns and issues immediately out in the open.
9. A. I feel that differences are not always worth worrying about.
   B. I make some effort to get my way.
10. A. I am firm in pursuing my goals.
    B. I try to find a compromise solution.
11. A. I attempt to get all concerns and issues immediately out in the open.
    B. I might try to soothe the other's feelings and preserve our relationship.
12. A. I sometimes avoid taking positions which would create controversy.
    B. I will let the other person have some of his positions if he lets me have some of mine.
13. A. I propose a middle ground.
    B. I press to get my points made.
14. A. I tell the other person my ideas and ask him for his.
    B. I try to show the other person the logic and benefits of my position.
15. A. I might try to soothe the other's feelings and preserve our relationship.
    B. I try to show the other person the logic and benefits of my position.
16. A. I try not to hurt the other's feelings.
    B. I try to convince the other person of the merits of my position.
17. A. I am usually firm in pursuing my goals.
    B. I try to do what is necessary to avoid useless tensions.
18. A. If it makes the other person happy, I might let him maintain his views.
    B. I will let the other person have some of his positions if he lets me have some of mine.

19. A. I attempt to get all concerns and issues immediately out in the open.
    B. I try to postpone the issue until I have had time to think it over.
20. A. I attempt to immediately work through our differences.
    B. I try to find a fair combination of gains and losses for both of us.
21. A. In approaching negotiations, I try to be considerate of the other person's wishes.
    B. I always lean toward a direct discussion of the problem.
22. A. I try to find a position that is intermediate between the other person's and mine.
    B. I assert my wishes.
23. A. I am often concerned with satisfying all our wishes.
    B. There are times when I let others take responsibility for solving the problem.
24. A. If the other's position seems important to him, I try to meet his wishes.
    B. I try to get the other person to settle for a compromise.
25. A. I try to show the other person the logic and benefits of my position.
    B. In approaching negotiations, I try to be considerate of the other person's wishes.
26. A. I propose a middle ground.
    B. I am nearly always concerned with satisfying all our wishes.
27. A. I sometimes avoid taking positions which would create controversy.
    B. If it makes the other person happy, I might let him maintain his views.
28. A. I am usually firm in pursuing my goals.
    B. I usually seek the other's help in working out a solution.
29. A. I propose a middle ground.
    B. I feel that differences are not always worth worrying about.
30. A. I try not to hurt the other's feelings.
    B. I always share the problem with the other person so that we can work it out.

. . .

SCORING GUIDE

SCORING THE DIFFERENCES INSTRUMENT

Circle the letters below which you circled on each item of the questionnaire.

I   = COMPETITION (Forcing)
II   = COLLABORATION (Problem-Solving)
III = SHARING (Compromise)
IV = AVOIDING (Withdrawal)
V   = ACCOMMODATION (Smoothing)

Item No.	I	II	III	IV	V
1				A	B
2		B	A		
3	A				B
4			A		B
5		A		B	
6	B			A	
7			B	A	
8	A	B			
9	B			A	
10	A		B		
11		A			B
12		B		A	
13	B		A		
14	B	A			
15				B	A
16	B				A
17	A			B	
18			B		A
19		A		B	
20		A	B		
21		B			A
22	B		A		
23		A		B	
24			B		A
25	A				B

Continued next page.

Contined from previous page.

Item No.	I	II	III	IV	V
26		B	A		
27				A	B
28	A	B			
29			A	B	
30		B			A

Total number of items circled in each column:

Competition	Collaboration	Sharing	Avoiding	Accommodation

. . .

METHODS OF DECISION MAKING

A decision is a collective agreement on a single course of action. It represents the best response to a current state of affairs, and presumably represents a consensus. A large part of decision-making is actually an attempt to find a common ground—to reach a decision all parties can live with. Although decisions deal with current situations, all decisions face in two directions: they remedy past problems; and they attempt to anticipate future ones.

The information explosion, the technological advances, and the shared complexity of the school district and its services have combined to create an apparent need for a complicated management system. Systems like PERT—program, evaluation and review technique, and PPBS—program, planning, budgeting systems—are only two examples of districtwide technological systems which evolved in the '60s. Unfortunately, much of the literature on problem solving and decision-making is either diffuse and mathematical, or too abstract for practical use. Basically, PERT and PPBS were much too complicated, and as a result did not receive widespread application. Theories are not often translated into easily understandable and applicable formulas; non-technological systems are especially difficult to formulize.

As an attempt to bridge the gap from the pure theory of decision making as an intuitive, unstructured process, I provide a list of non-technological models from the current educational literature.

One of my favorite methods of decision making is the Delphi model. I have written a separate chapter on the Delphi, Chapter 8, and I have referred to this model throughout this book. Besides the Delphi, a second effective method is force field analysis; force field analysis enhances the group's ability to visualize and to analyze the elements of a problem.

Another technique which I frequently use is the decision chart. I have included among the examples an unusual application of how the decision chart is used to resolve problems for maintenance management personnel. The decision chart can be adapted for almost any kind of a situation. In future chapters I discuss decision charts for the board and superintendent, for the superintendent and principals, and for the principal and teacher.

SAMPLE DECISION-MAKING TECHNIQUES

FORCE FIELD ANALYSIS

Purpose

Force Field Analysis provides a process for group problem solving. Through the identification of facilitating and hindering forces which are affecting a problem situation, strategies can be developed to move from a status quo to a potential solution.

Materials

Force Field Analysis handouts, butcher paper, markers, and tape.

Instructions

- Divide the participants into small groups; have the groups select a recorder.
- Provide all participants with a Force Field Analysis handout; have the recorder draw the diagram from the handout on butcher paper.
- Ask groups to quickly state an abbreviated version of the problem and to write it in the proper space.
- Ask groups to develop an abbreviated version of the ideal state and its opposite; record in appropriate spaces.

- Ask groups to brainstorm and record those facilitating forces which are assisting movement towards the ideal state.
- Ask group to brainstorm and record those hindering forces which are diminishing movement towards the ideal state.
- Ask the group to draw arrows based on assigned 1 to 5 values according to the following scale:
    1 - It has almost nothing to do with the problem.
    2 - It is of relatively little importance.
    3 - It is of moderate importance.
    4 - It is an important factor.
    5 - It is a major factor.
- Ask the group to select those facilitating and hindering factors which they want to work on.
- Develop action plans to strengthen the facilitating factors and weaken the hindering factors.

Time

Approximately 30 minutes for completing the Force Field Analysis handout and about 30 to 90 additional minutes for completing the action planning.

Comments

In developing plans to solve problems, groups frequently are uncreative and do not examine all of the factors. This process provides an easy tool for groups to examine in a systematized way all those positive and negative factors affecting a problem situation. This activity varies from the Polar Search activity in that there is an evaluation of the factors with a direct movement to action planning. Force Field Analysis is usually used with more limited and clearly defined problem situations.

Sample Chart

FORCED FIELD ANALYSIS

Facilitating Forces   Hindering Forces

Strengths

1 2 3 4 5   5 4 3 2 1

Opposite   Ideal
of Ideal   State
State

Problem

(Group recorder reproduces this on butcher paper)

. . .

DECISION CHART

Purpose

The purpose of this process is to assist groups of individuals who have varying responsibilities to predetermine roles and responsibilities in decision making. This process, after its initial implementation, needs to be continued on an ongoing basis so that decisions can be added or deleted as the need arises.

Materials

Butcher paper, markers, tape, and decision charts.

Instructions

- Discuss with the group the various limitations which affect local decision making. These limitations may be established by legislation, State Code, local board policy, local site policy, and employment contracts.

- Explain the general decision-making levels.
  - I - Complete Authority
  - II - Authority to decide or act, but must inform others of action.
  - III - Authority to act with prior approval.
  - IV - Consulted, but decision comes from someone else.
- Elicit from the group categories of actions. These categories at a local school site might include staff, classroom program, curriculum and evaluation, special programs, student discipline, supplies and textbooks, budget, and facilities.
- Use the Polar Search, Agreement Minus One, Clustering, and Clarifying techniques for determining specific actions for each category.
- Provide pre-printed Decision Charts or have individuals record the actions in the appropriate space.
- When all items have been selected for the Decision Chart, discuss each action and determine who has authority to make each decision. In making these determinations it may be necessary to consult policy or legislative manuals to determine final responsibility for completed action.
- Prepare a master Decision Chart for each participant.
- Add or delete actions as the need arises.
- Modify the authority column as legislation, policies or personnel change.

Time

Approximately 3 to 6 hours is required for the initial establishment of items for the Decision Chart. The time will vary depending on the number of actions and number of participants. Determining the level of responsibility for decisions depends on the number of items selected and the decision-making skills of the group.

Comments

While many people may look upon the establishment of the chart as an important product, the process used in the development of the chart is of greater significance. This process fosters team work and clarifies in advance potential problem areas. With modifications, this process can be used in determining the decision-making authority between boards and administrators, district administrators and site administrators, site administrators and teachers, teachers and students, and site staff and parents.

Sample Decision-Making Chart

The following is a unique application of the decision chart with maintenance management to clarify their authority in the school district.

MD UNIFIED SCHOOL DISTRICT
DECISION-MAKING CHART FOR MAINTENANCE MANAGEMENT
February, 1982

Maintenance Management Degree of Authority

I = COMPLETE AUTHORITY   I have complete authority to decide to act within the limits of district policy.

II = ACT AND INFORM   I have complete authority to act or decide but must inform my immediate supervisor.

III = PRIOR APPROVAL   I have authority to act with prior approval of my immediate supervisor.

IV = DISTRICT DIRECTION   I may be consulted but decision or direction comes from my immediate supervisor.

I   II   III   IV   (X = Authority Level)

				A. PERSONNEL SELECTION AND EVALUATION
X				1. Interview and select an employee to be under my direct supervision.
X				2. Assume the ongoing leadership responsibility associated with actively working with the Personnel Department in finding employees for my work force.
		X		3. Decide to terminate an employee.
	X			4. Reprimand an employee under my supervision and place a notation to that effect in his personnel file.
X				5. Evaluate the performance of a worker directly under my supervision.

I	II	III	IV	(X = Authority Level)

I	II	III	IV	
	X			6. Evaluate and decide to delay an employee's normal annual progression to the next highest step.
		X		7. Determine the type of employee—man, woman, student, full-time, part-time—for a specific vacancy in my area.
		X		8. Decide to advance an outstanding employee in my area to next highest pay step after only seven months in order to keep him from resigning and taking a higher paying job elsewhere.
X				9. Discipline—two-week suspension—an employee in my area for repeated violation of safety regulations.
		X		10. Decide to terminate an employee for unsatisfactory work performance.
			X	11. Determine pay level for various positions.
X				12. Discipline—two-week suspension—an employee for repeated tardiness.
		X		13. Select an employee for an existing vacancy from the eligibility list.
		X		14. Secretary tells me where to get off and I feel she has gone too far.
X				15. I find employees taking a 30 minute mid-morning break.
X				16. One of my employees tells me off.
X				17. I feel an employee needs in-service in a specific area.

B. WORK-RELATED RESPONSIBILITIES

I	II	III	IV	
		X		18. Reassign maintenance workers from one area (painting) to another area (carpentry).
X				19. At district expense, authorize employee to leave early.
		X		20. Select a worker to assume an acting supervisory role in the supervisor's absence.
		X		21. Set up morning arrival time and afternoon departure time for workers in my area.

I	II	III	IV	(X = Authority Level)
X				22. Reassign responsibilities—same area, same job classification.
		X		23. Change work hours from 7 a.m. - 3 p.m. to 3 p.m. - ll p.m., same job classification, for employees in my area.
		X		24. Authorize overtime pay for an employee in my area.
		X		25. Assign an employee to do maintenance work outside of job description.
X				26. Decide to have a specific job done in lieu of another job.
X				27. Truck breaks down and employees have no work to do at that particular school yet will be there for the next two hours.
X				28. Employee is spending time every day sharing non-job related information and it is costing valuable time.
X				29. Employee has done work of a poor quality and it needs to be done over again.
		X		30. Employees working under me are receiving oral working orders or instructions from an assistant superintendent.
		X		31. My decisions with employees working directly under me are being changed by others in the division.
		X		32. I have a new idea for changing the operational procedures within maintenance that would affect two other supervisors.
	X			33. Another supervisor has asked to use one of my employees for two days.
				C. GENERAL JOB-RELATED RESPONSIBILITIES
		X		34. Decide what level of building cleanliness and appearance to maintain.
X				35. Decide by priority of the 15 jobs I have received in which order I will do them.
		X		36. Decide if an item should be considered for an outside contract as opposed to being done in my particular area of responsibility.

I	II	III	IV	(X = Authority Level)
	X			37. Decide to modify a work order because I feel it should be changed.
X				38. Decide to modify a work order after consulting with administrator in charge and he agrees.
	X			39. Principal demands you make a minor repair not covered by a work order that I really feel should not be done.
		X		40. Secretary gives me a work order I feel is incorrect and demands I do it.
		X		41. Accept work orders directly from schools.
	X			42. Accept requests for work not covered by a work order, of an emergency nature, while at a school site.
X				43. Principal demands I make a minor repair not covered by a work order that I feel really needs attention.
		X		44. Principal demands a major repair not covered by a work order.
		X		45. Materials are, in my estimation, of poor quality.
	X			46. Superintendent requests that I do a little job (3 hours) for him not covered by a work order.
	X			47. Students are fighting on the playground and I feel someone is going to get hurt.
		X		48. The work order procedure being used is not working to my satisfaction.
			X	49. Decide whether a specific job that is requested by a school should be done or not be done.
			X	50. Decide which keys are to be given to which staff members within a school or area.
		X		51. Authorize the purchase of an item not contained in the district warehouse.
	X			52. Respond to the newspapers when they request information about a particular problem in my area.

I   II   III   IV   (X = Authority Level)

				D. IN-SERVICE EDUCATION
	X			53. Set up an in-service training program for the workers in my area to be held from 3:30 to 4:30 two days a week for two weeks.
	X			54. Retain a consultant for inservice training of staff in my area.
	X			55. I would like to attend an in-service meeting or conference that I feel has job value.

. . .

PAINT THE WALL

Purpose

The Paint the Wall Exercise is designed to illustrate the pros and cons of seeking total consensus.

Materials

None.

Instructions

- To carry out the exercise, the facilitator asks for eight volunteers. The eight volunteers and the facilitator sit in a small circle with the remaining people standing behind the circle.
- These eight people along with the facilitator attempt to make a decision by total concensus with equal input for all nine participants.
- All eight are told by the facilitator that they are teachers on a teaching team and the room in which they are now located is their open-space teaching area. The area is to be repainted next week. The decision to be made by total consensus is the color this room will be painted. The facilitator states that it must be only one color. "We cannot have one wall one color and another wall a different color, and we cannot wallpaper and have stripes or anything of that nature."
- The facilitator then gives these additional directions, "In order to insure equal and total input, you will not

be allowed to state why you want a given color nor will you be allowed to 'put down' someone else's color." The decision will be made by each person beginning with the facilitator stating the color he would prefer until everyone states the same color. Anyone may pass a given round, but if that person passes and the rest concur or name the same color, the decision is made.

• The group that is standing is told to watch for two things: (1) reaction of participants while the exercise is under way, (2) the quality of the decision being made. After a brief period of time, it will become obvious that the group has two or three colors to which they are gravitating. At this point the facilitator should stop the group and indicate to them that it is obvious they are considering several colors. "We want this decision to be made by total consensus. There-fore, if any color currently under consideration is not acceptable to any one person, all you have to do is indicate that by raising your hand or stating that you do not want that color when another person names that given color." "For example, is there anyone who could not stand this room if it were painted red?" If someone raises a hand, the color is eliminated. You do this with every color that was named in the last round.

• The facilitator says to the group, "Now we go back to the same process, but before we do, is there anyone in the group who does not care what color the room is to be painted and wants out of the process?" If someone indicates he wants out, then simply say, "Thank you. Please stay seated, but do not partici-pate." The point is simply that there should be an opportunity for input, but not forced involvement in a decision. Then the process begins again by naming any color that was under consideration before and which was not eliminated, any new color, but not any color that was excluded.

• This process is followed until the group agrees on one color. The color is generally in the neutral range—tan, sand, off-white. When the decision is finally reached, the facilitator asks the eight participants, "For how many of you was the color decided upon your first choice?" Almost always, no one chose this color as his first choice. The point is that in consensus seeking of any nature, the process dictates compromise; it reduces a chance for the more creative decision. However, in some situations the group must compromise to the point that enough people agree with the decision so it can be implemented. The decision that cannot be implemented is not a good decision.

- Ask the group how many people it took to block a given decision. Obviously, it took only one. In total consensus seeking this is exactly what can happen. One person can block the decision of the entire group. The point is that we should give the people the opportunity to choose not to be involved in a given decision or accept an 80 percent level of consensus.

- The facilitator should ask the entire group, "Were there any things that you observed during the process?" Many times those watching will comment about the obvious pressure felt from one person to another as the process continued. The second comment may be that many people will play games. In other words, if participant No.1 knocks out participant No. 3's color, participant No. 3 may knock out No. 1's color.

Time

The process usually takes about 25 minutes.

Comments

Total input eliminates the expertise that may be present within the group. For example, someone in the group may understand color and its effect on mood, and so on. This should be taken into consideration before the decision-making process begins. If this is not done, you are pooling ignorance, not taking advantage of expertise.

In most real situations if a committee or task force has done its homework, after a relatively short period of time—20 to 40 minutes, the group has a good idea of the general direction it is going. The time is then consumed, sometimes with a great deal of emotion and frustration, deciding the wording.

This Paint the Wall exercise is helpful for showing groups what actually happens in decision-making processes.

. . .

FIST TO FIVE

Purpose
This process is a convenient way to determine the degree of support within the group toward a given proposal.

Materials
None.

Instructions
- Once the task force or committee has indicated that they are moving in a clear direction, the facilitator states the proposal or direction as he perceives it. He then asks every member of the group to indicate how he feels about that direction based on a scale of fist to five.
- The fist to five simply means:

  Fist = That is not a good idea, and I am going to block you if you try to implement it (in other words, a no vote).

  One finger = I do not agree, but I promise not to block it.

  Two fingers = I do not agree, but I will work for it.

  Three fingers = I am neutral.

  Four fingers = It is a good idea, and I will work for it.

  Five fingers = It is a great idea, and I will be one of the leaders in implementing it.

  In other words, the Fist to Five is simply a scale from a no vote to a yes vote with varying degrees in between.

- Once every one in the group has indicated how he feels, the leader should turn to any blocker and ask, "What part of our current proposal do you object to?" The reason for doing this is two-fold. One reason for having input into decision making is that often one individual can see a particular problem with the current decision that the rest of the group has not seen. If that person holds up a fist, it is possible for the rest of the group to "see the light" and to compromise. Secondly, input is helpful because it places the responsibility or accountability where it rightfully belongs, with the person who has an objection. This forces that person to state openly to the rest of his colleagues exactly what he objects to and why. This reduces the possibility that the individual will object simply because he does not feel well that day, or because he does not like the person who proposed the idea.

Time
Approximately 5 minutes.

Comments
The leader should know that to implement a decision, the group should have no fewer than 70 percent in the three-to-five category, as long as there are not 20 percent organized against that decision. The closer the three-to-five category comes to 80 percent, the better the chance for smooth implementation.

The Fist to Five process also tells the leader where to spend his time. The greatest return will be realized if the leader spends the majority of his time with the 3's and 4's. The 4's are already predisposed to the idea and with more support and information, they can become a 5. The 3's, who are neutral on this issue to begin with, again with more support and information, can become 4's. The more who become 4's and 5's, the greater the chances are for smooth, strong implementation.

. . .

ADVOCATING

Purpose
This decision-making technique provides for debate in a structured manner concerning the pro's and con's of issues. Through this process arguments become focused: those who talk excessively are limited; and those who are reticent are encouraged. This activity is designed to deal with the importance of two or more issues; it should be carried out immediately before a decision is to be made by a

group, or before a group is to determine the relative importance of issues.

Materials

List of issues and a watch or clock with a second hand.

Instructions

- Post, in clear view of all participants, the list of issues to be considered or the issue to be adopted or rejected.
- Explain that each issue will be dealt with individually, that participants will be able to speak in favor or in opposition for 30 seconds, that no one can speak further unless someone else has addressed the issue, and that lobbying will continue until no one has anything to add.
- Proceed through the issues one by one until all advocacy has taken place.

Time

Variable depending on the number of issues, the number of participants, and the degree of controversy. When ten issues are being considered by 25 participants this activity will require about 45 minutes.

Comments

This activity usually fosters an animated discussion as individuals attempt to persuade the group to support or oppose issues. It is critical that the facilitator enforce the rules so there is no favoritism.

. . .

CONSENSUS BRAINSTORMING

Purpose

This form of brainstorming is much different from the usual brainstorming techniques. This process is used to generate general, acceptable responses. It is usually used to develop lists of items which can be readily accepted by a group.

Materials

Butcher paper, markers, and tape.

Instructions

- Write in clear, concise language the issue for the group to address, such as, "What are the criteria for determining effective schools?"

- Ask individuals to provide responses. When a response is given, ask, by a show of hands, for those who agree with the response. Record the response if at least 20 percent of the group are in agreement.
- Continue the process until there are no further responses which can obtain the 20 percent support.

Time
Approximately 20 minutes depending on the scope of the issue.

Comments
This process should never be used when there is a desire for creativity. It is only recommended for use when broad categories of familiar responses are discussed.

. . .

POLAR SEARCH

Purpose
This activity serves to diffuse strong emotions as well as to establish a base for the generation of quality ideas. By carrying out this process individuals are given permission not only to state but to see posted their favorite gripes as well as their pet causes. Once a group has completed this activity, participants are usually ready to proceed with the identification of alternate solutions.

Materials
Butcher paper, markers, and tape.

Instructions
- Select a general goal or solution statement, such as, "to make schools effective" or "to reduce drug abuse."
- Explain the rules for brainstorming by presenting CREATE.

    C ompile vast numbers
    R efrain from evaluating
    E xpect diversity
    A void discussion
    T itillate your imagination
    E laborate on other's ideas

- Form groups of 5 to 10.

- Have each group select a recorder to write ideas on butcher paper.
- Ask each group to brainstorm barriers or obstacles to reaching the goal.
- Ask each group to brainstorm facilitating or positive factors for reaching the goal.
- Ask the group to post and review their results.

Time

Approximately 20 minutes for the entire process with 3 - 5 minutes allocated for each brainstorm activity.

Comments

This activity is usually used to vent feelings and to spark creativity. Leave the brainstorming lists on the wall for the rest of the session. For on-going groups it is usually recommended to have the lists typed and reproduced.

. . .

AGREEMENT MINUS ONE

Purpose

This technique is similar to consensus brainstorming but is used with small groups. Through this process groups of four to six generate ideas which have the support of everyone in the group or at least everyone minus one. This activity results in quality ideas which have a high probability of being similar to ideas generated by other groups and having the support of a large portion of the total group.

Materials

Six by eighteen-inch strips of paper, markers, and tape.

Instructions

- Form groups of four to six. Have each group choose a recorder.
- Post a clear and simple question for the groups to address, for example, "What actions will help us achieve our goal?"
- Ask each group to think of actions. Instruct them to record an action on a strip of butcher paper when everyone in the group agrees to the action, or when there is only one person who disagrees with the action.

- Have groups continue the process until all action which follows the criteria have been recorded.

Time

Approximately 20 minutes.

Comments

This activity is frequently used following polar search, which usually serves as a trigger for the development of potential actions. High energy and spirited debate are usually found in groups as they attempt, through cooperation and compromise, to develop satisfactory objectives.

. . .

ENDS/MEANS WEIGHTING

Purpose

This activity provides a weighting of means according to their impact on ends. It can be used in diverse situations in which there is a series of alternative actions which have potential impact on another series of outcomes.

Materials

Ends/Means Weighting forms for each participant.

Instructions

- Have Ends/Means Weighting forms preprinted or have participants list the preselected list of means on the left side of the form and the ends across the top.
- Ask participants to take one end at a time, moving vertically, and to assess on a standard scale what kind of effect each mean would have in achieving the end. Post the following standard scale for participants to use:

    0 - 3 low impact

    4 - 6 medium impact

    7 - 10 high impact

- Ask participants to proceed by first selecting and scoring the lowest and highest valued means and then considering the mid-values represented by the other means. The score for each means should relate to the other scores in that column for comparison.
- Collect forms after they have been completed.

- Tabulate the sums for each cell on the matrix, putting the totals in the totals column.
- Add up the totals and compute the percentage of the total which each means represents, putting the results in the percent column.
- Rank order the means with the top percentage being one.

Time
   Approximately 15 minutes for most 10 x 10 matrices.

Comments
   This activity may seem laborious for some groups. Stressing the importance of the results usually assists groups in approaching the task in a positive manner. This process is different from most weighting or ranking activities in that it weights multiple means against multiple outcomes. The tabulating of the matrix is time-consuming but can usually move quickly if several people are assisting. In some situations, the ends may have been previously weighted. In these cases the scores in each vertical column should be multiplied by the weight.

Sample Form

ENDS/MEANS WEIGHTING FORM

MEANS	% RANK TOTALS	ENDS A B C D E F G H I J K L
1.		
2.		
3.		
4.		
5.		
6.		
7.		
8.		
9.		
10.		

. . .

PAIRED WEIGHTING

Purpose

Paired weighting is a technique through which individuals and groups can assign relative values to 10 or more issues. Through this process it is possible to determine not only how strongly an individual feels about a particular issue in relation to other issues but how the total group responds.

Materials

A list of 10 or more issues, paired weighting forms for each participant, a calculator, markers, and an Ends/Means Weighting Form.

Sample Score Sheet

PAIRED WEIGHTING SCORE SHEET

```
1  1  1  1  1  1  1  1  1  1  1  1  1  1  1  1  1  1  1
-----------------------------------------------------      1 = _____
2  3  4  5  6  7  8  9 10 11 12 13 14 15 16 17 18 19 20
   2  2  2  2  2  2  2  2  2  2  2  2  2  2  2  2  2  2
   ---------------------------------------------------      2 = _____
   3  4  5  6  7  8  9 10 11 12 13 14 15 16 17 18 19 20
      3  3  3  3  3  3  3  3  3  3  3  3  3  3  3  3  3
      ------------------------------------------------      3 = _____
      4  5  6  7  8  9 10 11 12 13 14 15 16 17 18 19 20
         4  4  4  4  4  4  4  4  4  4  4  4  4  4  4  4
         ---------------------------------------------      4 = _____
         5  6  7  8  9 10 11 12 13 14 15 16 17 18 19 20
            5  5  5  5  5  5  5  5  5  5  5  5  5  5  5
            ------------------------------------------      5 = _____
            6  7  8  9 10 11 12 13 14 15 16 17 18 19 20
               6  6  6  6  6  6  6  6  6  6  6  6  6  6
               ---------------------------------------      6 = _____
               7  8  9 10 11 12 13 14 15 16 17 18 19 20
                  7  7  7  7  7  7  7  7  7  7  7  7  7
                  ------------------------------------      7 = _____
                  8  9 10 11 12 13 14 15 16 17 18 19 20
                     8  8  8  8  8  8  8  8  8  8  8  8
                     ---------------------------------      8 = _____
                     9 10 11 12 13 14 15 16 17 18 19 20
                        9  9  9  9  9  9  9  9  9  9  9
                        ------------------------------      9 = _____
                       10 11 12 13 14 15 16 17 18 19 20
                       10 10 10 10 10 10 10 10 10 10
                       ------------------------------     10 = _____
                       11 12 13 14 15 16 17 18 19 20
```

Continued next page.

11 11 11 11 11 11 11 11 11

----------------------   11 = _____

12 13 14 15 16 17 18 19 20

12 12 12 12 12 12 12 12

--------------------   12 = _____

13 14 15 16 17 18 19 20

$$\frac{N\,(N\text{-}1)}{2}$$

13 13 13 13 13 13 13

------------------   13 = _____

14 15 16 17 18 19 20

14 14 14 14 14 14

--------------   14 = _____

15 16 17 18 19 20

15 15 15 15 15

------------   15 = _____

16 17 18 19 20

16 16 16 16

---------   16 = _____

17 18 19 20

17 17 17

------   17 = _____

18 19 20

18 18

---   18 = _____

19 20

19

--   19 = _____

20

20 = _____

Instructions
- Post the list of issues to be weighted and hand out the paired weighting forms.
- Explain that each item will be compared to every other item and that a decision will be made as to which is of greater value or comes first.
- Explain to the group that in the top row the first issue will be compared with every other issue.

- Inform the participants that you will read each compared issues twice and will then move to the next comparison which will be to the right.
- Ask participants to circle the number of the issue which is more important or comes first in each comparison.
- Proceed by reading the comparisons for the top row at a regular pace so participants do not ponder over judgments too long, become confused or indecisive.
- Proceed to the lower rows on the form in the same manner as the top row.
- Ask participants to score their own forms, if time allows. Explain that the scoring involves counting the number of times each number is circled. Show participants that all ones are in the top row, that the last number is in the right vertical column, and that all other numbers are in an L-shape, with some numbers in a column and some in a row. Ask participants to record their totals on a posted End/Means Weighting Form placed on the wall, or collect their forms and compile and reproduce the form. The relative values, and ranking for each issue may be calculated by totalling all the participants' scores. A more meaningful relative value may be established by calculating the percentage for each issue in the relationship to the total responses.

Time

Variable depending on the number of issues and the number of participants. Approximately 45 minutes is needed for weighting 20 issues by 15 participants.

Comments

This process works best with 10 to 20 issues, beyond 20 the process becomes laborious, but can be carried out with up to 30 issues. Paired Weighting is a tool which can be used for numerous purposes—weighting objectives, determining staffing assignments, and establishing budgets. Twenty item forms can usually be used for most situations.

SHARED WEIGHTING

Purpose

Shared Weighting is a technique in which individuals and groups can assign relative values to nine issues or less. Through this process it is possible to determine, not only how strongly an individual feels about a particular issue in relation to other issues, but how the total group responds. As can be seen, this process is similar to paired weighting.

Materials

A list of nine issues or less, shared weighting forms for each participant, a calculator, markers, and an End Means Weighting form, as used in Paired Weighting.

Instructions

- Post the list of issues to be weighted and hand out the Shared Weighting forms.
- Explain that each item will be compared to every other item and that a decision will be made as to which is of greater value or comes first.
- Inform the participants that compared issues will be read twice before moving on to the next comparison which will be to the right.
- Ask participants to divide five points between the two issues in each comparison. Explain that this allows participants to determine how much more important one issue is than another.
- Show participants that all ones are in the top row, that the last number is in the right vertical column, and that all other numbers are in an L shape, with some numbers in a column and some in a row.
- Ask participants to record their totals on a posted End/Means Weighting form placed on the wall or collect their forms and compile and reproduce an end/means weighting form. The relative value and ranking for each issue may then be calculated by totaling all of the participants' scores. A more meaningful relative value may be established by calculating the percentage for each issue in relationship to the total responses.

Time

Variable, depending on the number of issues and the number of participants. Approximately 15 minutes is needed for weighting nine issues by 15 participants.

Comments

This process works best with nine issues or less. Shared Weighting can be used for numerous purposes—weighting objectives, determining staffing assignments, and establishing budgets.

Sample Weighting Form

SHARED WEIGHTING FORM

$$\frac{N(N-1)}{2}$$

$\frac{1}{2}$	$\frac{1}{3}$	$\frac{1}{4}$	$\frac{1}{5}$	$\frac{1}{6}$	$\frac{1}{7}$	$\frac{1}{8}$	$\frac{1}{9}$	$1 =$ ___
	$\frac{2}{3}$	$\frac{2}{4}$	$\frac{2}{5}$	$\frac{2}{6}$	$\frac{2}{7}$	$\frac{2}{8}$	$\frac{2}{9}$	$2 =$ ___
		$\frac{3}{4}$	$\frac{3}{5}$	$\frac{3}{6}$	$\frac{3}{7}$	$\frac{3}{8}$	$\frac{3}{9}$	$3 =$ ___
			$\frac{4}{5}$	$\frac{4}{6}$	$\frac{4}{7}$	$\frac{4}{8}$	$\frac{4}{9}$	$4 =$ ___
				$\frac{5}{6}$	$\frac{5}{7}$	$\frac{5}{8}$	$\frac{5}{9}$	$5 =$ ___
					$\frac{6}{7}$	$\frac{6}{8}$	$\frac{6}{9}$	$6 =$ ___
						$\frac{7}{8}$	$\frac{7}{9}$	$7 =$ ___
							$\frac{8}{9}$	$8 =$ ___
								$9 =$ ___

. . .

SPEND A BUCK

Purpose

This technique is a simple activity for individuals and groups to use to determine the relative importance of several different issues. This activity is best used when weighting 5 to 10 issues, but could be used with up to 15 issues.

Materials

A list of 5 to 15 issues, enough 3x5 cards for each participant to have one card per issue, end/means weighting form, calculator, markers.

Instructions

- Distribute 3x5 cards to participants and have them write one issue on each card.
- Instruct them that they have $1 to spend on the issues according to their relative importance. Tell them that they must spend a minimum of 20 cents on an item. Have them write the amount, to total $1, on the cards.
- Have participants start with their top priorities, then go to their low priorities, and to finish with the middle-valued group. Adjustments in spending can be made as they go through the activity.
- Have participants record their spending on a relative value chart, or have them write their names on the cards, collect them and tabulate them after the session.
- Compute the totals, percentages, and rankings for the issues.
- Have the group analyze individual as well as group weightings.

Time

Approximately 30 minutes with 10 items and 15 participants.

Comments

Groups usually enjoy this activity because it provides a change of pace when it is necessary to weight several items. If there is a fairly large number, 10 to 15 items, it is appropriate to reduce the minimum expenditure to 10 cents.

. . .

MATCH BOOK WEIGHTING

Purpose

This activity provides a simple mechanism for individuals or groups to quickly determine the relative importance of several different issues. Best used with 5 to 10 issues, it could be used with up to 15 issues. This activity can only be used when a total group weighting is desired—individual ratings are anonymous.

Materials

One book of matches per participant, marked cups for each issue, a list of issues.

Instructions

- Post and review the list of issues with the participants.
- Instruct participants that each match is worth 5 cents. With normal match books they will have a dollar.
- Start with the first issue asking participants to remove the number of matches equivalent to the value they place on the issue. Collect all of the matches in the appropriate cup.
- Continue until all issues have been addressed.
- Inform participants that it is all right to have some unspent matches. This is preferable to going back to issues or over-rating the final issues due to a miscalculation of spending.
- Total the value for each issue by counting the matches and multiplying by 5 cents.

Time

Approximately 30 minutes for 10 issues and 20 participants.

Comments

Participants usually enjoy this change of pace weighting process. The process may be varied by using a substitute for the matches—beads, pennies, or toothpicks. This weighting process should not be used where a careful analysis is required because the fast pace makes it difficult for participants to accurately compare each item with the other items.

. . .

STACKING THE DECK

Purpose

This process is used with individuals and groups to determine the priority of a list of items. The physical munipulation of the cards facilitates the process of determining priorities.

Materials

Three by five cards for the number of participants times the number of ideas for which a priority must be determined.

Instructions

- Distribute preprinted or blank cards. When using blank cards ask participants to write one item from the list on each card.
- Ask participants to select the most important card. Have them write a number on the card equal to the total number of cards. If they should be ranking 10 items, a "10" would go on this card. Have them set this card aside.
- Ask participants to select the least important card and write a "1" on the card. Have them set this card aside.
- Ask participants to select the most important card which remains, and as in the case of 10 cards, to write a "9" on it.
- Have participants continue the process until all cards have been given a number.
- Tally the results by totaling the values for each item. The highest number is the top priority. To facilitate the tallying when individual rankings want to be maintained, participants can place their data on a master chart.

Time

Approximately 15 minutes.

Comments

This process should only be used when an arithmetic progression rank order is required; the resulting data does not allow for an individual to show how much more important some item is than another. Most groups enjoy this process because it moves quickly and is a change from the normal written or verbal process techniques.

. . .

NEGATIVE VOTING

Purpose

This technique is used to reach consensus on an issue when time, interest, or value does not allow for prolonged discussion. Through this process consensus can be quickly reached to include those who agree, those who are not sure, and those who do not agree, but do not feel upset by the group's decision.

Materials

Butcher paper, markers, and tape.

Instructions

- Write the issue in clear, concise language on butcher paper and post. This issue may have been generated previously by the group or by a member or members of the group.
- Review the issue and clarify as needed.
- Ask who cannot accept the statement. If no one responds, assume that the group accepts the statement, even though there may not be strong commitment.
- Ask for suggested modifications from negative votes until negative voting consensus is reached.

Time

Approximately 15 minutes.

Comments

This process should be used in gaining consensus on extremely broad or extremely minute issues. It is especially useful in adopting broad, general goal statements. If there is a strong negative vote, the facilitator should be prepared to switch to an extended consensus decision-making process.

. . .

CLUSTERING

Purpose

This process makes it possible for a large group to consolidate similar ideas into categories. Through this process all ideas are accepted, posted, and included in the final idea categories. This activity usually follows Agreeing Minus One.

Materials

Butcher paper, markers, and tape. Strips of paper with actions.

Instructions

- Divide the total group into small groups of six to eight; have each group select a recorder.
- Ask each group to generate ideas and to write each one on a separate strip of paper.
- Ask a group to present one of the actions they have recorded on a strip of paper. Post it on the wall.
- Ask other groups to present strips which have the same or similar actions. Post them together when the total group agrees they are the same or very similar. If there is disagreement, ask for clarification from the contributing group. If there is any disagreement about similarity, do not force the issue. Instead, start another category.
- Ask for a different action after all similar actions have been offered. Continue through the process until all strips of paper have been posted.
- Go through each group of actions asking the group for general titles or categories. When a title is suggested, use negative voting to obtain consensus.
- Record the general titles over each category and also on a separate butcher paper which serves as a summary sheet.
- Ask if any other categories have been omitted. Accept only those categories which have the support of a group of people equal in number to that required for an idea to be accepted in a small group. Individuals who had an idea which was not supported in a group may obtain the necessary support from the total group.
- Continue the process until all suggestions are exhausted.

Time

Approximately 30 minutes for a group of 25.

Comments

Groups usually enjoy this process as they compete to see who has the most different or the greatest number of actions. Following this

process the categories with subtopics should be typed and reproduced so that all contributions are recognized and can be used for
future planning.

. . .

CLARIFYING

Purpose
   This activity is designed to provide groups with a process through
which they can gain clarity about issues being considered. This process is especially significant when issues have been contributed to a
master list from small groups. Because of differing terminology, issues
which seem clear may need clarification.

Materials
   List of issues.

Instructions
   • Put the list of issues discussed in clear view of the
     group.
   • Explain that they are not to be concerned with debat-
     ing the importance of an issue at this time.
   • Tell the group that they will proceed through the list
     one issue at a time. Explain that if they are uncertain
     about the meaning of an issue, to raise their hand.
     The person or group who contributes the issue will
     then explain what they meant.
   • Continue through each issue until the list is ex-
     hausted.

Time
   Approximately one minute per issue.

Comments
   This process is important because disagreements frequently arise
from confusion about intent or meaning. Make certain that no value
judgments are made during this activity.

. . .

CORRELATED PLOTTING

Purpose
   This process is used to graphically analyze a list of actions when
data has been gathered according to two different criteria. When ana-

lyzing the objectives, plot them according to their importance in reaching a goal and according to their current usefulness.

Materials
A list of actions which have been weighted according to two different criteria, butcher paper, markers, and tape.

Instructions
- Draw a graph with one criteria used for the vertical axis and the other criteria used for the horizontal axis. Place the positive values at the top of the vertical and at the right of the horizontal axis.
- Place the average for each axis at the intersection.
- Plot the individual items using the two scores.
- Analyze the location of the items according to the following example:
  — high value/high performance - maintain
  — high value/low performance - opportunity
  — low value/high performance - overskill
  — low value/low performance - gripes
- Proceed with action planning which usually stresses those items which have been determined to be opportunity actions.

Time
The graph and plotting can be done outside of the meeting with subsequent analysis done by the group. This takes approximately 20 minutes.

Comments
This activity is usually best done when the items and values have been agreed upon by the group and when it can be repeated to show movement or trends.

. . .

INTERACTIVE CLARIFICATION

Purpose
This activity is an ongoing communication tool employed by group facilitators to ensure that the content and feelings of participant responses are understood by the group.

Materials
None.

Instructions

- Listen carefully to responses which participants offer making sure that the feelings and content are clear.
- Ask participants clarifying questions if it seems that there is unclear communication. Examples of clarifying questions include:
  — It sounds like you are feeling _____ about this issue?
  — It seems like you are saying (paraphrase content)?
  — Is what you are saying the same as _____?
- Ask clarifying questions when other participants raise questions about someone else's statement.
- Move on in the discussion as soon as clarification is reached.

Time

Approximately one minute per episode.

Comments

This activity should be carried out in an incidental way so participants do not feel insecure about unclear communication. The best use of this technique occurs when participants are unaware of the facilitator's intervention. The facilitator should never offer a personal value about statements being clarified.

. . .

HERE AND NOW

Purpose

The purpose of this activity is for participants to clarify their personal feelings related to the session and to share on a voluntary basis those feelings with the group. This activity assists facilitators in quickly assessing how participants are feeling about the session.

Materials

Copies of here and now worksheet.

Instructions

- Hand out worksheet to participants.
- Suggest that participants sit as quietly as possible for about one minute to get a sense of themselves, where they are, what sensations they are having, and their state of mind.

- Ask participants to write one word in each of the four sections of the worksheet that best describes their current feelings.
- Ask participants to select the word that describes their strongest feeling and to write it in the space at the lower left. Ask them to expand on the word in free form writing.
- Ask volunteers to share their written response with the group. Do not pressure anyone to share and do not comment on the responses unless there seems to be some general unrest which needs to be addressed.

Time
  Approximately 20 minutes.

Comments
  This activity is a quick process check which can be used when the facilitator detects that there may be some need to change the schedule or the approach. This activity is also helpful in obtaining informal evaluative feedback from a group.

Sample Worksheet

HERE AND NOW WORKSHEET

1 _____   2 _____

3 _____   4 _____

* _____   _____
_____
_____

. . .

SENTENCE COMPLETION

Purpose
  The purpose of this activity is to obtain personal, open-ended feedback from participants about the session. This activity can serve as a quick process check to determine the general status of the participants.

Materials
    Butcher paper, markers, tape.

Instructions
    - Tell participants that you are interested in obtaining
      feedback about the session.
    - Present the following incomplete sentences on
      butcher paper:
      I learned _____
      I wish _____
      I would like to _____
      I am feeling _____ because _____
    - Ask participants to write out the completion of one of
      these sentences.
    - Ask volunteers to share their sentences with the
      group. Do not pressure volunteers and do not allow
      specific discussion or comments about the responses.

Time
    Approximately 20 minutes.

Comments
    This activity provides quick feedback to the facilitator as well as the
group. This technique could be used during a session to obtain feedback which may help the group to vent concerns, or could be used at
the end of a session to obtain informal evaluative feedback. To
encourage feedback, the facilitator must show acceptance and of support for the participants.

· · ·

RULE OF ONE-THIRD

Purpose
    This technique is used to obtain a quick and reliable high, medium,
low ranking as related to individual and group perception of needs or
to their interest in pursuing action with a stated objective.

Materials
    Butcher paper and markers.

Instructions
    - List all goals, objectives, and actions to be considered
      on butcher paper.

- Divide the total number of statements by three to determine how many each participant may choose (15 divided by 3 = 5).
- Ask the participants to select five statements and record their choices (numbers) on scratch paper.
- Ask participants to indicate their choice for each statement with a show of hands, and record the total for each statement.

Time

Approximately 15 minutes.

Comments

This technique is especially useful when time is limited, and is effective with groups who have high trust and are skilled in group decision making. It also gives the less sophisticated group an easily managed technique.

· · ·

GROUP GOAL SETTING

Purpose

This process makes it possible for a large group to consolidate similar ideas into categories. Through this process all ideas are accepted, posted, and included in the final goal statements. This activity is also appropriate for determining objectives.

Materials

Butcher paper, markers, tape, and strips of paper (about 18 x 4).

Instructions

- Ask participants to record their goals on the strips of paper (only one goal per strip).
- Ask a participant to share one goal recorded on a strip of paper. Post it on the wall.
- Ask other participants to present strips which have the same or similar goals. Post them together when the total group agrees they are the same or very similar. If there is disagreement, ask for clarification from the contributing group or person. If there is any disagreement about similarity, do not force the issue; instead, start another category.

- Ask for a different action after all similar actions have been offered. Continue through the process until all strips of paper have been posted.
- Go through each group of goals asking the group for general titles or categories. When a title is suggested, use negative voting to obtain consensus.
- Record the stated goals over each category and also on a separate memory paper which serves as a summary sheet.
- Ask if there are any other categories which have been omitted. Individuals who had a goal that was not presented may add it to the list of goals. Obtain consensus for new goals through negative voting.
- Continue the process until all suggestions are exhausted.

Time
Approximately 20 minutes for a group of 25.

Comments
Following an advocacy period, the rule of one-third may be used to rank high, medium and low interest. Following the process, the ranked categories with subtopics should be typed, reproduced and shared so that all contributions are recognized and can be used for future planning.

. . .

GANTT CHART

Purpose
The Gantt chart can be used by groups to generate action plans which show tasks, timelines, and individual responsibilities. This chart provides a concise format in which plans can be easily communicated and monitored.

Materials
Gantt charts for each participant, butcher paper, markers, and tape.

Instructions
- Post the ranked list of objectives or activities. This may be a result of a Force Field Analysis activity or some list other series of activities.

- As a group, determine the target date for completion of each major action. Form groups of four or five to discuss each activity or objective.
- Ask the small groups to identify subtasks necessary for accomplishing the activity. This may be done through general discussion and consensus, brainstorming, clustering, advocacy and weighting, or force field analysis.
- Ask the small groups to share the task analysis of their action plan. When all plans have been accepted by the total group, they then determine the appropriate time for each subtask to be completed. If it is a single task, ask them to place an "X" in the appropriate space; if it is an ongoing task, ask them to start with an "X" and to draw a continuous line.
- Ask the group to indicate those who will be responsible for each task by writing names in the appropriate spaces and to indicate responsibility with an "X."
- Reproduce the groups' charts and distribute to the total group or make a master chart and post in staff room.

Time

Approximately 60 minutes depending on the number of high priority objectives.

Comments

Gantt planning charts provide opportunities for group members to be voluntarily and equally involved in the implementation of a school plan. These charts provide a visual dimension to measure ongoing progress, a ready reference to assist in monitoring and adjusting the plan throughout the implementation, and a process for self-evaluation.

Sample Chart

GANTT CHART

Objective: School Site Council Decides To
Administer Climate Survey

Date	ACTION	A	B	C	D	E	F
_____	1. Notify teaching staff.			X			
_____	2. Notify classified staff.	X					
.	3. Notify all families.					X	
.	4. Notify all students.			X			
.	5. Select every fourth family for survey.				X		
	6. Select every fourth student for survey.	X					
	7. Prepare self-addressed stamped envelopes.					X	
	8. Prepare family addressed envelopes.				X		
	9. Mail surveys to families.				X		
	10. Set time for staff to complete survey.			X			
	11. Set time for students to complete survey.			X			
	12. Notify community if it is to be minimum day.				X		
	13. Administer survey to:						
	a. teaching staff.			X			
	b. classified staff.				X		
	c. students.		X				
	14. Survey return date.				X		
	15. Return all collected data to R & D.						X

Person/Group Responsible (columns A–F)

Date	ACTION	A	B	C	D	E	F
	16. Teachers and Administration complete self needs assessment.				X		
	17. Send self assessment data to R & D.						X
	18. Upon return share data results with:						
	a. staff.				X		
	b. community.		X				
	c. students.						X
	d. site council.				X		
	19. Analyze data.	X					
	20. Prioritize need.	X					
	21. Prepare plan:						
	a. objectives for each need.						X
	b. activities for each objective.						X
	c. budget for each need.				X		
	d. timeline for implementation.		X				
	e. evaluation design.		X				
	22. Update plan.				X		

. . .

COMMENTS

This variety of decision-making techniques should provide numerous alternatives for a leader to meaningfully involve people who are going to be affected by a decision. Shared decision making is undoubtably the most difficult form of leadership; it requires the highest level of leadership skills.

The effectiveness, as well as the difficulties of shared decision making, are discussed in such recent books as *Search for Excellence, Megatrends, Corporate Cultures, Theory Z,* and *One Minute Manager.*

In education, these decision techniques, should assist the leader in involving people in a highly productive manner, and in placing decision making as close to the learner as possible.

Chapter 11
The Delphi

Over the years I took a complex procedure, the Delphi technique, and gradually experimented and refined it. This technique can be used in numerous and varied circumstances within education, business, and industry. I have had the privilege of conducting workshops using the Delphi in most states of the country as well as in Canada, and Southeast Asia, where I served as a consultant for the United States State Department to the American International Schools in Singapore, Kuala Lumpur, Malaysia, and Bangkok, Thailand.

Of all the decision-making techniques that are available and are used in school districts, I think this one has been by far the most practical and the most frequently used.

WHAT IS THE DELPHI?

HISTORICAL BACKGROUND

In response to the need for a process to help make decisions when the best answer was highly uncertain, the Rand Corporation of Santa Monica developed the Delphi technique. Originally it was used to help make predictions about the future. While Robert McNamara was secretary of defense he used the Delphi as a process of bringing together ideas of experts from several knowledge fields who were working on the space exploration program. Educators first used this technique to help determine desirable educational goals.

When the original Delphi technique was used for goal setting, the information generated by this process was organized into five different indices: 1) an educational goal index; 2) a quality of life index; 3) a perceived achievement index; 4) a priority index; and 5) an education trend index.

These index results were not meant to determine decisions but rather to provide decision makers with vital information. The indices identified the common goals for education from a scientific sampling of the community people, the students, and the educators. The indices also identified the different goals for these sub-populations. This original procedure in the use of the Delphi technique can still be valuable if you wish to spend the time and the effort. However, current uses of the Delphi technique can gather almost the same quality of information in far less time.

CURRENT USE OF THE DELPHI TECHNIQUE

Simply put, the Delphi technique is a method for collecting judgments which help people make decisions. The process has become so efficient that it can be used to arrive at complex decisions in a matter of minutes. It is highly usable in determining goals for education in curriculum, personnel, finance, community relations, student activities, management, and organizational decisions. It has been used to evaluate both the current effectiveness of organizations as well as of personnel and educational programs.

WHY USE THE DELPHI?

To involve others in decision making an administrator could employ one of three techniques: ask a single expert, which would provide only one person's judgment and might not be sufficient input; ask several experts, which could be a helpful method, but does deny the individual consultants the benefit of hearing other responses that might encourage refinement of their contributions; or ask a round table for consensus, which might be inadequate because group decisions reflect the special characteristics of group dynamics and their potential distortions more often than the objective truth. The Delphi, on the other hand, is an expeditious and efficient technique to derive input from 6 to 300 people at one time.

This technique is based on three simple premises: anonymity of respondents, controlled feed back, and statistical response. It allows for divergent viewpoints without distructive criticism by other members of the group; for a realistic or feasible solution rather than a socially accepted accord; and for a quick consensus without excessive, wandering discussions. The Delphi process avoids domination of the discusssion by vocal "ax grinders," by verbose participants, and by status leaders.

This process encourages both divergence and convergence in planning. In its initial stages, what seems like an abundance of goals are generated. However, this stage is essential for reaching the concerns and insights of all the participants. In the subsequent stages, the technique forces an emphasis on a half dozen or fewer items to which the group has given high priority. Most people in organizations cannot deal effectively with dozens of tasks in a highly efficient manner; using the Delphi technique ensures a focus on half a dozen of the top items. In the meantime members can still work on minor areas of interest that have been identified by this process. However, the group should understand that you are only going to write performance objectives and give progress reports on the priority items. Group members using the Delphi understand before beginning that they are both generating and selecting goals.

Two important points should be kept in mind before beginning this process. First, determine a specific problem or question to be considered by the group. This must be succinctly and clearly stated to allow members to know exactly what they are expected to answer. Second, select participants who have a stake in the outcome. The process is sensitive to the input and the priorities of each individual; therefore, the result should not be distorted by uninterested participants.

JMS DELPHI PROCESS

STEPS
DETERMINE THE QUESTION (as explained above)
SELECT THE PARTICIPANTS
EXPLAIN THE PROCESS
At this point in the process you should indicate precisely what will follow: how statements will be written; how cards will be collected; how responses will be clustered; all the way through to the final steps.
WRITE STATEMENTS
Use 3x5 cards on which the participants will write their statements. Participants must be specific and must write only one statement on each card. If participants are establishing one-year goals and three-to-

five-year goals at the same time, color-coded cards should be used. For example, use white cards for the one-year goals, and another color card for the three-to-five-year goals. Or, if you are conducting a personnel evaluation of "I like" and "I wish you would," the "likes" and the "woulds" should each be on a different colored card.

The size of the group determines how many cards each participant generates. The total number of cards that will appear on the printout should be no more than 100. I have used the process with up to 300 people, but I restricted them to one card, and also explained that we would be eliminating all items that were similar in an attempt to reduce the total number of statements under 100. This should be understood ahead of time. However, if the group is under 20, let each person generate as many cards as they wish. It does not make any difference whether one individual generates more cards than another. At this point in the Delphi process, the purpose is to generate as many ideas as possible, no matter where the ideas come from. If the problem is sensitive, such as an evaluation of a person, make sure that all the cards are left in. After participants have gone through the process a half a dozen or more times, the integrity of the process can still be maintained if the elimination of similar responses is allowed. However, in the beginning it is best to leave everything in, no matter how often an item is repeated.

Maintaining the credibility and integrity of the process is important. Sometimes, when the process is first used in a sensitive area, an individual will test the process by purposely misspelling a word to identify his card in the printout. The first few times the process is used duplicate all cards exactly in the printout—misspelling and all.

COLLECT THE CARDS

As people write their statements on 3x5 cards, they should put the completed card face down in front of them. Each person participating in the process should use the same type of writing instrument so no identification as to who generated the statement is possible.

Usually, if the group has been alerted ahead of time to be thinking of their input for the Delphi technique, the cards can be generated in 15 to 20 minutes. Large groups, generating from one to three cards, can usually do this in five minutes or less. As people complete their statements on the cards and are putting them face down in front of them, a trusted member of the group who has completed his cards can pick up the others. As he picks up each participant's group of cards, he shuffles them into the cards already collected. The collector should be careful to keep the cards face down and thoroughly shuffle them so that they are well mixed and cannot be traced, thereby maintaining the integrity and the anonymity of the process.

CLUSTER RESPONSES

Two options can now be used to cluster the responses once the cards are collected and well mixed. The participants could be divided into groups; the group size should not exceed six in number. The second option is to have one or two people cluster the responses while the rest of the group goes on with other items of business on the agenda.

In option one in which the participants have been divided into groups of six or fewer, the collected and mixed cards are redistributed evenly among the groups established. These groups will cluster the cards into categories and label the categories. No responses are dropped at this point. As the group distributes the cards that are similar in nature, labels for each category will become apparent. A category can have one card if it does not fit any of the other categories.

NEGOTIATE FINAL CLUSTERS

Whether you use option one, which is using groups of six people or fewer, or whether you use option two, in which a couple of people do the clustering, representatives from each group need to negotiate the final clusters. The final label must be meaningful for each of the clusters. It does not matter how many statements are in each cluster. A category might have only one card, or it may have several cards. The important thing is that the cards be similar in nature and fit under the label given to that cluster.

REPRODUCE COPIES

At this point a break should occur in the process, while the clusters are typed. All responses are typed under a label and, for clarity, each statement is numbered consecutively throughout the clusters. If you have a dozen or so clusters, and a hundred statements, number straight through the clusters from one to 100.

Each participant gets two copies of the printout, one for establishing priorities to turn in, and one to keep to see how his ratings compared later with the group. The break in time to type the printout for rating by the group can take a few hours, a few days, or even a week or two. I have conducted this with a break of over a month because the particular group that was doing the Delphi technique only met once a month. I would not suggest any longer break in time than that. I have also had the group do the input session with a break of a couple of hours while the typed printout was done by a number of secretaries so that the printout could be brought back to the group for rating before they left that day. In the meantime, during the two-hour break for typing, the group discussed other items on the agenda.

ADVOCACY TIME

As the printout of responses comes back to the group, and before the group actually rates the responses, one option, if you do not mind certain members of the group influencing others, is to intervene at this point with an advocacy procedure. Members of the group may say anything pro or con about any item on the printout for 30 seconds. The participants may have as many 30 second turns as they like; however, others get their 30 seconds before the participant speaks again. The advocacy time can be 30 seconds, 60 seconds, or whatever you wish. I have found, over the years, that 30 to 60 seconds is ample time for participants to succinctly state a pro or con rationale for any item. This is one option that may be used at this point in the process. However, normally *I would recommend that any discussion be saved until after the particiants have rated all the responses and can see the results.*

RATE RESPONSES

The rating form should be titled with identification of the group that is doing it, the date, and the question. The printout should contain the directions for rating. The items to be rated appear in the middle of the page. One rating method, the five-point, strongly-agree-to-strongly-disagree technique, appears on the right side of the printout, and a second rating method, top ten goals to top one goal, appears on the left side of the printout.

Example of Rating Methods

(See chapter 13 for a more complete example)

HIDDEN VALLEY SCHOOL DISTRICT ONE YEAR GOALS
April, 1983

1 - Top Goal		SA - Strongly Agree
2 - Top Two Goals		A - Agree
5 - Top Five Goals		N - No Opinion
10 - Top Ten Goals		D - Disagree
		SD - Strongly Disagree

1 2 5 10   SA A N D SD

(List Goals Here)
1. Goal one
2. Goal two
.
.
.
. . .

On the right side of the printout are five columns: strongly agree, agree, no opinion, disagree, and strongly disagree. For each item listed, participants check the column that best agrees with their opinion.

On the left side of the printout are four columns: top goal, top two goals, top five goals, and top 10 goals. It does not matter whether the 10 goals are from one category or various categories. However, once the participant has identified his top 10 goals, he must stay with those as he starts the reduction process toward his top goal. From these original 10, he checks his top five; from these five he checks his top two; and from these two he checks his top goal.

COMPUTING THE STATISTICAL RESULTS

Collect one of the two copies from each participant with their completed ratings. At this point a trusted member of the group can take all the rated forms from the participants and compute the statistical results. On the right hand columns, the strongly-agree-to-strongly-disagree category, a compilation of the total responses in each of the five columns is made. The completed statistical response will state the number of people in the group who strongly agreed, agreed, no opinion, disagreed, and strongly disagreed. A numerical total is written in each of the five columns after each statement.

In computing the top 10 goals rating method, the person doing the computation should proceed as follows: Each of the top 10 goals checked receives one point; items checked in the top five goals receive two points; items checked in the top two goals receive five points; an item checked as the top goal receives 10 points. A statement that was checked as one of the top 10 goals and then moved through the five-goal column and the two goal column to the top goal would only receives 10 points as the top goal, rather than getting point credit for each of the preceding columns. Therefore, the highest point total a particular statement can receive on a participant's rating sheet would be the point value of the highest checked column.

For each rating form, the scorer now totals the number of points attributed to an item from each of the participants. The item receiving the highest number of points, becomes the number one priority, and so on through the top half dozen items. Fewer items than six are acceptable if a decided gap exists between any of the first half dozen priorities. For instance, if the third highest goal received a total of 105 points and the fourth highest total received a total of 24 points, only the top three goals should be considered. I have made a rare exception by including more than six goals if the seventh or eighth top-rated goal was close to the other six.

I generate a printout showing the total scoring for every item, so the participants can see how each item fared in the establishment of priorities. I put a cover letter on the printout summarizing the top goals, and list other top goals in numerical order to a reasonable level so the group can get an idea of what other items were determined to be important along with the top half dozen.

REPORTING THE STATISTICAL RESULTS
OF THE DELPHI PROCESS AND DISCUSSION

The accumulated totals are returned to the group and discussion is invited. It should be understood that the participant now has the master copy to use only for reference. Discussion is beneficial at this time because some members will have opinions about certain items, either in agreement or disagreement.

TRANSLATING OUTCOMES
INTO SIMPLE PERFORMANCE OBJECTIVES

Appropriate staff write simple performance objectives for each of the top half dozen items. These objectives should succinctly and precisely state what is going to be accomplished. Everyone will then be able to tell whether or not the objective is being accomplished, how it is being accomplished, and who is being held responsible for completing it by a specific date.

PERIODIC PROGRESS REPORTS

Those responsible for carrying out the performance objectives should make periodic progress reports. Such reports should be given every six months, or in some situations, once a year. These reports should be simple and succinct.

REDOING THE PROCESS

Depending on the nature of the question in the Delphi, the exercise should be repeated every so often. If the Delphi was being used to determine the goals of the school district by the board of education, it should be redone every time a new board member is elected. If you have continuity of the participants, then the process should be done every two or three years. Every time a new member is elected it is important for him to have the opportunity to participate in the goal-setting sequence. In one school district, during a tumultuous period of time, we had 13 different board members on a five-member board in a two and a half year period of time. We were redoing our goals frequently.

OUTLINE

1. DETERMINE QUESTION—Determine the specific question to be considered.
2. SELECT PARTICIPANTS
3. EXPLAIN PROCESS—Explain purpose of the process. Indicate how this process will assist in action or decision making.
4. WRITE STATEMENTS—Have participants write 5 to 10 statements (or fewer). Be specific. Use 3x5 cards. One card per statement.
5. COLLECT CARDS
6. CLUSTER RESPONSES—Option 1. Break participants into groups. (under six). Number of groups depends on number of participants. Mix all cards and redistribute evenly to groups. Groups will cluster cards into categories, give a name or label to each cluster. No response is dropped. Option 2. Have two members of the group do all the clustering.
7. NEGOTIATE FINAL CLUSTERS - Representatives from each group meet to negotiate final clusters. Label each final cluster.
(A break in time to type responses.)

8. REPRODUCE COPIES—Clusters are typed. All responses are typed under a label. Two copies are made for all participants.

9. ADVOCACY TIME—(OPTIONAL) Participants get 30 to 60 seconds to address any items.

10. RATE RESPONSES—Typed responses are distributed to all participants. Participants rate the responses two ways -strongly agree to strongly disagree, and identification of top 10 items reducing them to one item.

(A break in time.)

11. COMPUTE STATISTICAL RESULTS—Responses are collected. Compute an accumulated total for each item.

12. DISCUSSION—Further discussion period if necessary.

13. ACTION—Have top staff write simple performance objectives. State who does what by when.

14. PERIODIC PROGRESS REPORTS—Every six months or at least annually.

15. RE-DO ANNUALLY—Or every two or three years depending on topic.

VARIOUS USES

SETTING GOALS

One of the major uses of the Delphi process is to establish goals for the organization. The questions posed are usually: what should this staff or organization be doing next year to improve our programs? What should we be doing for the next three to five years? In each case a different colored card is used for the input process; one color for one-year goals, another for the three-to-five-year goals. I have used the Delphi innumerable times in whatever organization I have been in. I have also helped many other school districts and organizations though the use of the Delphi. When I was president of the 11,000-member Escondido Chamber of Commerce, I used it to set goals with the board of directors. When establishing one-year goals, it is necessary to redo them annually at a set period of time during the year. Usually, three-to-five-year goals are done every other year, or every three years.

EVALUATION OF INDIVIDUALS AND PROGRAMS

The second major use of the Delphi is to evaluate individuals and programs. A principal in a school, a president of an organization, an executive director, or a superintendent might ask the group to complete two phrases: "I like" and "I wish you would." The "I like" statements should appear on one color 3x5 card, and the "I wish you would" statements should appear on another colored 3x5 card. When this process is used to evaluate an individual, it is necessary to have his consent. If the individual receives a number of "I wish you would" cards, it is possible that he might be upset. One principal who received a negative evaluation, took the cards home and did the clustering himself. He managed, by process of deduction, to determine that most of the negative comments were made by a teacher who had used a certain writing instrument, and he took retaliatory measures. The integrity and credibility of the Delphi process was destroyed.

Another individual using the Delphi process sued the school district for liable because he maintained his career advancement had been injured by the use of the Delphi process which had been negative and had been revealed outside the circle of participants. Make certain that the individual is totally supportive of using the Delphi process for his evaluation before you use it. The process is meant to be helpful and constructive, not a means to dismiss a person from the job. If you need to take disciplinary action as a result of an evaluation, then I suggest you use the more traditional evaluations that eventually could lead to a dismissal action.

Whenever I entered a new administrative assignment or district, I would evaluate the present programs. I would usually do this with the board of directors as one group to get its input; with my superintendent's cabinet, or executive group as a second input group; and, if in a small district, with teachers and general staff. Thus, I would have a three dimensional input on what others liked about their organization and what they wished I would be doing to improve it as their new leader. Some school districts have a districtwide parent advisory group which could be involved in suggesting goals. In the Association of California School Administrators, I used the 130-member Delegate Assembly to gather input in the goal-setting process. By using this approach, you find out the things that people like in the organization and that you certainly will want to continue and enhance. In other words, "If it ain't broke, don't fix it." You will identify enough items that they wish you would improve and appear to be broken and in need of fixing. By getting the employees and participants in the organization involved and by following their lead you have a definite commitment to improve and to succeed.

REORGANIZATION OF DISTRICT
ADMINISTRATIVE SERVICES

I once asked site administrators what the district office could be doing better to serve their needs. The identification of several concerns led to the establishment of a research and development position which kept the site administrators current with research techniques that could be implemented in their schools. They received assistance in developing programs from the district office on the basis of research. Because ownership for the position came from all the site administrators, the board of education was more readily convinced that the administrative post should be added to the district office staff. I also continued to evaluate that position by asking what the principals liked about what was being done as well as the things they wished the director of research and evaluation would do to continue improving that service to local schools.

OTHER USES

The Delphi process can be used in many ways to resolve various concerns. The following are more examples of questions that can be asked and answered through this process.

"How would you like to see our inservice day used?" was another question posed by a local school to its staff.

During the establishment of a multimedia center in an elementary school the question was asked, "What services should a multimedia center provide for the educational program at this school?"

In determining the essential ingredients in a participative management system, the question asked was "What are the issues critical to operation of a participative management system?"

A question asked of teachers was "What are your concerns and needs related to our newly established special education program?"

In determining the priorities of a local school site budget allocation, the staff was asked "How should we allocate our $5000 in the school budget?"

OTHER QUESTIONS

"What are the critical issues in public education?"

"How can we reduce vandalism in the school, or reduce absenteeism of students and staff?"

"How shall we improve the discipline in the school?"

"How can we improve the positive relationships on our elementary playground during recess and the lunch hour?"

COMMENTS

I found through the years that the status leaders many times will discourage the use of the Delphi process because it takes away from their unilateral influence with the group. The Delphi process gives everybody an equal determination in the outcome, without undue influence from the power merchants within the group. Therefore, you will hear some interesting rationales by those in power as to why the Delphi process is inadeaquate and lacks quality of input or outcome.

Using the Delphi process has helped me be an effective leader, has involved staff in a meaningful way, has identified key problem areas, and has ensured successful outcome of goals. I certainly recommend the process.

Chapter 12
How to Conduct and Enjoy Effective Meetings

Leaders who have the philosophy and attitude necessary to develop their staffs into cohesive problem-solving teams can use meetings positively and constructively in school management. Such meetings can be dynamic, productive, and quick; but to take on these qualities, meetings must have the orchestration of an effective leader.

TYPES OF MEETINGS

There are several types of meetings. The more common is task-oriented. Such a meeting is used for:
- Developing a plan through group consensus.
- Problem solving through analysis and selection of a solution from alternatives.
- Decision making through a group decision and recommendation.
- Data gathering to obtain information, opinions, and consensus.

A second major type of meeting is for information giving or for training sessions which are used to disseminate "the word" or to explain a process. This may involve either one-way or two-way communication.

The third common type of meeting is a rap session which encourages feelings and attitudes to surface, and to be handled in a constructive manner.

MEETINGS FOR DECISION MAKING

I will concentrate on *decision-making or problem solving meetings.* I will not discuss establishing procedures for an information meeting for the typical kind of group in which the administrator calls the staff together to make announcements and to explain or to sell decisions already made. Nor will I discuss "consultive management" meetings in which the administrator merely gets imput from the individual members and then uses the data as a basis for making his own decisions.

This chapter focuses on meeting techniques for regularly constituted groups such as an executive board, an administrative council, or a faculty or student senate. These techniques are designed for a meeting group size of 5 to 25 people, with 8 to 12 people being the optimum size for participation and decision making.

The meeting techniques in this chapter are for those leaders and staff who have the philosophy and attitude to become a cohesive problem-solving and decision making team. This can be accomplished through regularly scheduled meetings in which every member as well as the leader assumes the responsibility for:

- Bringing in problems for inclusion on the agenda.
- Deciding priorities of agenda items.
- Offering alternative solutions.
- Making a final decision as to the best solution.
- Determining what needs to be done to implement each decision.
- Establishing follow-up methods to evaluate the eventual outcome of their problem-solving efforts.

These are techniques for participatory management meetings whose members have been given the opportunity by the leader to join with him in the management of the activity for which the administrator is accountable. As a group participates in these decision-making meetings, each member should be sensitive to feelings that are apt to occur such as:

- Irritation among group members towards someone for not listening or being empathetic.
- Resentment over not being allowed to participate in decision making.
- Resentment at being manipulated.
- Apprehension towards being open about personal feelings and opinions.

- Boredom because too much time is being spent on a particular subject.
- Anger or conflict among group members because of lack of concern for each other's needs.
- Anger because opinions are not objectively explored by the group.
- Apathy and indifference because of irrelevance of tasks to personal needs.
- Confusion because of unclear agenda.
- Discomfort with the meeting environment—temperature, lighting, length of meeting.
- Satisfaction from being productive and accomplishing group task.
- Warmth and appreciation towards group members because of their supportiveness.

DECISION-MAKING STYLES

There are three major types of decision-making styles.

UNILATERAL

The advantage of this style is that it is quick. The disadvantages are minimum input, slow implementation, creation of possible conflict, little commitment by participants, and a sense of being treated undemocractically.

MAJORITY RULE

The advantages of this style are that it is quick and that it is seen as democratic. The disadvantages of majority rule are devisive polarities of positions, waste of potential contributions by those holding minority positions, slow implementation, and the possible sabotage of plans by an upset minority group.

CONSENSUS

The advantages of this style are involvement by everyone, total use of group assets and resources, and a synergistic force through group commitment which ensures success in implementing the decision. The disadvantages are that it takes time, it does not avoid confrontation, it requires a high degree of skill on the part of the facilitator, and consensus may not even be possible in situations in which basic principles are diametrically opposed.

Of the three major procedures of decision making indicated above, the one which generally results in the most satisfaction to all concerned, and which provides the greatest commitment for follow through is decision making by consensus.

What is meant by consensus and how can one achieve it? Consensus does not necessarily mean unanimity, but it does mean striving for a win-win situation in which all parties win instead of a win-lose situation in which one part of the group wins and the other loses. When an impass exists, the participants can look for alternatives acceptable to both groups, find out what particular elements are causing the disagreement, strive for alternatives to these elements, and check the language used. Does it mean the same to both groups? Are some words emotional? Participants can determine if some reactions are to particular people rather than issues, and can avoid techniques such as majority vote which might end the impass but result in a win-lose situation.

Consensus attainment is not compromise. Compromise means both partners give up on certain principles. Consensus is finding alternatives generally acceptable to all parties without either one giving up what they desire. When differences of opinion are taken into account in working out a consensus agreement, the result is superior to that based on one-sided opinions only.

ROLES OF THE DECISION-MAKING TEAM

Four major roles are performed in a shared decision-making meeting.

- Leader or the boss
- Facilitator (instead of the chairperson) who conducts the meeting
- Recorder
- Participant

I strongly recommend that the leader or the boss become a regular participant of the group rather than the chairperson. A facilitator should run the meeting, and a recorder from among the group members should take minutes instead of an outside secretary.

I have found over the years that rotation of the recorder and the facilitator among all group members becomes a tremendous learning experience and makes the entire group more effective. It usually takes two rotations of serving as recorder and facilitator before the group starts to mature and become highly effective. The group should receive training in the development of skills for conducting a meeting.

When I enter a school district as its new superintendent, I assume the role of the facilitator for the first six meetings; I then schedule—on a volunteer basis—each member of the group as recorder for two meetings and then as the meeting facilitator for the next two meetings before rotating him back to being a regular participant of the group.

The function of the chairperson should be carried out by a facilitator who concentrates on keeping the group moving on the problems, listens closely, makes certain that group members are hearing each other, stimulates each individual to contribute ideas and to join in the discussion, protects members from personal criticism, and concentrate the group's attention on issues.

As the group becomes engaged in problem solving activities the facilitator must be certain that these activities take on the following characteristics:

- The problem must be a situation someone wants to change.
- Only one problem should be solved at a time.
- The problem should be stated as a question.
- Key words should be clarified.
- The time needed should be taken.
- The topic should be agreed by everyone to be a real problem.
- Participants should restate the problem in their own words.
- Brainstorming should take place.
- The solution should be guided by appropriate criteria.
- Impossible or unrealistic solutions should be eliminated.
- "Musts" and "wants" should be differentiated.
- A solution should be chosen.

AGENDA GUIDELINES
Executive Staff Meetings
Agenda Guidelines
1. Three categories of agenda items:
(a) **Information:** Three minutes or less.
(b) **Discussion:** Bring any written information you wish to pass out or explain.
(c) **Decision:** Action item. Have a proposal—oral or in writing. If we need background information to make the decision, get to the staff in writing.

- As you enter the meeting room, write your topics on the board—under one of three categories, as outlined above.
- Also, include your initials in parentheses next to your item.
- Indicate with an asterisk any items which require a decision that day.
- The first 6 minutes of each meeting will be given to agenda sign-up.

2. Meeting time: 8:29 a.m. to 11:59 a.m.

3. Fines: (to finance social activities)

Absence (only terminal illness excused)	$1.00
Tardiness (.01 per minute, minimum of .10 and a maximum of .50)	$.10-.50
Discipline fines by facilitator (maximum of .50)	$.10-.50
Addition of agenda items during meeting	$.25

4. Facilitator Responsibilities - subject to fines:

Not starting meeting on time	$.50
Not providing break every 1 1/2 - 2 hours	$.50
Not ending meeting on time	$.50

5. Schedule

Schedule	Recorder	Facilitator
Monday, Sept. 13	Elmer C.	Pat H.
Monday, Sept. 20	Elmer C.	Pat H.
Monday, Sept. 27	Marilyn H.	Elmer C.
Monday, Oct. 4	Marilyn H.	Elmer C.
Monday, Oct. 11	Al Z.	Marilyn H.
Monday, Oct. 18		Marilyn H.

One of the first things that should be done is to establish a system of fines set at monetary levels that are comfortable for the group. Fines should never make members of the group feel uncomfortable. The monetary fine is designed to be a fun way of reminding the group of certain obligations that the members have to make the meetings run more smoothly and effectively. Also, the fines could be accumulated to finance a social get-together by the group once or twice a year.

The facilitator incurs fines for not starting on time, not providing a break, or not ending the meeting on time. Members of the group are fined for missing a meeting or being tardy, usually $1 with the only excuse being "terminal illness." Tardiness is fined at the rate of 10 cents for every 10 minutes late with a minimum fine of 10 cents and a maximum fine of 50 cents, no matter how tardy as long as the individual arrives at the meeting. The maximum of 50 cents is to encourage members to attend no matter what time they arrive, otherwise they might be inclined to just pay the $1 for being absent and be discouraged from attending.

Members are also fined for submitting an agenda item after the deadline of 8:35 a.m. The member pays 25 cents for each additional agenda item after that time. The facilitator also has the opportunity of fining a member from 10 to 50 cents for meeting disruptions, sarcasm, put-downs, or other violations that take away from running the meeting smoothly and effectively.

I have found the fining system adds enjoyment to the meeting as long as the fines are not punitive by being higher than the members can comfortably afford.

Executive Staff Agenda

Information	Discussion	Decision
*Item - SH	*Item - SH	Item - JS
Item -HM	Item -WN	*Item - DR
*Item - LF	Item - HC	*Item - JS

The agenda is set by placing items on a chalkboard under three columns. One column is for information items of two or three minutes duration that tend to be announcements. The second column is for discussion items which may require lengthy discussions, but no decisions. For example, this might be for the purpose of introducing an item which would be carried over to the next meeting for a decision; it might be that the originator of the item seeks information necessary for a decision he has to make later; or he might be seeking reaction to a decision already made and needing discussion and reaction. The third column on the chalkboard is for decision items.

If an item in any of the three columns must be taken up at this meeting, the originator needs to put an asterisk in front of the item to indicate to the facilitator that it has to be addressed at this meeting and not carried over. All members must put their initials after their item so the group knows who initiated it. Failure to do so incurs a fine from 10 to 50 cents.

GENERAL GUIDELINES

FREQUENCY OF MEETINGS

How often a group needs to meet depends on the number of problems a group has to solve, the complexity of the problems, and the effectiveness of the group. Groups should meet at the same time, on the same day, and on a regularly scheduled basis— usually once a week. Newly formed groups often have to meet more frequently at first because of their inexperience and a full agenda. A group will build up experience that will tell how frequently it needs to meet in order to get its problems solved.

DURATION OF MEETINGS

Meetings should have a specific beginning and ending time which should be rigidly enforced. Groups should not meet longer than two hours without a break; it is better to set up additional meetings rather than have a single meeting that is too long. After some experience the group should be allowed to decide the length of its meeting, taking into consideration organizational needs and fatigue factors. I have personally found that meetings of three hours or less are the most effective.

I start a meeting at a precise time—8:29 a.m. rather than 8:30 a.m. Setting the meeting time at a precise time such as 8:29 a.m. implies that everyone is to be on time. Setting the time at a common hour such as 8:30 encourages people to drift in, and delays the start of the meeting or necessitates repeating certain items for latecomers, which is unfair to the group who is on time. It should be well understood that the meeting will last no longer than three hours unless the group completes its business sooner. Any extension of the meeting should be by group consensus; and then only for a short period of time to complete an item or two that is of utmost importance.

PRIORITY OF MEETINGS

Few other organizational requirements should have greater priority than attendance at the group meeting. If the meeting is not important enough to require everyone's attendance at every meeting then it should not be held. Each group member should assume responsibility for instructing secretaries and staff as to the priority of the meeting and as to procedures for handling phone calls and interruptions which should only be for an absolute emergency.

MEMBERSHIP OF THE GROUP

Generally, all line executives should be members. It should be the leader's responsibility to determine which of the staff should be members. Certain staff, who are not members of the group, may be asked to attend when matters falling within their area of operation are discussed, and only then for a specific time after which they should resume their other responsibilities.

ALTERNATES FOR MEMBERS

If the group decides to use alternates, it should be the responsibility of each group member to appoint one to attend group meetings in the member's absence. Each group member should assume responsibility for keeping the alternate informed at all times so that if he is needed he will have sufficient knowledge to be a responsible group member. When attending the group meeting, the alternate should have full authority to speak for the department.

It is important that membership be regular and continual for a least a year in order to build a cohesiveness in the group and a synergistic effort in the shared decision-making process. Alternates attending the meeting create a definite lack of continuity. My personal preference is not to use alternates at all, but to inform the absence member through another member of the group.

THE PLACE OF THE MEETING

The conference room should have adequate seating facilities, privacy, and comfort. The meeting should not take place in the leader's office. Meetings held in connection with lunches and dinners are seldom effective.

PHYSICAL ARRANGEMENTS

Chalkboards or chart pads should be available at all meetings. Tables should be provided to enable group members to write notes. The members should be seated so each person can be seen by every other person. The leaders should minimize status by not always sitting at the head of the table.

RECORDING FUNCTION

The group should set its own methods of recordings its proceedings. Some groups prefer to have a permanent recorder; others rotate the recording function. The leader should not be the recorder; his time should be free for carrying out leadership functions. The group should decide what it wants recorded. After recording a specific action of the group, the recorder should check his understanding of that action with the total group to make certain that he has recorded it accurately. My personal preference is that all minutes should be brief—one or two lines indicating what is going to be done by whom and by what time. The briefer the record of the group proceedings, the more likely it will be used by group members.

DEVELOPING THE AGENDA (refer to agenda example)

The group, rather than the leader, should develop the agenda. Formal agendas can be prepared ahead of time in which case members assume responsibility for submitting agenda items to the person who sends the agendas to all members prior to the meeting. My preference is for the group to develop its agenda at the start of each meeting by placing their items on the chalkboard. For any agenda item that might require a decision at that meeting, the originator of the agenda item has the responsibility to send out material in advance of the meeting so the members are properly informed to make the decision. If the member of the group just wishes to introduce the item for further discussion or decision at a subsequent meeting, the material can be handed out during the meeting and discussed for clarification.

RULES FOR SPEAKING

The group should work out its own rules for handling communications during the meeting. These rules should be kept to a minimum or be none at all. Effective problem-solving groups usually function quite informally, permitting any group member to speak when feeling like it without getting permission from the facilitator. In mature problem solving groups, each member assumes sole responsibility for the appropriateness and timing of their own contributions as well as for facilitating communication from others. The facilitator of a meeting must be careful not to inhibit contributions through unintentionally dominating or controlling the group's communication. He must also encourage members to communicate openly even in the presence of the leader.

PROBLEMS APPROPRIATE FOR THE GROUP

Every member of the group should always have a clear notion of the kinds of problems that are appropriate for that group. Generally such problems are those which require data from, which may affect, or which may be implemented by all members of the group. Each member assumes responsibility for determining the appropriateness of problems brought to the group and for screening out problems that effect only his or her own area of responsibility.

Groups should always be alert to items that are not appropriate to the total group and quickly assign them to an appropriate individual to be resolved outside the group meeting. Each person, including the leader, should tell the group at the beginning of the discussion of the agenda item exactly what is wanted from the group. Using the three column approach— information, discussion, or decision—helps clarify the intent of the item. Further clarification can be made with the group: a clear decision is wanted; ideas are being sought for a final solution which will be made by the originator; or the group is being used as a sounding board to test out a solution that has already been chosen.

PROBLEMS INAPPROPRIATE FOR MEETINGS

The group should not use its time for solving problems that concern only a few of its members, that are too unimportant for the level of the group, that require preliminary staff study and data gathering, or that are outside the area of authority of the group. Members should assume responsibility at all times for identifying a problem which they think is inappropriate.

RESPONSIBILITY OF GROUP MEMBERS
BEFORE EACH MEETING

Each group member should assume responsibility for submitting their own agenda items, being fully prepared with documents or data that might be required to help the group solve the problem, and for making their own recommendation, if one is ready, to the total group. Each member should study the material ahead of time to determine if any preparation needs to be done in order to intelligently discuss the problems the group will be dealing with at its next meeting. Each member should review previous minutes to make sure all the task assignments from previous meetings have been completed; the minutes may also indicate agenda items that are carried over from the previous meeting.

RESPONSIBILITY OF GROUP MEMBERS
DURING THE MEETING

Group members should assume primary responsibility for leadership of the discussion on their agenda items. Each group member should assume responsibility not only for making content contributions but also for making process contributions— suggestions and observations for improving the effectiveness of the group's problem-solving procedures. In other words, each group member should be as responsible as the leader or the meeting facilitator for the conduct of the group. Responsible group members are those who play an active role in clarifying objectives, providing information, offering alternate solutions, evaluating alternative solutions, observing limits, giving feedback to clarify communications, summarizing, testing to see if the group is in agreement, calling for a decision, keeping the group on track, protecting the rights of minority point of view members, encouraging hesitant members, asking questions to seek information, and making suggestions that will move the group ahead in its search for the best decision to a particular problem.

RESPONSIBILITY OF GROUP MEMBERS AFTER THE MEETING

Group members should assume the responsibility for transmitting to their staff all decisions or information that staff should know in order to do their jobs most effectively or to keep informed of what is going on at the level above them. Members should review the minutes of the previous meeting as soon as they receive them in order to refresh their memory concerning specific task assignments. They should carry out those task assignments given to them by the group. In their communications with their own staff, they should accept their share of the accountability for all group decisions rather than communicate that they were not in favor of some group decisions and, thus, not accountable. *Group members should never attempt to reverse a group by making appeals to the leader after the meeting is over.* When members, after some reflection, feel that a decision does not seem to be a good one, they should reopen discussion of the problem at the next group meeting; or in the case of something urgent, they should ask the leader to call a special meeting to reopen the problem. *The leader should never reverse a decision of the group after the meeting.* If the leader feels a problem needs reopening, the group should be called together again.

RULES FOR DECISION MAKING

The total group should arrive at a set of rules to identify when a decision is reached. Preferably, groups should strive for consensus on all problems. If there is sufficient time, the group should keep discussing the problem until it reaches a solution agreeable to everyone. When group members feel strongly about the correctness of their position, they should keep advocating it.

When group members do not feel strongly about the correctness of their position, they should be willing to go along with the majority. Group members should be particularly sensitive when further advocacy of their position is unlikely to change the position of the majority. Effective problem-solving groups seldom call for a vote unless it is in the nature of a straw vote to determine how the group is lining up on a problem. For some kinds of problems, the group members should be willing to defer to those members who will have more responsibility for implementing a solution or to those members in whose area the problem most logically falls. When time does not permit enough discussion to obtain consensus, the group may delegate the final decision to one member, to two or three members acting as a subgroup, or to the leader.

CONFIDENTIALITY OF GROUP MEETINGS

It is extremely important that each group member assume responsibility for keeping confidences. Effective problem-solving groups are those in which each member feels that they may express their feelings or opinions in the group and be assured that the other members will not report their comments to people outside the group. In some cases, the group may definitely decide that a particular decision should not be discussed outside the group, or they may wish to establish certain conditions governing discussion of a particular item outside the group.

A basic rule must be that a member of the group should not discuss a matter outside the group that is likely to hurt any individual. By following this one rule you can usually know what should and should not be discussed outside the meeting. A basic attitude of each group should be that they are members of a family and confidential matters in a discussion should not be communicated to people outside the family.

DISPOSITION OF AGENDA ITEMS

At each group meeting, every agenda item should be resolved in one of the following ways.

- A solution is reached.
- The problem is delegated for further study outside the group.
- The problem is delegated to an individual or subgroup for a recommendation to the total group.
- The problem is taken off the agenda by the member who submitted it.
- The problem is redefined into a different problem. In no case should a problem be left unresolved.

MINUTES OF A MEETING

Minutes should be typed and distributed to all members of the group as soon as possible after the meeting. The group should set up definite rules as to who should be permitted to see the minutes, and who, in addition to the group members, should receive copies. Individual members of the group should personally communicate to staff what they should know, rather than running the risk of misunderstanding the minutes. Minutes of each meeting should contain at least the following: all decisions reached by the group, all items of information that were discussed, and topics that were placed under discussion; dispositions of every agenda item; and all tasks assignments including due dates.

PROCEDURES FOR CONTINUOUS EVALUATION OF GROUP EFFECTIVENESS

Groups, as well as individuals, have to learn how to function effectively. Learning is facilitated by immediate feedback of results. Thus, effective groups usually build in specific procedures for evaluating their own effectiveness. The group should adopt or devise some method for evaluating its own functioning. Some groups do this at the end of each meeting, others may do it periodically. Some groups use written evaluation sheets, others do the evaluation orally. I recommend setting aside the last 10 minutes of every meeting to evaluate that meeting according to the standards you have set; and that you use a Delphi procedure once a year asking the question "How can we make our meetings more effective?"

SUMMARY OF GENERAL GUIDELINES

For a decision-making meeting to function effectively, all members must learn to carry out certain functions and responsibilities. Just as effective leadership must be learned so must effective membership be learned.

The following summary of general guidelines for decision-making meetings should be duplicated and distributed to all of the staff who are members of a regularly scheduled decision-making group. Discuss each item at one of your early meetings.

PREPARATION

- Read the minutes of the previous meeting before going to each meeting.
- Come to the meeting having clearly in mind what problems or items you want to put on the agenda.

- Arrive at the meeting on time.
- Bring all needed materials.
- Arrange to have phone calls intercepted.

BEHAVIOR IN THE MEETING

- Submit your items for the agenda at the beginning of the meeting. State them briefly.
- State your opinions or feelings honestly and clearly, do not hide them.
- Stay on the agenda item being dealt with and help others stay on it.
- Ask for clarification when you do not understand someone.
- Participate actively; when you have something to say, say it.
- Take responsibility for saying things that will help the group function effectively; it is your meeting, not just your leader's.
  - Start on time.
  - Set the agenda.
  - Stay on the subject.
  - Keep order.
  - Listen to others.
  - Keep records.
  - Write items on the board.
  - Arrive at decisions.
  - Quit on time.
- Protect the rights of others to have their opinions or feelings heard. Encourage silent members to speak.
- Listen attentively to others. When appropriate, clarify what others are saying.
- Avoid communication that disrupts a group—humor, sarcasm, diversions, asides, jokes, digs, or put-downs.
- Think creatively about solutions that might resolve conflicts. Share them with the group.
- Keep notes on things you agree to do after the meeting.
- At all times, keep saying to yourself, "What right now would help this group move ahead and get this problem solved? What contribution can I make to help this group function more effectively? What does the group need? How can I help?"

AFTER THE MEETING

- Carry out assignments and commitments.
- Inform your staff of decisions affecting them.
- Keep confidential things that are said in the meeting that might hurt a member of the group.
- Do not complain about a decision to which you agreed.
- Refrain from "out of meeting appeals" to your leader. Your feelings should be expressed in the group.

COMMENTS

I have found that over time groups can achieve a tremendous sophistication in participating in and facilitating meetings. A superintendent's cabinet of 25 members who used the facilitation meetings that I have been describing became not only self-sufficient but capable of continuing the operation of the school district through the once-a-week superintendent's cabinet meeting even if the superintendent or leader could not be present. Because the assignment of recorders and facilitators is posted at the beginning of the year for the entire year, everyone knows their responsibility and role. Critiquing each meeting for 10 minutes at the end is a constant reminder of the criteria that contribute to enjoying and conducting effective meetings.

This approach has proven, over the years, to be highly successful and enjoyable. I recommend it to all leaders who are interested in sharing decision making with a management team and who want to improve the effectiveness of the group or organization.

Chapter 13
Board-Superintendent
Relations and Decision Making

School districts have been experiencing increasing political activity and increasing societal pressures. The traditional roles of the board of education and of the superintendent are being challenged; the 1980s and 1990s will bring significant change in the way they complement each other in their educational responsibilities. To establish efficient and effective relationships between the board and the superintendent, good communication and decision-making procedures are essential.

HISTORY OF RELATIONSHIP

TRADITIONAL ROLES

The roles of the board and of the superintendent were created during the early 1900s and remained the same until about 1954 when school districts merged and became more centralized, and the concept of scientific management substituted for political influence. Between 1900 and 1954, the goal of education was to harmonize the immigrant population into a cohesive society. During this time the board developed policy, and the superintendent administered the district.

SUPERINTENDENT POWER

Beginning about 1954, the position of superintendent took on more power due to increasing centralization. Policies suggested by the superintendent were approved by the board 85 percent of the time—a success rate that would be the envy of any president, governor, or mayor. As a result, many superintendents took an intensive, personal involvement in the success of the district, and actually felt that they "owned the store."

CHANGES BEGIN

From about 1954 to the present, an era of nationalization of education began to emerge. This brought with it two dichotomous schools of thought for public education. The first stated that schools were to serve as an agent of social change; while the second stated that schools should be returned to the people. Whereas superintendents had formerly gained control from the citizens, they now lost a large portion of this control to the federal government. They had to comply with the demands of the Department of Health, Education and Welfare, and court judgments, such as Brown vs. the Board of Education. Additionally, the federal government launched such programs as the Education Act of 1965—ESEA and Title I, which enticed school districts to accept free dollars.

RETURNING THE SCHOOLS TO THE PEOPLE

When Reagan became president, an emphasis to return the schools to the people increased, and the financing of schools became a responsibility of each state instead of the federal government. If schools are truly returned to the people, what happens to the control of the districts that passed from local superintendents and boards, to Congress, the Federal Courts, and other national and state agencies presents an interesting dilemma which might disrupt and challenge the relationship of the board and superintendent. Even with the reduction of federal mandates and court rulings considerable pressure—through state statutes, state department of education regulations, individual values, philosophies and living styles, taxpayers, board member turnover, teacher union demands, pressure group demands, and community expectations—continues to affect school boards and superintendents. These pressures contribute to stress and possible conflict.

A NEW SOCIETY

As described in Alvin Toffler's *Third Wave* and John Naisbett's *Megatrends*, we are emerging from an industrial society into a service and information society. Characteristics of this new society are diverse living styles, a desire for freedom and independence, and high expectations for services. New leadership and management skills, as well as procedures for establishing board-superintendent relations, are required. Superintendents no longer "own the store;" the board of education through the electorate does. The superintendent must assume the role of a highly skilled leader and manager for the "owners."

CONSUMERISM

School districts must respond to the consumer of the service. Consumerism is strong throughout this nation. This becomes obvious when a large conglomerate such as General Motors must call back a new automobile to replace a 20-cent part in the car's transmission, costing GM millions of dollars in labor; in decades past that expense would have been bourne by the consumer. It follows that parents are going to demand that school districts do a better job of making certain that their most beloved possession—their child—will receive a successful education. If not, public school parents will seek other means of educating their children, such as private schools.

BOARD-SUPERINTENDENT ROLE STATEMENTS

All this affects the relationship between the board of education and the superintendent in their decision-making roles. District board policy, administrative procedures, and a job description for the superintendent can help minimize the ambiguities in this relationship and in decision making.

NSBA-AASA JOINT POSITION STATEMENT

What follows is a joint position statement of the National School Boards Association (NSBA) and the American Association of School Administrators (AASA) on roles and relationships.

> Today, effective public education requires strong school boards and strong superintendents who willingly assume leadership roles. To an important degree, educational success is dependent upon a good working relationship between the school board and the chief administrative officer it employs.
>
> Basic to this relationship is a clear understanding that the board and superintendent constitute a team. Neither can operate effectively without a thorough knowledge of and support for the other's role.

It is increasingly important for the board and superintendent to delineate their respective roles. A superintendent is expected to display excellence as an educational leader, to be politically sophisticated, to be aware of and active in legislative developments, and to have an extensive knowledge of federal and state laws. A school board is asked to be responsive to its constituencies in governance; sensitive to the special needs of all learners in the district; a more active advocate for learners to the people, other local governmental entities, and state and federal levels of government; and a vigorous ambassador explaining the instructional programs to the people.

To accomplish these tasks, the board must serve as a legislative body in the development and evaluation of policies. The superintendent must be primarily responsible for the administration of the school district in accordance with board policies.

The board and superintendent must recognize that the distinction between strictly legislative and strictly administrative functions is not always clear-cut. If ambiguity is to be kept to a minimum in the working relationship between the board and superintendent, each should be aware of three influences that bear on this important division of responsibility:

1. The nature of policy development and administration.

Serving as a professional adviser to the school board is one of the key roles played by the superintendent. While the board is not bound to accept the superintendent's advice, it nonetheless should not establish policy without first consulting the superintendent, its chief professional adviser. In the same vein, the superintendent should not institute far reaching administrative procedures without first affording the board an opportunity to review proposed rules and their adherence to board policy. Moreover, the board should be given a regular opportunity to review existing administrative procedures to test whether they do conform to policy. The emphasis must be on communication—the sharing of information between board and superintendent. The process should not focus on approval to be sought or won, but on the development of mutual understanding.

2. The increasing influence of external factors on local school district governance and on the board-superintendent relationship.

Legislative mandates, for instance, frequently require the board to adopt detailed rules in implementing new laws or mandated curriculum. And the superintendent must meet unanticipated events with actions that establish policy by precedent in areas in which the board has no formal written policy.

3. The discretionary authority boards grant their chief administrators.

The board by law is responsible for school programs and operations. Nevertheless, all boards delegate some portion of that authority to the district superintendent. Without sufficient authority delegated from the board, the superintendent's ability to discharge responsibility is diminished. Where to draw the line of delegated authority is a matter each board and superintendent must determine individually and review periodically. Here is one guideline: The board must give the professional school administrator enough authority to carry out designated responsibilities, and the administrator must give the board adequate assurance that the job the board designated is being accomplished.

School Boards: Specific Responsibilities

Within this general framework, school boards have these specific responsibilities:

• To delegate to the superintendent responsibility for all administrative functions, except those specifically reserved through board policy for the board chairperson. Those reserved areas might include: conducting board meetings and public hearings, approving the agenda and minutes and other activities incidental to, and associated with serving as presiding officer of the board.

• To support the superintendent fully in all decisions that conform to professional standards and board policy.

• To hold the superintendent responsible for the administration of the school through regular constructive written and oral evaluations of the superintendent's work. Effective evaluation is an ongoing effort and should be

linked to goals established by the board with the assistance of the superintendent.

• To provide the superintendent with a comprehensive
employment contract.

• To give the superintendent the benefit of the board's
counsel in matters related to individual board members'
expertise, familiarity with the local school system, and
community interests.

• To hold all board meetings with the superintendent
or a designee present.

• To consult with the superintendent on all matters, as
they arise, that concern the school system and on which
the board may take action.

• To develop a plan for board-superintendent
communications.

• To channel communications with school employees
that require action through the superintendent, and to
refer all applications, complaints, and other communications, oral or written, first to the superintendent in order
to assure that the district processes such communications
in a effective, coordinated fashion and is responsive to
students and patrons.

• To take action on matters only after hearing the
recommendation of the superintendent.

• To establish a policy on the effective management of
complaints.

• To provide the superintendent with sufficient administrative help, especially in the area of monitoring teaching and learning.

Superintendents: Specific Responsibilities.

In keeping with the division of effort, superintendents
have these specific responsibilities:

• To serve as the board's chief executive officer and
adviser.

• To serve as the school system's educational leader.

• To keep the board informed about school operations
and programs.

• To keep the community informed about board policies, programs, and district procedures.

• To interpret the needs of the school system to the
board.

- To present and recommend policy options along with specific recommendations to the board when circumstances require the board to adopt new policies or revise existing policies.
- To develop and inform the board of administrative procedures needed to implement board policy.
- To provide leadership for the district's educational programs.
- To develop an adequate program of school-community relations.
- To manage the district's day-to-day operations.
- To evaluate personnel and keep the board informed about evaluations.

Communication a Key

An efficient and well-understood system of communication between the school board and superintendent is vital to a successful working relationship, based upon the general responsibilities contained in this statement. The first step toward achieving this relationship takes place when a board and superintendent put in writing what they agree to be their respective roles and responsibilities.

SUPERINTENDENT JOB DESCRIPTION

As stated earlier in this chapter, a well-stated job description helps to minimize ambiguities between the board and superintendent. The following is a job description I once used.

SAMPLE SUPERINTENDENT JOB DESCRIPTION

1.0 **Conditions of Employment.**

1.1 The superintendent shall be appointed by the board of education and the conditions of employment shall be specified in the contract.

2.0 **Qualifications.** The superintendent must:

2.1 Be dedicated to the belief that the finest ideals of American life depend significantly on the schools for their realization.

2.2 Be determined that, through the schools, the potentials born in people will develop for every student, whatever his background.

2.3 Possess the skill in human relations to stimulate consensus and action.

2.4 Know the ever-changing community well enough to keep the schools in tune with its varied and often conflicting desires.

2.5 Be able to align the community's desires with the needs of the times.

2.6 Be a person of considerable knowledge, academically, socially, and culturally, with a vision of what the future is likely to require of young people.

2.7 Possess a thirst for learning throughout his professional career in his search for ways to improve the school system and solve its problems.

2.8 Be able to accept criticism of all aspects of the school system graciously.

2.9 Seek throughout his career to benefit from the thinking of his colleagues.

2.10 Deal always in an honest, professional, open, and above-board manner with the board, staff, and community.

2.11 Be able to accept the responsibility for results.

3.0 **Resonsibilities**. The superintendent serves as the chief adminis-trative official of the board of education, providing overall leadership and direction of the schools, in accordance with board policies and the state education code. In fulfilling his responsibilities, the super-intendent:

3.1 Serves as secretary to the board and supervises preparation of the agenda, supporting papers, and minutes for all special and regular meetings of the board of education.

3.2 Plans and formulates policies, procedures, programs, and deci-sions needed in the conduct of the schools and presents such pro-posals to the board for its consideration and action.

3.3 Shall be responsible for the research, preparation, and presenta-tion of the annual budget, based upon the appropriate requests of the several schools and departments in the district and commensurate with the basic authorizations granted by the board of education.

3.4 Assumes general control for all purchases and expenditures within limitations of the budget as approved by the board.

3.5 Shall maintain an appropriate and complete system of accounting so that the board of education and public shall, at all times, be able to ascertain the costs of education in the district.

3.6 Recommends to the board the appointment, suspension, promo-tion, or dismissal of all employees of the school district.

3.7 Supervises the assignment and transfer of all employees according to the needs of the district.

3.8 Assumes complete responsibility for the evaluation of personnel who report directly to the superintendent.

3.9 Plans for the professional growth of all employees.

3.10 Develops and supervises the operation of a constructive program of inservice education for all employees of the school district.

3.11 Recommends to the board courses of study, and orders textbooks, supplementary books, library books, equipment, and supplies necessary for the conduct of the schools.

3.12 Prepares, or has prepared for his approval, the content of each course of study authorized by the board of education.

3.13 Enforces the proper use of the adopted courses of study and textbooks.

3.14 Directs that instruction be given for at least the minimum time in all subjects required to be taught by the state education code.

3.15 Prepares long-term plans and estimates for the schools covering properties, finance, personnel, and instruction and keeps these plans coordinated and under continuous study and revision.

3.16 Oversees the general operation and maintenance of school facilities and equipment, and the purchase, storage, distribution, and inventory of all supplies.

3.17 Determines the boundaries of school attendance areas, subject to the approval of the board.

3.18 Provides periodic reports to the board in order that the members may be informed of the status of all major functions of the district's operation and how their policies are being implemented.

3.19 Keeps the board informed of the progress of the school district toward achieving its goals and objectives.

3.20 Devotes a proportionate amount of time for study, travel, and association with colleagues which does not impair his primary responsibility for day-to-day operation of the school district.

3.21 Informs the board of developments that may significantly affect the operation of the school system, including regulations or instructions affecting staff personnel management, instruction of the pupils, safety of pupils and employees, custodial service, financial status, and relations of the schools to other branches of government.

4.0 **General Functions.** The superintendent:
4.1 Creates the conditions in which other people can get things done

and above all in which the teacher in the classroom can perform to
the best of his ability.
4.2 Seeks a consensus of the board, community, and staff on the goals
of the schools as a basis for decisions on the instructional program.
4.3 Seeks opportunities to create conditions in which the climate for
learning and the work of teachers may be improved.
4.4 Interacts with the staff to create and work within a general framework of professional and participatory relationships.
4.5 Considers the public's views since those views influence the quality of the schools. In particular, the public's willingness to pay taxes
constantly influences the choices of the schools, and public tolerance
is an essential foundation of academic freedom.

NEED FOR CLARITY

A closer analysis of the joint statement and the job description
indicates that many ambiguous areas remain which could cause a
degree of uncertainty as to the strategy a superintendent should follow in the decision-making process.

Other variables that affect the board-superintendent relationship
are the size of the district, the social status of the board, and the levels
of community tension. If one accepts that the board "owns the store"
then a more successful relationship can be engendered by the superintendent with the board if he regards his role as one of leadership
and management, and endeavors to be as politically sophisticated as
possible.

SIZE OF DISTRICT

Superintendents will face more opposition from school boards and
other organizations in large urban and suburban districts than in rural
districts. Even though turmoil and dissension in urban and suburban
districts are greater, superintendents are more likely to overcome it.
Usually, the larger school district is so complex that only the superintendent has a comprehensive view; through the professional expertise of his role, he can greatly assist the board in overcoming the
political pressure it faces. However, cities are more likely to have
"factional" boards that split on major issues.

The superintendent can maintain a good working relationship with
board members by continuing to provide them with a professional
analysis of the data. This can assist them in making better decisions
even in the face of political pressures from vested interest groups
within the community.

Rural districts provide a better opportunity for a closer relationship between the board and the superintendent because organizational and group opposition is less. Because of a more homogeneous population and a commonly shared sense of social values, rural boards and the superintendent can conduct business with greater consensus. Because the rural district is generally smaller and less complex, technical expertise counts for less than in larger urban or suburban districts. Rural boards oppose their superintendents less often, but when they do, the action is likely to be unanimous, effective, and detrimental to the superintendent.

STATUS OF BOARDS

Also affecting the relationship between the board and superintendent is the educational, social, or economic status of the board. High-status boards are more likely to oppose superintendents than low-status boards, although the former are less likely to press through to victory than the latter. The low-status board usually regards the superintendent as an employee rather than a professional; upset low-status boards indicate trouble for the superintendent. High-status boards are more likely to become involved in the important decisions of establishing curriculum, determining evaluation procedures, and determining budget categories for expenditures; while low-status boards tend to become involved in day-to-day operations such as personnel selection, evaluation, and the internal transfer of funds from one account to another.

COMMUNITY TENSION

Another variable that affects the board-superintendent relationship is the amount of community tension that exists. The relationship between the board and the superintendent is closest when public demands are low. Involuntary departures of superintendents are usually associated with political heat within the community. In large cities community tension can work for the superintendent because his role controls many resources and because urban boards tend to be factional. In small communities, on the other hand, tension of any sort works against the superintendent.

THE WEEKEND STUDY SESSION

After working with 50 board members throughout a 20-year period, I have found that a two-day study session with the board, beginning Friday evening with dinner and going through Sunday afternoon, provides an effective opportunity to establish basic directions and decision-making roles for the board and superintendent. The weekend study session is usually attended by the board and the superintendent's cabinet, which is representative of all the employees in the school district and ranges in size from 6 to 15 members.

ARRANGEMENTS

THE MEDIA ATTENDS

A representative of the media is invited to attend this study session to comply with the "sunshine laws" that exist in many states—particularly California. It is preferable to invite the editor. If numerous media are present in the community then representatives of those media should be included in the invitation. Because the study session is devoted purely to study and discussion and is completely void of any formal decisions by the board, the press usually does not attend more than the first evening, unless it is the editor. Weekend assignment of reporters for the study session is expensive due to the overtime.

LOCATION OF THE STUDY SESSION

Study sessions can be held in a comfortable surrounding such as a hotel or a religious retreat where the participants can be housed and fed for the weekend. There seemed to be fewer objections from the taxpayers and from the news media when the local board and administrators held their study session at a "religious" retreat rather than a "resort."

TIME FOR STUDY SESSION

The study session with the board and the superintendent's administrative cabinet is usually held once a year.

AGENDA FOR STUDY SESSION

Five major agenda items are addressed during the study session: short- and long-term goals, decision chart for the board and superintendent, plans for keeping the board informed, efficient board meetings and agendas, and discussion of programs.

I believe that discussion in these five major areas enhances the effective and efficient working relationships between the board and superintendent, no matter what the variables are in a particular school district.

Agenda item one: Establish the district one-year and three-to-five year goals through a Delphi process which is described in Chapter 11.

Agenda item two: Resolve the decision chart for the board and superintendent, considering about 100 different decision situations that might occur during the year for decision by the superintendent and the board.

Agenda item three: Develop plans for the superintendent to keep the board informed by identifying situations about which the board wishes to be informed in addition to those contained in the decision chart. The smaller the school district the more detailed is the information about which the board wishes to be informed. Usually, the best arrangement is agreement between the board and the superintendent on a procedure of alerting each other to rumors or to matters that they think the others should be informed about in addition to the regular written and oral communication that takes place in the district. Board members like to be apprised of what is going on instead of reading it in the newspaper as a surprise. Because it is especially difficult for a superintendent to know when reporters are making inquiries into district school matters it becomes imperative that board members assume a responsibility, if they hear rumors or activities taking place that might be of interest to the others, to alert the communication network so the information can be relayed to the rest of the board and to the superintendent.

Agenda item four: Plan for the most effective way the board meeting can be held in public. Agenda techniques and procedures should be thoroughly discussed and agreed to so the board can put its "best foot forward" during board meetings.

Agenda item five: Discuss topics and programs for which the board members would like to have an orientation and more information. Those items are usually generated by board members, though the superintendent can present a list of possible topics.

SHORT- AND LONG-TERM GOAL SETTING

One of the first activities the board engages in during the study session is the identification, through a Delphi process, of the board's one-year and three-to-five-year goals. Because participants have prepared their ideas beforehand, the input session of the goal-setting process usually takes 20 to 30 minutes.

As each participant completes a goal statement, he turns the card upside down and places it in front of him. Usually the participants sit around a square or rectangular table so they can see each other. After seven or eight minutes, a staff person collects the cards, and, as he picks them up, shuffles them to help protect the identity of the originator. After the cards are gathered and shuffled, two members of the staff put them in clusters according to common topics and prepare print-outs. An example of a print-out follows.

SAMPLE ONE-YEAR GOALS

ONE YEAR GOALS FOR SUPERINTENDENT AND STAFF
1983-84
SET BY BOARD OF EDUCATION

Directions:

5 columns on the right: For each item listed, check the rating in the column best reflecting your opinion.

4 columns on the left: From the entire list of items, select your top 10 items; from those 10 items, select five; from those five items, select two; and, finally, from the top two items, select your top item.

Scoring:

To determine the high priority items, it is necessary to score each individual item on the Delphi separately. The following point system is used:
- The top item equals 10 points.
- The remaining item of the top two items equals five points.
- The remaining three items of the top five receive two points each.
- The remaining five items of the top 10 items receive one point each.
- Total the points across for each item.

Chart:

1. Top Goal	SA -	Strongly Agree
2. Top Two Goals	A -	Agree
5. Top Five Goals	N -	No Opinion
10. Top Ten Goals	D -	Disagree
	SD -	Strongly Disagree

1   2   5   10   SA A N D SD

G
(5pts.)
	ATTENDANCE & DISCIPLINE
	1. Focus on attendance and
	   discipline, apply for
	   Title IV-C Grant.
		G Y
		M S
		    L

S Y M (9pts.)	**COMMUNICATION** 2. Improve communication.	S Y G M L

L M G Y
      S
(19pts.)
	3. Encourage all staff to become
	   more responsive to public at
	   all times.
		L Y
		M S
		G

M Y
G S
(6pts.)
	COMMUNITY RELATIONS
	4. Continue to improve board and
	   administration image.
		G Y L
		  M S

G L S (22pts.)	5. Increase parent participation in the decision-making process.	G L Y M S
M L Y (17pts.)	6. Review the community response to a second academics plus site.	M Y S G L

(etc.)	**CURRICULUM**
	7. Complete a curriculum guide for
	   science, K-6. Bring to board of
	   education in the fall.
	8. Develop a curriculum guide for health
	   education, K-6.
	9. Complete a curriculum guide for
	   written expression, K-12; and
	   complete a curriculum guide for
	   spelling, oral expression, and listening
	   skills, K-6.
	10. Continue emphasis on curriculum
	   articulation.
	11. Adopt a grading policy with a clear
	   definition.
	12. Continue clinical supervision training.
	13. Examine, explore, develop second
	   academics plus site.
		(etc.)

14. Designate curriculum as your top priority.
15. Integrate efforts to serve borderline "drop-out" students at all levels.
16. Continue to improve academic achievement, learning climate, and parent involvement.

DATA PROCESSING

17. Update data processing capabilities and services.
18. Implement a data processing system to meet demands of the district.
19. Increase supervision over data processing, its organization and output.
20. Allocate money for temporary personnel to update the data processing system.

EMPLOYER/EMPLOYEE RELATIONS

21. Conduct back to school meeting at the Community Pavilion.
22. Conduct employee awards night.
23. Develop programs to enhance employee motivation and morale.
24. Improve staff morale.
25. Improve affirmative action policy for promoting women.
26. Develop a policy of affirmative action to hire adult handicapped individuals in larger numbers.
27. Employ a person to work full time in staff development.

FACILITIES MAINTENANCE AND PLANNING

28. Institute an ongoing study of possible economies such as school closure.
29. Improve landscaping at all schools.
30. Improve maintenance services.
31. Make certain that two real estate sales are completed and all other usage of surplus property is determined.

32. Establish energy conservation program to realize a savings of $100,000.

FINANCE

33. Establish non-funded categorical program income and expenditures relationship.
34. Investigate the possibility of private funding by an athletics foundation.
35. Adopt different preliminary budget processes.
36. Develop a balanced budget with a one percent reserve.

INTERNAL RELATIONS

37. Consider paying board members.
38. Participate in training seminars for school board members.
39. Promote better personal relations among staff, administration, and board.
40. Conduct spring conference, lunch and awards meeting at the Pavilion.

MISCELLANEOUS

41. Improve long-range planning; perhaps we need a planner.
42. Establish a formal procedure for board accountability.
43. Consider policy adoption process.
44. Improve special education programs.
45. Improve bus service for special education students.

. . .

DECISION CHART FOR BOARD AND SUPERINTENDENT

While participants are waiting for print-outs of the goals, which would be typed that evening and be ready for the group Saturday morning, they begin to discuss the second major portion of the study session which is determining the decision chart for the board and the superintendent.

Much of the superintendent's day is devoted to decision making. Often the superintendent asks the question "Should I decide on my own or should I involve the board in some way?" District policy together with administrative procedures and a job description usually help minimize ambiguities in decision making.

However, many "undefined areas" exist which cause a degree of uncertainty as to the strategy a superintendent should follow in the decision-making process. Discussing these areas of ambiguity among the board and the superintendent beforehand helps identify decision-making responsibilities. Having done so, energy previously expended in efforts to determine the extent of involvement as to who makes the decision can be rechanneled into finding the solution.

To clarify the working relationship between the superintendent and the school board, I used a decision chart. An example of this chart follows.

INSTRUCTIONS

1. The general purpose of this chart is to clarify the distribution of *operational*—not legal—authority within the district organization. A more specific purpose is to clarify to what degree powers which are vested in the district as a whole have been delegated to the superintendent. We are not concerned with limitations that have been imposed upon the superintendent or the district from external sources, such as by law or contracts. Rather, we are interested in limitations that have been imposed internally, such as by district organization, board policy, regulation or "practice", upon a superintendent's flexibility to decide to act in various situations. In going through this chart, we are not concerned with whether the particular decision (or action) proposed is a wise one. The question at issue is: "Assuming the superintendent wanted to make that decision, does he have the operational authority to do so?"

In some cases, responsibility and authority are vested in a particular body or position by law or administrative regulation, and for this reason certain actions and decisions must go through the formality or approval by that body or position. For example, all appointments of teachers to fill established vacancies are usually approved by boards, but a board does not generally study and review the decision to hire specific applicants. For purposes of the present analysis, *if a superintendent can make a decision with virtual assurance that approval will follow as a formality, then the superintendent should be consid-*

ered as having the authority to make the decision (operational authority).

2. On the following pages situations are proposed for decision or action. To complete the chart, select for each situation the one degree of operational authority you believe most closely describes the authority the superintendent has in connection with that situation.

> DEGREES OF OPERATIONAL AUTHORITY are as follows:
>
> I. Superintendent has complete authority to decide or act (within limits of law, board policy, contracts, and budget).
> II. Superintendent has complete authority to decide or act, but must keep board informed about the decision made or action taken.
> III. Superintendent has authority to decide or act only with prior approval of the board.
> IV. Superintendent may be asked for recommendations, but decision, responsibility and direction come from the board.

3. In some cases the superintendent may not exercise his operational authority personally, but may delegate it to one or more members of the staff. Such cases, when the superintendent has the authority to permit the staff to take action or make decisions, should be considered no differently than when the superintendent exercises the authority personally.

4. Assume that availability of funds is not a limiting factor—any funds necessary have already been budgeted, are within tax limits, or will be made available through budgetary transfers.

5. Please add any questions, which you feel should be resolved, at the end of the chart.

6. Your superintendent and staff will be more efficient and effective if they know their operational authority. It is important to have a systematic management plan for the school district.

. . .

SAMPLE CHART

DECISION CHART FOR SUPERINTENDENT/BOARD
UNIFIED SCHOOL DISTRICT
April, 1983

I Complete Authority
II Act/Inform
III Prior Approval
IV Board Direction

I	II	III	IV	
	x			1. Put a new program in mathematics into the district's curriculum in several of the schools.
x				2. Permit a school to replace a major portion of the maps, films, and written materials (other than books) for the social studies-history curriculum in order to better meet district goals.
		x		3. Establish a School Site Council.
		x		4. Initiate (or abandon) a program of decentralized management throughout the district.
x				5. Have students meet with teachers for considering curriculum changes.
x				6. Permit a choral group to compete at a festival out of the San Francisco Bay Area that would require staying overnight.
x				7. Approve a field trip to an electronic equipment assembly plant in San Jose (same day).
x				8. Select map and globe materials for all schools.
	x			9. Promote a teacher who has a reputation of being a militant to a principalship.
	x			10. Initiate (or abandon) a districtwide flexible scheduling program at the high schools.

I	II	III	IV	
x				11. Approve a staff request for a foreign-made brand of tape recorder that has not been used in the district prior to this time.
x				12. Exchange teaching assignments between two teachers at different schools without their consent.
		x		13. Initiate a new and sensitive (i.e., family life) program.
	x			14. Retain a consultant, not on district staff, to assist four principals in setting up a remedial reading program within general purpose budgeted funds.
		x		15. Increase the district student-teacher ratio.
			x	16. Initiate a 12-month school year.
		x		17. Agree to a Regional Occupation Program contract with county offices for a 10 percent increase over last year.
x				18. Establish an additional class rather than increase size of existing classes (even though there would be no penalty in state support if class sizes were increased).
	x			19. Formulate and publish administrative regulations to implement board policy.
	x			20. Suspend publication of a student newspaper.
		x		21. Provide district lifetime passes for athletic and other school events to distinguished community citizens.
		x		22. Discontinue an interscholastic sport in all district schools.
		x		23. Allow each school to have courses and subjects not taught at other schools in the district.
		x		24. Establish a districtwide testing program beyond the state testing program to determine the progress of students in the district.

I	II	III	IV	
		x		25. Abandon report cards in favor of parent conferences in several of the district schools.
		x		26. Set attendance, achievement, and subject requirements for graduation from high school.
x				27. Determine rules for dress.

Authorize district staff to have individual student tests carried out for diagnostic or placement purposes in each of the following categories:

I	II	III	IV	
x				28. Aptitude.
x				29. Achievement.
x				30. Psychological.
x				31. Psychiatric.
	x			32. Under emergency conditions, impose administrative rules about unauthorized assembly, riots, etc., more stringent than adopted by the board.
		x		33. Determine type and number of district office administrative positions—how many assistant superintendents, directors, coordinators—to comprise the central office staff.
	x			34. Transfer a principal to a different school.
	x			35. Authorize a district staff member to fly to Atlantic City for a workshop (from general purpose funds).
	x			36. Permit an assistant superintendent to undertake paid consulting assignments for private gain from other school districts two days a month, with the understanding that any time spent on these assignments during normal district working hours will be taken from his vacation time.

I	II	III	IV	
			x	37. Appoint an individual to an existing assistant superintendent, business services vacancy.
		x		38. For the next school year, decide to add an additional coordinator at the district office level.
	x			39. Establish salaries for assistant superintendents (not on salary schedule).
		x		40. Establish a new position entitled Director, Research and Development.
		x		41. Terminate a principal.
			x	42. Retain a negotiator to represent the district.
		x		43. Demote a management employee.
	x			44. Send a principal to a three-day leadership conference in Las Vegas on school time and at district expense.
		x		45. Select a person for an existing vacant principalship.
x				46. Reprimand a principal and place a notation to that effect in his personnel file.
	x			47. Temporarily remove a principal from his position, for arriving at "back-to-school" night under the influence of alcohol, until an investigation can be made.
x				48. Establish rules allowing teachers to leave campus during the school day as long as their assignments are covered.
x				49. Authorize giving coaches one less class assignment, so they can start practice early.
x				50. Set up an inservice training program for about five percent of the district's teachers after school four days a week for eight weeks with extra pay.

I	II	III	IV	
		x		51. Terminate a tenured teacher because of continued policy violations.
x				52. Notify a non-tenured teacher that unless improvement is made, action will be taken to terminate his services.
x				53. Grant a request for a two-week leave of absence, without pay, for a teacher to accompany spouse on a business trip.
x				54. Grant a teacher request for one day off, with pay, for personal leave.
	x			55. On a day that two-thirds of the teachers are absent and on strike, decide to close a school and send students and all other teachers home.
	x			56. Send a teacher out of state to a four-week concentrated course on new instructional methods, paying salary and all expenses.
		x		57. Designate the administrative representatives for the negotiation process.
		x		58. Terminate a permanent secretary for unsatisfactory work performance.
x				59. Authorize employment of custodians for all schools.
		x		60. Cut custodial force by layoff of 10 percent in order to provide funds for additional library books.
x				61. Demote a maintenance supervisor for unsatisfactory performance of supervisory assignments.
x				62. Suspend a bus driver for two weeks due to repeated violations of safety regulations.
x				63. Transfer a student from a teacher's class because of a parent's demand.
	x			64. Accept a gift of black history books from the Black Panthers.

I	II	III	IV	
x				65. Grant demand of parents to have student transferred to another school within the district because of alleged widespread drug abuse in present school.
		x		66. Change attendance boundaries that will cause 10 percent of the population to attend different schools the following year.
			x	67. Recommend unification of Walnut Creek which would result in losing five schools.
	x			68. Invite a controversial organization to make a presentation to a school student body.
x				69. Cooperate with the AM-Vets concerning sponsorship of an essay contest on citizenship.
x				70. Provide a board agenda with supporting papers to a known member of a group who unjustly criticizes the schools.
		x		71. Represent the board at a city council meeting exploring the possibility of selling a school to them.
x				72. Establish level of grounds quality and appearance to be maintained in the district.
		x		73. Lease four portable classrooms for temporary use until completion of a new school that is seven months behind construction schedule.
		x		74. Authorize extensive landscaping additions to an existing school.
x				75. Establish level of building cleanliness to be maintained in the district.
		x		76. Agree to waive the penalty clause against a contractor for being late in completing a building contract, because of extenuating circumstances not contemplated in the contract.

I	II	III	IV	
x				77. Retain a consultant for inservice training of all custodial staff of the district.
x				78. Have the exteriors of one-third of the district's schools repainted.
		x		79. Put automatic lawn sprinklers in all schools.
x				80. Authorize weekend use of school facilities for activities by a religious organization charging only the actual out-of-pocket costs for their use.
		x		81. Have the superintendent's office redecorated and refurnished.
x				82. Authorize districtwide master keys to be given to all district office administrators.
x				83. Determine what deterrent or detection systems for vandalism are to be used for district schools.
x				84. Decide not to seek restitution from a student apprehended breaking windows at a school.
		x		85. Select the architect for rehabilitating a school.
		x		86. Decide how the money is to be allocated among various budget categories (e.g., how much for teachers, teacher aides, clerks, equipment, supplies, grounds, etc.) within a total amount acceptable to the board.
		x		87. Transfer funds from one series to another.
		x		88. Authorize a school principal to exceed the total school budget, with funds to come from reserves.
		x		89. Contract for busing by a private company rather than purchase an additional bus.
			x	90. Announce to the community that another tax election will be necessary next year.

I	II	III	IV	

	x			91. Place an order for a new bus that is needed but not budgeted, with funds to come from reserves.
	x			92. Authorize the purchase of a district car to be assigned to an assistant uperintendent.
	x			93. Select the auditing firm to audit district records for the current school year.
	x			94. Institute a budgeting system to be operational districtwide within two years.
	x			95. Expand a district data processing center to handle services from other school districts.
	x			96. Initiate a district fee schedule which charges students for direct costs of educational programs.
x				97. Accept a major grant to the district from a private organization.
	x			98. Employ any new unbudgeted positions.
		x		99. Establish an educational foundation to raise supplementary funds.

CONTENTS OF THE DECISION CHART

Depending on the school district and the members of the board, the chart will usually contain a hundred potential decision situations. The items—drawn from actual circumstances that require decisions—occur in such areas as curriculum, personnel, finance, community relations, and internal school operations. Authority is fluid, a matter of degree, but for convenience we have calibrated the overall range of authority into four distinct levels.

Level one: The superintendent has complete authority to decide or act within the limits of the law, the board policy, propriety and conscience, negotiated contracts, the educational code, and the budget.

Level two: The superintendent has complete authority to decide or to act but must keep the board informed about the decision or action.

Level three: The superintendent has authority to implement or act only with prior approval from the school board.

Level four: The school board initiates the action and may encourage the superintendent to make recommendations. The difference between level three and level four is that in level four the board of education has the responsibility to initiate the action or to ask the staff for recommendations; whereas in level three the initiation of the action comes from the superintendent to the board. However, in both level three and four the board has the final authority.

GETTING STARTED

During discussion by the board members and the superintendent, consensus—regarding which decision situations to list on the chart, and the appropriate disposition of authority level in each situation—is the goal. To begin this process, each board member is asked to review a list of proposed decisions and to amend the list if they wish. Next, the board members and the superintendent go through the list independent of one another. Each participant indicates what, in their opinion, is the appropriate level of authority for each potential situation. This is done prior to the weekend study session. Before going on retreat, the individual results are compiled and a composite is made showing each person's judgments.

SAMPLE RESULTS OF THE DECISION CHART

General Analysis

DECISION CHART ANALYSIS

The report and analysis of the board-superintendent decision chart follows:

In general, there was a high degree of agreement (85 of the 99 items).

It was significant that there was only one item (No.41) in which each sees the other as the decision maker.

Item By Item Analysis

I only list five sample items; an actual analysis would have all 99 items.

Item	Board Member					Board		Consensus	Supt.
	A	B	C	D	E	Mode	Mean		
	Decision Level								
1.	2	3	1	2	1	2		2	2
2.	1	1	1	1	1	1		1	1
14.	1	3	4	1	2	2		?	1
25.	2	3	4	4	2	3		?	1
41.	1	2	1	1	1	1		?	3

Summary Analysis

SUMMARY—DECISION CHART ANALYSIS

Board Member	Raw Score	Mean	Decision Level Score			
			I	II	III	IV
A	175	1.7	50	31	9	9
B	245	2.5	13	38	36	12
C	211	2.1	46	14	19	20
D	263	2.6	27	20	12	40
E	282	2.8	14	31	10	44
Superintendent	185	1.9	47	23	24	5

Board Member	Superintendent as Decision Maker (Level I-II) Number of items	Board as Decision Maker (Level III-IV) Number of items
A	81	18
B	51	48
C	60	39
D	47	52
E	45	54
Superintendent	70	29

Matched agreement (Mode/Mean equal)   53 items

General agreement (Mode/Mean I-II)   18

General agreement (Mode/Mean III-IV)   14

Agreement Total 85

Each sees the other as being the decision maker   1 item

Both board and superintendent see themselves as the decision maker   14 items

Member A scores indicate an approximate 4:1 ratio in favor of superintendent as decision maker, even exceeding the superintendent's perception of himself as decision maker.

Member B scores in terms of decision making have a slight weighting toward the superintendent.

Member C scores indicate an approximate 3:2 ratio in favor of the superintendent as the decision maker.

Members D and E have similar scores in terms of decision making being nearly equally divided between the board and superintendent with a slight weighting in favor of the board.

One item
Each sees the other as being the decision maker
    #41 Terminate a principal

14 items
Both board and superintendent see themselves as being the decision maker
#13 Initiate family life program
#25 Abandon report cards for conferences
#27 Designate rules for dress
#29 Achievement testing program
#48 Establish rules allowing teachers to leave campus
#50 Set up inservice for teachers
#52 Implement evaluation process for teachers
#56 Authorize teachers study trips out of state
#73 Lease portable classrooms
#74 Authorize landscaping
#79 Installation of lawn sprinklers
#80 Authorize use of school facilities
#87 Budget transfers
#88 Authorize principal to exceed budget

     4   Curriculum Items   13, 25, 27, 29
     6   Budget Items   73, 74, 79, 80, 87, 88
     5   Personnel Items   "41," 48, 50, 52, 56
         Public Relations Items   ----

. . .

REACHING CONSENSUS

At the retreat the board members and the superintendent discuss their selections. Often, areas are identified in which both the superintendent and the board members feel they should exercise maximum authority. Additional areas are found in which neither the board or the superintendent claims authority. Responsibility in these latter instances is usually assigned to the superintendent as the item tends to be quite difficult to administer such as terminating a principal.

Some items have marks by the participants in all four decision categories, but as the discussion proceeds, usually at considerable length, clarification occurs and consensus follows. The advantage of using this process is the development of a solid understanding concerning philosophic differences among board members, and between the board and the superintendent regarding methods of school system operation. Because no absolute answers exist, the final outcome is the consensus.

In a relaxed and tranquil setting, a thorough understanding is achieved about who should have what degree of authority for the various aspects of operating the schools. Everyone learns where the other stands, not just on abstract issues, but in terms of actual school functions.

The board generally prefers to delegate the majority of decisions to the superintendent with the proviso that they be kept informed. This is an attitude common among large complex systems. School boards in small systems ordinarily prefer to retain more direct decision-making authority.

HOW OFTEN IS THE CHART DONE?

Whenever new members are elected to the school board the chart is redone. If board composition remains unchanged the chart should be redone every two or three years to ensure that the school system is being operated in accordance with current conditions and attitudes.

AUTHORITY CAN BE DELEGATED TO OTHER STAFF BY THE SAME CHART PROCESS

Areas of authority given to the superintendent may subsequently be delegated to other members of the administrative team. A similar decision chart is developed by the superintendent and school principals. A third decision chart is developed by the principal at the building level.

MAINTAINING HARMONIOUS RELATIONSHIPS

School board members and superintendents can maintain close and harmonious working relationships even during times of high emotion and intense controversy. The key to survival is a simple management plan that addresses school problems in a systematic way. Organization development and systems management are essential to running an effective school district. Equally vital are frequent exchanges of feelings and views among school board members and the superintendent, especially in situations of stress.

ASSISTS IN UNDERSTANDING BOARD POLICY

The fact that the school board and the superintendent's cabinet set one-year and three-to-five-year goals and then subsequently resolve a decision chart for every conceivable decision that might come up between the board and the superintendent helps to build an understanding of how the policy of the board of directors will be carried out in detail by the administrative team. I have also noted over the years that board members who have been successful in business or who work in large organizations tend to give the superintendent and the staff more authority. The longer the board and the superintendent work together, the greater the tendency of those board members to give their superintendent and staff more authority. If this does not happen, the superintendent should consider that his job may be in jeopardy.

HOW LONG DOES THE PROCESS TAKE?

Resolving the decision chart takes from 90 minutes to 4 hours depending on whether the repsonses seem to reflect wide differences or consensus.

SOME EXAMPLES

An interesting example from the decision chart is the matter of conference attendance by staff. Instead of coming to the board for approval each time a staff member wants to attend a workshop, the board allows the superintendent to submit a report to the board every six months or annually on conference attendance. Concerns the board may have are changed for the future.

It is essential for participants to understand that there are no right answers on the decision chart. Rather it is an exercise of consensus, so the superintendent and staff can understand how the "owners of the store" want the business of the school district conducted. It is far better to know what the board wants in the area of decision making ahead of time, before matters become controversial and the superintendent is surprised that the assumed authority is not there. This proves to be an embarrassment because the board does not support the recommendations of the superintendent during critical times.

In one instance when I was superintendent, the board decided that as long as they were informed I should have transfer authority. Because they were informed regarding a controversial high school principal transfer, the board upheld the decision of the superintendent even though many parents and students were demonstrating and objecting to losing their principal by the transfer.

HOW OFTEN DO YOU REFER TO THE CHART?

You probably will not look at the chart often because a basic understanding exists that was engendered when you developed the chart. You should resolve the decision chart during times of calm and peace when participants can be objective.

WHAT AREAS ARE THE MOST SENSITIVE?

The most sensitive items occur in the areas of budget transfers, personnel, and conference attendance.

KEEPING THE BOARD INFORMED

THE FRIDAY REPORT

The third area discussed during the weekend study retreat is keeping the board informed about pertinent situations occurring in the school district. Even though participants can indicate on the board-superintendent decision chart items about which the board needs to be informed, those tend to be routine informational items. Each Friday, the superintendent should mail a report to the board regarding the highlights of that particular week.

BOARD AND SUPERINTENDENT ARE EQUALLY RESPONSIBLE FOR INFORMATION

For years I let the board make it my sole responsibility to keep them informed of things that were happening within the district; this usually occurred by way of a phone call to all five or seven board members and became a difficult responsibility to achieve. Invariably something would happen in the school district and board members would hear about it before I could contact them. After the Watergate incident, during the Nixon administration, reporters and local newspapers styled themselves as inquiry reporters looking for scandal, hoping to find some newsworthy event that would appear on the front page of the local newspaper. It became impossible for me to know everything that was happening within the district before others did. This was especially true in larger districts.

As a result, I informed the board before the weekend study session that they needed to be thinking about items about which they wished to be informed. Did they want to know about significant happenings to personnel such as someone being in the hospital? About a death that had occurred among students or staff? Did they want to know

about fights of significance on campus, or drug related arrests, or
knifings, or shootings?

I could usually convince the board to assume equal responsibility
for any events they might have heard of by rumor, by grapevine, by
some person on the staff, or by a student informing them. It was their
responsibility, if they thought an item was newsworthy, to alert my
office, so the rest of the board could be informed. We would either
place the information in the Friday report, or, if I felt it were highly
significant, I would immediately initiate the phone tree to inform the
board so they would not be surprised later.

INFORMATION VARIES

Depending on the size of the district, the amount of information
the board wanted varied. In small districts, the board wanted to know
when there was an objection to a bus stop or when a bus did not pick
up students and we had a complaint by a parent. In large districts, the
board only wanted to know about major happenings such as a shoot-
ing on the campus, or a drug bust by the police, or when a school had
been burned or vandalized, rather than personnel incidents or parent
complaints.

Additional items about which the board wanted to be informed
were added to the decision chart.

EFFICIENT BOARD MEETINGS AND AGENDAS

The fourth major area discussed during the weekend study retreat
is the efficiency of board agendas and public meetings. During my 17
years as a superintendent in four different school districts, and as a
consultant in many other school districts, I was concerned with board
agenda formats that were not compatible with the public interest.

Many board agendas were obviously arranged to prevent the public
from participating or even knowing what was going on. Much work
was done either by phone before the board meeting or at executive
sessions. This was in violation of the "sunshine law" which states that
only certain personnel matters and items of confidentiality between a
negotiator and an attorney could be discussed in executive or private
session. I became aware of situations in which the majority of the
board members were meeting for coffee or at someone's home to
discuss items of importance.

DECIDE HOW TO HANDLE CONTROVERSIAL AUDIENCES

In order for the board members to conduct effective, efficient
board meetings, it was essential during the weekend study session to

talk about what their agenda format would be and to encourage them to involve the public in a systematic way. This could be done by publishing board meeting procedures in advance and by having them available as the audience came in to avoid surprises as the meeting proceeded.

At times, when controversial items such as closing schools or reducing transportation attracted large numbers of emotionally distraught people to meetings, procedures for addressing the board were essential. Usually, if the audience was large, it was stated that a person would have three minutes or less to address the board. The opportunity to speak would come at a convenient time on the agenda so the public would not have to wait around until midnight before they could speak to the board.

Usually the board agenda was set up cooperatively with the board president and the superintendent. On those occasions when we knew we had controversial items to be decided, we would try to conduct most of our business on the routine items portion of our agenda. Board members could always remove an item from the routine agenda if it warranted more discussion. We preferred to call this part of the agenda routine business items rather than consent items to avoid the negative psychology of the board being viewed as rubber stamping which the term consent might imply.

The most efficient method for working with any agenda would be to regard the entire agenda as a package and move to adopt it all at one time—unless a board member, superintendent, or a member of the audience wanted to identify a particular item for discussion.

SPEAKING TO THE BOARD

The length of time that each person in the audience was allowed to speak was usually determined by a show of hands as to how many people wanted to speak that evening, and by dividing the time so everybody would have equal opportunity.

When closing a dozen schools is the issue and more than 800 emotional people are in the audience, or when you are deciding an employee contract following a bitter eleven-day teacher's strike and a 1,000-member audience attempts to disrupt the meeting by cat-calling, board meeting procedures must be enforced. It becomes impossible to conduct a meeting when people are unruly and disruptive. Occasionally, police protection was necessary to provide the board and superintendent with an atmosphere in which the meeting could continue.

In those cases in which it was almost impossible for everybody to speak in an evening, people were encouraged to let spokespersons represent them, so groups would have more time to address the board. Usually we allowed 2 or 3 minutes per person if the audience was large; if only a few people wanted to speak, they were allowed 5 to 10 minutes.

It is important for board members to understand that they are not to argue with members of the audience after an audience presentation, but rather ask questions for clarification. Also the board needs to show interest in what is being said. What follows is an example of a typical board agenda including a routine items section.

Sample Agenda
SCHOOL DISTRICT BOARD OF DIRECTORS MEETING
May 13, 1983
7:00 p.m.

AGENDA

1.0 CALL TO ORDER (white pages)
    1.1 Members Present
    1.2 Visitors Present
    1.3 Next Meeting Date: June 21, 1983, District Headquarters
    1.4 Communications-Correspondence
    1.5 Approval of Minutes of April 2, 1983
    1.6 Adoption of Agenda

2.0 REPORT OF PRESIDENT (white pages)

3.0 REPORT OF SUPERINTENDENT (white pages)

4.0 Routine Items (white pages)
    4.1 Receipt of Reports
        4.1.1 Membership and Cash Flow Reports
        4.1.2 Budget Summary Report
    4.2 Actions
        4.2.1 Resolutions to Amend Retirement Plan
        4.2.2 Curriculum Conference Committee

5.0 INTERNAL OPERATIONS (pink pages)
    5.1 Funding for Extra Committee Meetings
    5.2 CM/CE Request for Transfer of Funds
    5.3 Executive Session - Professional Standards
    5.4 82/83 Audit Contract

6.0 POLICY/ACTIONS (yellow pages)
    6.1 Opposition to Tuition Tax Credit
    6.2 Performance Objectives for Board Goals
    6.3 Length of Time in School
    6.4 Propositions on June Ballot

7.0 REPORTS/DISCUSSION (blue pages)
    7.1 City Council Liaison
    7.2 Board Liaison to Schools
    7.3 Update on Legislation
    7.4 Unfavorable Media Coverage
    7.5 Study of School District
    7.6 Suit Against Legislature
    7.7 Task Force on Secondary & Post Secondary Education

8.0 ADDITIONS TO THE AGENDA (white pages)

9.0 ADJOURNMENT

. . .

HOW WE ARE JUDGED BY THE PUBLIC

It must be remembered that the board agenda format and the procedures for the public meeting are important. This is probably one of the few times the board members are viewed by the public and, as a result, it is essential that the "owners of the store" who represent a voting constituency make a favorable impression with those who are observing them in action, whether it is the public or the staff.

I have been in districts in which the board meetings were regularly broadcast over local radio and television. This had a bearing on the manner in which the board members conducted themselves; they knew that the constituency which had put them in office was observing them. Much posturing took place during the board meeting under these conditions.

Despite such posturing the superintendent and the staff should help the board members present themselves well during the board meeting by having a carefully planned agenda and by having reasonable procedures for public involvement. The weekend study session is an excellent time to discuss the merits of how board meetings will be conducted.

DISCUSSION OF PROGRAMS

The fifth and major area addressed during the weekend study session is a list of selected topics to be discussed in depth. These topics are usually submitted by board members, and, if not, topics are suggested by staff. This approach allows considerable in-depth orientation and discussion of such major areas as special education, family life education, or science education. If the board only wants information concerning various programs, a presentation is made by the proper staff member who may not be a participant in the study session but who is brought in for this special presentation.

Items which the board may want to discuss might include the transportation system and how the buses are scheduled throughout the district, or a preliminary discussion of growth or declining enrollment issues. Often emerging from these discussions is a request by the board to bring a proposal to a board meeting for a formal decision.

You should indicate on the study session agenda a time allotment for each of the topics.

ADDITIONAL SUGGESTIONS

As indicated earlier, it is important for the study session to occur in a comfortable and relaxed environment—a hotel or a religious retreat. However, I have had boards who were reluctant to spend any extra money for housing or food during the weekend.

After a recall of the board—three new members were elected who were antagonistic toward the other two members and the superintendent—the weekend study session was held in the board room. Participants made their own arrangements for meals. Four television stations and nine newspapers were present, however they all left by Saturday noon.

The weekend study session contributed to a better working relationship between the newly constituted board and the superintendent. Staff made it clear that the board "owned the store" and that the professional staff was there to carry out the policies and directions of the board that were further clarified through the goal-setting process and the board-superintendent decision chart. During the next year, the board and superintendent worked well together.

The skills of working with a diverse or factionalized board are much like those which city managers use in working with city councils who usually are elected by partisan, vested-interest groups. Seldom does a city council have complete unanimity of philosophy among the members. More frequently now, school boards are elected by partisan, vested-interest groups; the chances of having philosophical unanimity among the members are becoming less likely.

SHOULD SPOUSES ATTEND?

The consideration of spouse attendance depends on whether or not the board and staff are compatible. If you are able to hold the weekend study session at a retreat in a comfortable environment that can accommodate everyone, spouses could be included and could participate in the social activities.

If compatibility exists and if you want to establish a close rapport among board and staff, I recommend that spouses be invited to all sessions and that the weekend agenda allow for socializing and recreation. This creates a spirit of team unity, yet allows the board to carry out its policy function.

WHO IS ON THE SUPERINTENDENT'S CABINET?

The superintendent's cabinet is a representative group which includes principals, representatives from transportation, food services, maintenance, and other departments. Depending on the employee unions, it can be desirable to have a representative from their group which could be the president.

RECREATIONAL ACTIVITIES LEAD TO RAPPORT

I have sponsored a number of activities to encourage closer working relationships among the various groups within the school district. We have sponsored recreational activities such as bowling leagues, golf and tennis tournaments, and ten kilometer races. Board members, administrators, teachers, and support staff, all with their tents or recreation vehicles, have also enjoyed a relaxing and fun weekend camping in state parks. Recreational activities can help engender closer working relationships among various members of the school district.

COMMENTS

Although many other areas can be considered in board-superintendent relations and decision making, the practical activities I have mentioned in this chapter can definitely contribute to a stronger board-superintendent relationship, to greater cooperation within the educational community, and to improved educational programs for all learners in our schools.

Chapter 14
Superintendent-Principal
Decision Making

The message of the research and literature seems clear: schools are not helpless in the face of the forces that influence students before they get to school. Schools can, and do, make a difference in the achievement of the student. Schools effect change by creating a set of expectations that support achievement. The one person in the school who has the most influence on the establishment of the environment that will produce this achievement is the *principal.*

HISTORY OF THE PRINCIPALSHIP

Approximately two centuries elapsed from the time the principalship was created until the principal was released from all teaching duties. Studies conducted in the early 1900s underscore the changing role of the principal. A principal's business management functions were contrasted with descriptions of the principal as a teacher of teachers; the ultimate knowledge of "best" practices resided in these status leaders. No matter what differences there were about a principal's primary role, there was agreement that the principal was an authority.

By the early 1940s the traditional authoritarian view of the principalship began to erode; effective leadership emerged as a philosophy. Involvement of all school personnel in policy and decision making was encouraged. This thrust for participative management came not only from contemporary management theorists, but from federal and state legislatures as well. Legislation called for school site councils or

advisory committees which required staff, student, parent, and community involvement in policy development and decision-making
processes affecting individual school programs. The demand on the
principal increased as these requirements were imposed on public
schools.

In the 1970s the intensity and the complexity of the demands upon
the principal's skills, and the time required to fulfill all these responsibilities had greatly increased. Because of the numerous pressures
placed upon a principal, it became necessary that he be given as
much authority as possible and that resources be made available to
help him solve his local school site problems at that level rather than
having to go through a hierarchy of decisions before adequate solutions could be reached.

CONCERNS OF MIDDLE MANAGERS
OR PRINCIPALS

A report published by the American Management Association in
their forum newsletter, *Management Review*, May 1981, stated that
two-thirds of the managers surveyed believed their job performance
to be adversely affected by the decisions and actions of their immediate supervisors. The group complained repeatedly that they lacked
the information needed to do their jobs properly. Managers were also
disturbed by the lack of feedback on job performance. When feedback was delivered, it was usually negative and derogatory in tone and
content—what you are doing wrong, not what you are doing right.
More than a third of the managers thought that bosses were
indecisive—a surprisingly high figure considering that decision making is a main task. Forty-one percent of the respondents claim that
they were not provided with the information they needed to do their
jobs properly. Many complained about getting information in bits and
pieces, only when they asked for it, or secondhand.

More than half of the respondents agreed with this statement:
"When a major decision is taken in the organization it is influenced
more by the status of the individual proposing a solution than by the
logic of the argument." This would imply that decision makers are not
receptive to available information, that the information on which
decisions are based is distorted by status differentials, and that decision makers are more interested in justifying their decisions than in
making the right ones.

ATTITUDINAL CHANGES OF MIDDLE AND TOP MANAGEMENT

The following excerpts, taken from *Management Review,* May 1981, published by the American Management Association, further substantiate concerns of middle managers.

> The Opinion Research Corporation of Princeton, New Jersey, has been conducting attitude surveys among American companies since the 1950s. In its latest study, which included 19,500 managers in 200 companies, ORC discovered an increasing estrangement between middle and top management. The following are just a few of the attitudinal changes that have occurred during the past few decades:
>
> • Only 33 percent of managers currently see their companies as responsive to their problems and concerns (1978-80), compared with 50 percent in 1960-64.
> • Only 37 percent see their companies as fair in making promotions, compared to 55 percent in 1960-64.
> • Only 50 percent rate high-level management as "good" or "very good", while 70 percent gave high marks to top executives in 1960-64.
> • Sixty-seven percent of managers rate their companies as an above average place to work—compared to 84 percent in 1960-64.
> • In the absence of corrective measures, this crack in the corporate management hierarchy will almost certainly spread during the 1980s. Even allowing for the fact that there will be fewer young workers as the post-World War II "baby boomers" enter middle age, middle managers are likely to become increasingly disillusioned unless ways are found to involve them meaningfully in the decisions they have to implement.

The concern of middle management is not just contained in American management circles in industry and business. To substantiate the concern of principals and assistant principals who manage school site operations and to justify delegating as much decision-making authority to the school site as possible so solutions to learning problems can be solved close to the learner, I am including an article which an elementary principal and I wrote for the *Executive Educator* magazine.

WHEN UNIONS START WOOING PRINCIPALS,
YOU'D BEST HAVE A BETTER ANSWER —
HERE IT IS
By Bob Boone
and Jim Slezak

School principals and other site-level administrators are
very much like people. Feeling isolated and ignored by the
superintendent and headquarters staff, they can take just so
much grief from parents, pupils and teachers, just so much
insensitivity and red tape from the central office—then they
seek solace.

Guess who's ready with the velvet mitten? Your friendly,
would-be principal union. Perhaps a group noted for
empathy and understanding—like, for instance, the International Brotherhood of Teamsters.

Principal unions need not be public education's latest
dilemma. Consider our case:

Principals and vice-principals in the Mt. Diablo Unified
School District in California were meeting with the Teamsters. Site-level administrators wanted to explore the possibility of being represented by that union in negotiations
with our school board. And as though disgruntled principals weren't enough, the current superintendent—who
had just come into the school system—was greeted by the
litany of woe common to California public schools: plum-
meting enrollment, budget deficits, staff reductions, school
closings, transportation cutbacks, political attacks, and an
impending teacher strike. Immediate action definitely was
indicated on several fronts—but a united management
team would be essential in dealing effectively with any of
the difficulties.

Site-level administrators had a list of concerns: They swore
that they were excluded from crucial decision making, that
they were poorly represented at the bargaining table, that
board members and central office administrators were out
of touch with the bleak realities of school-site management. The monthly meetings with the central office staff

were laughable, they insisted—autocratic exercises in communication from on high. In a shameful variety of ways, the principals were precisely right.

Today, much of that justifiable dissatisfaction has evaporated. Here's how:

The Mt. Diablo school system (K-12; enrollment: 50,000) asked principals to nominate three candidates at each level—elementary, intermediate, and high school—to represent them as full-time directors of education at the central office. Because these principal directors serve a three-year term and are rotated back to the field periodically, the other site-level administrators tend to trust them. The site administrators know that their representatives at the central office remain in touch with front-line reality.

From among the nine principals nominated in the field, the superintendent and the central office administrators chose two elementary, one intermediate, and one high school director. What follows is a description of how those rotating principal-directorships work to improve the decision-making process—and front-line management morale.

The four principal-directors sit on the school system's negotiating team, participate in the weekly meetings of the superintendent's 13-member cabinet and attend all regular and executive sessions of the school board, including the annual school board/cabinet retreat which is held in April.

By having four principal-directors on the negotiating team, the school-site managers are assured that their interests are being protected by people who understand their circumstances. The principal-directors hold weekly meetings (usually when school is not in session) with the administrators they represent, so the principals and other building-management personnel also know they are being kept fully informed of developments throughout the school system. Effective two-way communication now exists between site-level and central office management. The four principal directors receive the same salary as principals in the field. The directors, however, get five more than the ordinary allotment of per diem days to cover special duties and meetings.

Two other major steps ensure that every management layer in the Mt. Diablo system has a significant decision-making role:

* Each August, before school starts, all 200 members of the management team take part in a three-day planning workshop. Object: to set one-year and three-year goals for the school system. To put it simply, we seek answers for these two basic questions: "What should the superintendent and his staff accomplish during the coming year?"; "What should we accomplish during the next three years?" The specific answers developed by management then are compared to the larger objectives established at the April retreat by the school board and superintendent's cabinet. At the end of the subsequent school year, the superintendent publishes a report on the progress made toward the various goals set by the total management team, the superintendent's cabinet, and the school board. This process, taken as a whole, ensures unity of purpose, mutual understanding, and accountability.

* Every two years—or more frequently if necessary—we take time out to clarify who is responsible for what. We use the Central Office/Site Administrator Decision Chart. At a three-day retreat, the superintendent's cabinet and half a dozen principals work through approximately 130 typical decision situations. Each situation is rated on a scale of from one to four, as follows: 1.-The principal alone decides. 2.-The principal alone decides, but someone in the central office must be informed. 3.-The principal's decision must be approved in advance by the central office. 4.-The central office makes the decision, and the principal implements it.

In our first close encounter with the decision chart, we identified an unsettling number of situations in which no one had assumed the decision-making authority. We also discovered situations in which both site-level and central office administrators assumed ultimate authority—to the severe consternation of all concerned.

Our overriding goal was to invest as much decision-making power as possible in site-level administrators, because as part of our basic philosophy we believe that the closer to the students a decision can be made, the better for the students that decision is likely to be.

During our three days of discussion, we eventually found ways to resolve all major disagreements and to perfect the decision-making process. As a result both of using the decision chart and of having the four principal-directors in the central office, we've developed improved procedures in purchasing, budgeting, maintenance and many other areas. We've clarified educational goals, reduced paper-work, and restored appropriate authority to the site-level administrators.

But in an inlet or two, the tide has reversed, and we've decided to increase central office responsibility. Transpor-tation, for instance, has benefited from greater centraliza-tion. By staggering school opening and closing times, each bus can be used more efficiently to serve additional schools. In a system forced to cut its transportation budget, this increased efficiency is a godsend.

Principals aren't the only ones getting a healthier slice of the action. School-site advisory councils also are being formed to involve parents, teachers and—at the secondary level—students in the decision-making process. Certified and non-certified staff members increasingly are joining with principals in controlling day-to-day school operations as well.

Salutary as all this certainly is, two knotty problems still elude solutions:

One remaining difficulty is the assignment of evaluation responsibilities. Currently, administrators engage in self-evaluation, and an assistant superintendent conducts more-formal appraisals of site administrator performance. One person alone is hard-pressed, however, to render adequate judgments about every building-level administrator in a school system the size of ours. Consequently, we're temp-ted to ask the four principal-directors to take on this vital task.

Then again, we'd rather not. Much of the essential open-ness and candor that now exist between the principal-directors and the administrators they represent would be irredeemably lost under such threatening circumstances.

The second stubborn problem is the rotation process itself. The director's job is complex enough that it takes at least a year to get the hang of it thoroughly, to establish new working relationships, and to develop effective routines. To forfeit the acquired central office expertise after only three years seems a pity. Yet, to keep a principal-director in the central office too long defeats the program's very purpose.

In spite of these two chronic faults, the program generally is a success. But remember, we've been talking here about only the organizational and decision-making facets of Mt. Diablo's comprehensive program—the Individual School Management System (known affectionately to us as I.S.M.S.). The whole management system comprises six parts: planning, organization, monitoring, staff development, learning climate, and decision making.

Common goals and mutual respect among all strata of governance and management have stood Mt. Diablo in admirable stead during hard times. We've weathered a bitter teacher strike, a $1 million budget deficit (now recouped), a precipitous and unabated enrollment decline of 15,000 students, layoffs of 400 staff members, a total transportation cut—and a brush with a would-be principal union.

Would we have survived without our principals' loyalty to the management team? Well, at Mt. Diablo, we have just one more thing to say: Teamsters, keep on trucking.

As the article from *Executive Educator* magazine indicated, a complete organizational development or management system was used in that large school district in California where I was superintendent. One part of that system was a decision chart for school principals.

Because I strongly believe that the principal does make a difference in the school site setting, I transfer to the principal as much of the authority and decision-making power that has been delegated to me as superintendent by the board as I possibly can.

I use the superintendent-principal decision chart to identify and to transfer as much delegated authority to the principal as possible, working with central office administrators to accomplish that end result. The most difficult part of achieving this is to persuade central office administrators, who are often held accountable by the board for the success of the programs which they administer, to delegate some of that authority to the principals. The feeling of the central office administrators is that they lose control, which they in fact do. I find the best solutions are made as close to the learner as possible. Therefore, as much authority as possible for finance, personnel, equipment and material resources need to be given to the principal.

A DECISION CHART FOR SCHOOL PRINCIPALS

Many items that have been decided by the board and the superintendent when they did their chart are repeated in this chart. This is done to help clarify for the principal his decision-making authority. Many times he is precluded by the board from having complete authority because they want to be informed or to make the decision; the superintendent must require the principal to at least inform the district office, so the information can be transmitted to the board.

SAMPLE CHART

MD UNIFIED SCHOOL DISTRICT
DECISION CHART FOR SCHOOL PRINCIPALS
May, 1983

Principals' Degrees of Authority

I.   I have complete authority to decide or act within the limits of the law, Education Code, board policy, contracts and budget.   (COMPLETE AUTHORITY)

II.   I have complete authority to decide or act, but must inform _____ of my action.

                name   (ACT/INFORM)

III.   I have authority to act only with prior approval of _____ .   (PRIOR APPROVAL)

        name

IV.   I will be consulted, but decision or direction comes to me from _____ .

                name

                (DISTRICT DIRECTION)

Implementing the Degrees of Authority

Column I through IV are labeled for each decision and/or action according to the degree of authority and the implementation focus for each listed decision/act. The final authority source follows using the location of implementation below:

(DR)	- Appropriate directors in educational services are also included as contact and consult sources.
(HM)	- Appropriate directors in administrative and personnel services are also included as contact and consult sources.
(LF)	- Appropriate directors in business services are also included as contact and consult services.
(S)	- Superintendent

I Complete Authority   *Indicates decision from
II Act/Inform   board-superintendent
III Prior Approval   decision chart
IV District Direction

I	II	III	IV	
		DR		*1. Put a new course into your school's curriculum.
X				2. Change the objectives of a course already being taught at your school.
			DR	*3. Establish School Site Council.
X				4. Permit a teacher to replace a major part of the subject content of a course in order to better meet the objectives.
X		LF		5. Select and purchase instructional material
matl.		equip.		or equipment which is not on your standard equipment list.
		LF		6. Determine items to be placed on standard requisition list.
X				*7. Approve a teacher taking a one-day field trip.
	DR			*8. Approve a teacher taking an overnight field trip.
X				*9. Select and pay a consultant to assist in school inservice activities within district guidelines.

I	II	III	IV	
		DR		*10. Initiate (or abandon) a specific program throughout the school—Academics Plus, open education, community school, modular scheduling.
X				11. Permit your staff to make a change in textbooks within district guidelines.
		DR		12. Decide the year that the school will apply for and implement categorical programs.
			DR	13. Determine the assigned school site of special programs.
X				14. Decide when to hold kindergarten registration.
X				15. Approve registration forms beyond student master file requirements.
X				16. Approve enrollment cards used at a school.
		DR		17. Set minimum days for staff development within district policy.
X				18. Determine "Slip Schedule" at a school.
		HM		*19. Suspend publication of a student newspaper for inappropriate statements.
X				20. Set AIM teacher schedule (G/T Program).
X				*21. Establish priorities within the school for diagnostic assessments of students potentially in need of special education services.
		DR		22. Place children into special education classes when they have been in special classes in another district or county program.
		DR		23. Cancel a special education program with insufficient number of qualified students.
		DR		24. Authorize placement of special education students after the EAS has been held.

I	II	III	IV	
		DR		*25. Decide to abandon report cards in favor of a program of parent conferences, or visa versa.
	DR			26. Authorize placement of special education students after the SAT has been held.
X				*27. Determine rules for dress.
	DR			28. Designate special education personnel to prepare for SAT paperwork and scheduling.
		DR		*29. Set requirements for graduation from your school which exceed those for any other school in the district.
		DR		30. Designate special education personnel to prepare for EAS paperwork and scheduling.
X				31. Refuse non-district programs that take principal and/or staff time.
X				*32. Decide to administer standardized tests (beyond the state and district testing program) to determine the progress or achievement of students in your school.
X				33. Determine variety and extent of intramural sports programs at your school.
X				34. Determine what clubs or other student organizations will be permitted at your school.
X				35. Determine variety, extent, and restrictions for all school-associated social functions.
X				36. Establish evening open house schedule and format for school.
			LF	37. Set transportation schedule for a school.
			HM	*38. At district expense attend an out-of-state conference.
X				39. Decide what is an acceptable program of study for an individual student in your school.

I	II	III	IV		
			DR	*40.	Participate in professional responsibilities beyond the district during school hours.
X				41.	Assign work priorities for school supersonnel port passigned to the school.
X				42.	Institute remediation of students not passing competency tests.
X				43.	Determine rules for tardiness and attendance within state requirements.
X				44.	Discipline students by detention.
	DR			45.	Discipline students by suspension.
		DR		46.	Discipline students by expulsion.
			S	*47.	Select subordinate administrative staff members.
X				48.	Report and prefer charges to police or juvenile authorities for violations of laws by students on school grounds (not a riot situation).
DR				49.	Call police on campus to prevent or quell mass disturbances or riots.
			HM	50.	Create classified campus supervision time from certificated personnel allocation.
X				*51.	Exchange teaching assignments between two appropriately credentialed teachers—P.E. and math, or kindergarten and third grade.
		DR		*52.	Assume ongoing leadership responsibilities outside the district during school hours.
			DR	*53.	Decide on use of psychologist's time onassigned days.
		HM		*54.	Decide to give some of your teachers an additional period for class preparation.
			S	*55.	On a day that two-thirds of your teachers are absent and on strike, decide to close school and send students and all other teachers home.

I	II	III	IV	
		HM		56. Grant a request for a two-week leave of absence, without pay, for a teacher to accompany spouse on a business trip, in keeping with board policy.
		HM		57. Select a teacher for an existing vacancy in your school.
		S		58. Send student body home early due to emergency.
		DR		*59. Decide to send teacher to a four-week concentrated course on new instructional methods, with district paying salary and all expenses.
HM				*60. Send a teacher home for arriving at back-to-school night under the influence of controlled substance.
		HM		*61. Decide to terminate a teacher
		HM		*62. Decide to terminate a custodian, groundsperson or secretary for unsatisfactory work performance.
		HM		*63. Select a secretary, head custodian or groundsperson from eligibility list for an existing vacancy in your school.
	HM			*64. Reprimand a teacher for administering corporal punishment to a student and place a notation to that effect in his personnel file.
	DR			*65. Forbid specific support services personnel from the district staff to work with one of your students because you lack confidence in that person.
		HM		*66. For the next school year, decide to replace two non-teaching positions with an additional teacher.
			HM	*67. Formulate the certificated staffing pattern at a school: nurses vs. music vs. resource teacher, etc..
X				68. Call faculty and staff meetings as frequently as is reasonable.
		DR		*69. Select support personnel for a school.

I	II	III	IV	
		HM		*70. Evaluate the performance of a clerk, custodian, or groundsperson on your school staff and decide to delay his normal annual progression to next highest step.
		HM		71. Demote a secretary, head custodian, lead groundsperson for unsatisfactory performance of duties.
X				72. Reassign responsibilities (same school, same job classification).
		HM		73. Change working hours from 7 a.m. - 3 p.m. to 3 p.m. - 11 p.m. (same job classification) for custodial, groundsperson, maintenance personnel.
		HM		*74. Decide to advance an outstanding custodian or groundsperson to next highest pay step after only seven months in order to keep him from resigning and taking a higher paying job elsewhere.
		HM		*75. Discipline—two-week suspension—a custodian or groundsperson for repeated violation of safety regulations.
X				*76. Decide on areas of maintenance needed at a school.
X				77. Retain a consultant for inservice training of your custodial or groundspersons staff.
	HM			78. Require secretary to perform a task outside his job description such as supervision of loading of buses.
			HM	*79. Determine pay level of various classified positions.
		LF		*80. Decide on extensive landscaping additions or changes.
X				*81. Change working hours of your secretary so that he comes to work a half hour earlier, and has a half hour longer lunch period.

I	II	III	IV	
X				*82. Decide what level of building cleanliness and appearance to maintain.
		HM		*83. Decide by mutual agreement of principal at another school in the district to exchange secretaries.
	HM			*84. Discipline—two-week suspension—a clerk for repeated tardiness.
X				*85. Decide color scheme school is to be painted.
	HM			86. Give a clerk-typist time off, with or without pay, to take a refresher course in shorthand during working hours— two hours a day for 12 weeks.
			LF	*87. Decide to have eight classrooms repainted.
X				88. Authorize compensatory time for school secretary.
		HM		89. Authorize overtime pay from general fund for school secretary.
		HM		90. Move a clerk into a secretarial job classification.
X				*91. Decide what keys are given to which staff members.
	LF			92. Assign a custodian to do emergency maintenance work outside of job description.
			LF	*93. Decide what deterrent or detection systems are to be used.
X				94. Decide not to seek restitution from one of your students apprehended while breaking a window at your school.
X				95. Assign an on-site gardener to alternative duties on a rainy day within job description.
	LF			96. Decide how money is to be distributed and transferred among various non-personnel budget categories at your school.

I	II	III	IV	
		LF		97. Decide to make a double-sized class-room by tearing out a wall between two rooms.
		LF	*98.	Contract outside agency for alterations if cost does not exceed district estimate.
X			99.	Require all off-site district employees to report to the office prior to visiting classrooms or performing maintenance and repair tasks.
	LF		100.	Assign district gardening crew to assist custodian to move picnic tables.
	LF		101.	Assign plumber to fix faucet when he comes to repair toilet.
	LF		102.	Implement work with community to repair playground equipment on school property.
X			103.	Initiate dialogue with community to repair playground equipment.
		LF	104.	Decide to go to outside agencies on a contract basis for equipment repair or emergency adjustments to buildings or grounds.
			LF	*105. Determine schedule for glaziers.
X			*106.	Approve requisitions and expenditures within budget limitations for your school.
		HM	*107.	Decide how money is to be distributed and transferred among various person-nel categories at your school.
		LF	108.	Authorize purchase to be made after April deadline date.
			LF	*109. Decide format of budget printouts.
	HM		*110.	Approve installation of additional phones paid from local budget or other sources.
			LF	*111. Approve concept of monetary credit for low incidence of vandalism.
		DR	112.	Determine how federal monies can be spent at a site.

I	II	III	IV	
	LF			113. Approve outside purchase of warehouse stored items if available at a cheaper rate.
	LF			114. Use instructional account to send teacher to conference.
	LF			115. Carry money over to coming year's budget.
X				116. Buy a copy machine on a multiyear contract.
X				117. Decide to put student body funds into a checking or interest-bearing account which is registered with the district.
X				118. Use principal's discretionary fund furnished by parent club to buy plants for faculty lounge.
		HM		119. Have a report on an alternative program typed in word processing department and duplicated by the duplicating department.

Respond, as a spokesperson for the district, to inquiries, proposals, demands, or actions of the following groups on the subjects noted.

I	II	III	IV	
X				120. The parents of a white student in your school demand to have him transferred out of a black teacher's class.
X				*121. A voter or parent within your attendance area wants information about group testing scores for your school.
X				*122. The parents of a student in your school demand to have him transferred to another school within district because of alleged problems.
X				*123. The local newspaper requests information about the suspension of one of your students for repeated use of obscene language.

I	II	III	IV		
	DR			*124.	A controversial group asks to present to your student body a one-hour program on the importance of truth and freedom.
X				*125.	Determine role of School Site Council.
					Initiate dialogue or program designed to influence opinion and actions of the following groups on the subjects noted.
X				126.	With parents of your students, concerning the dangers of drug abuse.
			S	*127.	With voters in your attendance area, concerning a tax override election or initiative.
X				*128.	With the local TV or radio station, concerning dress requirements at your school.
X				*129.	With local organizations, concerning sponsorship of an essay contest on citizenship.

PROCEDURE

The procedure for using the decision chart for school principals starts with the superintendent and a half dozen representatives of the principals who review a sample decision chart to determine if all the items in that chart are appropriate for that particular school district. Some items are eliminated from the sample copy, other items are added. The language is changed so the representative group of principals feels comfortable with the examples which usually number well over a hundred and occur in various areas—curriculum, academic performance, extra curricular activities, behavior and discipline, personnel, administrative, teacher, secretarial, custodial, aides, community relations, physical plant, budget, and transportation. The chart is then sent to every school principal in the district as well as to the central office administrators. Each person, independent of the others, is asked to indicate on the decision chart where he thinks each item should be decided.

The chart designates four levels of authority. The first level gives the principal complete authority to decide or act within board policies and school law. The second level gives the principal complete authority to decide or act, but he must inform someone of the action, usually a central office administrator. The third level gives the principal authority to act only with prior approval of someone at the central office. The fourth level states that the principal may be consulted, but the decision or direction comes to him from someone, usually at the central office.

After the principals and central office administrators have completed the chart, it is then returned; the results are tabulated and consolidated on a summary decision chart, and copies are made for the subsequent study session.

The total number of choices indicated by the principals under each of the four levels of authority for each item are tabulated. The initials of the central office administrators are placed in the proper authority column to indicate what their choices were. In a small school district with very few principals, the initials of principals could be put in. In a large district just the numbers will suffice on the summary chart before going into the study session.

STUDY SESSION

At the study session, participants make final decisions as to where the level of authority shall be placed. Each participant must receive a summary chart showing where various principals and central office administrators felt the level of authority should be made.

In a large district, representatives of each level of principals should be part of the study session, but in a small district, all the principals and central office administrators should be involved. Groups of a dozen or fewer work best to resolve the chart; by keeping the group to under a dozen everyone is able to enter into the discussion.

It takes 15 to 30 hours to resolve the chart the first time it is done. The process usually takes less time in subsequent years. It is important to reach a consensus as to where the final authority will go for every item; in cases in which consensus is hard to obtain or virtually impossible, the superintendent has to make the decision.

It is often difficult for central office administrators, who are held accountable to the board, to relinquish authority to the principal. The business manager, in particular, is reluctant to allow too much flexibility in the expenditure and transfer of funds in the school budget. It should be clearly established that the role of the business manager is that of accounting, not of decision making as as to what money can or cannot be spent for particular items. Once the budget is set for the school district and for each school, it is then the responsibility of the principal and the school staff to allocate funds from that budget; these expenditures are reported to the business office, so they can be properly accounted for and placed in the appropriate budget accounts established by state law.

ADVANTAGES OF THE SUPERINTENDENT-PRINCIPAL DECISION CHART

Often principals indicate items for the superintendent to decide, which are the same items the superintendent thought the principal should decide. Without a decision chart, confusion can result as to who makes the decision. Items on which everyone thinks they have authority can be resolved better at a study session where logical, intelligent discussion can take place, than during a time of crisis which can engender controversy, misunderstanding, and irritation.

I have found that even though I did not get as much authority from the board as I thought I should, I was able to administer the area of responsibility and authority I did have more adequately because I clearly understood what I could or could not do. The same would be true of the principal's relationship with the superintendent. When a controversial issue arises and one assumes they have the authority to resolve it, only to be overruled by higher authority, it is embarrassing and frustrating. It is better to have authority clarified before a crisis situation occurs, so misunderstandings and embarrassment from being overruled are avoided.

FREQUENCY OF COMPLETING THE DECISION CHART

In an organization which has stability, little turnover, and a large number of administrators, a chart should be redone at least every three years for clarification, deletion, and addition of items that are pertinent to the current situation. In a small district with less than six or eight administrators, the chart should be redone each time a change occurs in even one of those positions.

You may not have to refer to the chart that often once it is completed, however, it should be placed close at hand for easy reference. The time you spent resolving the authority levels often clarifies the general operation of the educational program sufficiently, so little reference is needed.

COMMENTS

The principal is the most important individual at the school site in determining the quality of the program and the learning level of the students. Middle managers in business and industry as well as school site principals and assistant principals have concerns about the authority of their role. One way of relieving those concerns and of alleviating the constant pressures on the school site principal is to delegate as much decision-making authority to the school site level as possible where solutions can be accomplished close to the learner.

Chapter 15
Elementary-Middle School Decision Making

Evidence indicates that the basic element of an effective school is strong leadership by the principal. What contributes to his high degree of professional leadership? An outstanding leader has:

- An excellent record of academic achievement in college.
- Effective interpersonal communication skills.
- A strong motivation for service.
- A commitment of off-duty time to his job.

Among necessary interpersonal skills is knowing how to involve the staff in the operation of the school and in the decision-making process. This is not to imply that the staff makes the decisions, but that the principal and the staff need to work out a clear understanding of who makes which decisions. Many decisions are given to the teacher; placing decision making as close to the learner as possible gives the greatest results.

As much flexibility should be given to the teacher as possible to allow a stimulating learning environment to take place. If the teacher knows that many of the decisions can be made at the classroom level, he will save a considerable amount of time that would have been spent clearing decisions with the administration. This time can now be spent developing effective instruction.

DECISION-MAKING CHART

One of the elements of decision making at the school is the involvement matrix on which the staff can indicate whether they wish to be involved in a particular school decision or just be informed of the solution. The staff lists the various decisions that need to be made at the school on the left hand side of the matrix and indicates under their name, which appears at the top, whether they wish to be involved in each decision.

SAMPLE INVOLVEMENT MATRIX

BEL AIR ELEMENTARY INVOLVEMENT MATRIX

Please indicate how you wish to be involved by marking a "1" or a "2" after each decision item. You may add decision items if you wish.

    1) Involved in decision or recommendation

    2) Do not wish to be involved—inform me of final decision

Decision Items	A	B	C	D	E	F	G	H	I	J	K	L	M	N	O
1. Teacher grade-level assignment	1	1	1	2	1	1	1	1	1	1	2	1	2	1	1
2. Teacher duty schedule	2	2	2	2	2	2	2	2	2	2	2	2	2	2	2
3. New programs to be implemented	1	1	1	1	1	1	1	1	1	1	1	2	1	1	2
4. Selection of textbooks	1	1	1	1	1	1	1	1	1	1	2	1	1	1	2
5. Selection of materials	1	1	1	1	1	1	1	1	1	1	1	1	1	1	1
6. Warehouse orders	2	2	1	2	1	2	2	2	2	1	2	1	2	1	1
7. Staff development	1	1	2	1	1	1	1	1	1	1	1	1	1	1	2
8. Writing school plan	2	2	2	2	2	2	1	1	1	1	2	1	1	1	2
9. Determine capital outlay budget	1	1	2	2	2	2	1	1	1	2	2	2	1	1	
10. Determine school policy	1	1	2	2	2	2	1	1	1	2	1	2	1	2	
11. Setting goals and expectations	1	2	1	1	1	1	1	1	1	2	1	2	1	1	
12. Attendance procedure	2	2	2	2	2	2	2	1	1	2	2	2	2	2	
13. SAT referral procedure	2	2	2	2	2	2	2	1	1	1	2	1	1	1	
14. Hiring of staff	1	1	1	2	1	1	1	2	1	1	2	2	2	1	1
15. School beautification	2	1	1	1	1	2	2	2	1	1	2	1	2	2	2
16. Expenditure of student fund	1	1	1	1	1	1	1	2	1	1	2	2	2	1	2
17. Room allocation and use	1	1	1	1	1	1	1	1	1	1	2	1	2	1	1
18. Communications to parents	1	2	2	1	2	1	1	1	1	1	2	2	2	1	1
19. Procedure for retention	2	2	2	2	2	2	2	1	1	1	2	2	2	1	1
20. School schedule	1	2	2	1	1	1	2	1	2	1	2	1	1	1	2
21. Site Council	2	2	2	2	2	2	2	1	1	1	2	2	2	1	2
22. PTA funds and programs	2	2	2	2	2	2	1	2	1	1	2	2	2	1	2
23. Responsibility for programs	2	2	2	2	2	2	2	2	1	1	2	2	1	2	2
24. Develop school budget	1	1	1	1	1	1	1	1	1	1	2	2	2	1	1
25. Develop school goals	2	2	2	2	2	2	2	1	1	1	1	2	1	1	1

. . .

SAMPLE SUMMARY OF INVOLVEMENT MATRIX

BEL AIR ELEMENTARY

TO: Staff
FROM: Dee
RE: Involvement Matrix Summary

1. The following categories were rated No.1 by the staff—the staff wants to have a major role in the decision.
   - Teacher grade-level assignments
   - Staff development
   - New programs to be implemented
   - Selection of textbooks
   - Selection of materials
   - Determine capital outlay budget
   - Setting goals and expectations
   - Hiring of staff
   - Expenditures of student funds
   - Room allocations and use
   - Develop school budget
   - School schedule

2. The following categories were rated No.2 by the staff—the staff wants to be informed of the decision, but not necessarily be the prime decision-maker.
   - Teacher duty schedule
   - Warehouse orders
   - Site Council
   - Responsibility for programs
   - Attendance procedure
   - PTA funds and programs

3. The following categories were evenly divided between No.1 and No.2 by the staff. These are the areas where teachers who indicated their wish to be involved will be given that opportunity. We will keep the rest of the staff informed. Writing of school plan (by necessity teachers have decisions in this area, since classroom teachers are responsible for implementation.)

   - Develop school policy
   - SAT referral procedure
   - School beautification
   - Communications to parents
   - Procedure for retention
   - Develop and publish school goals

. . .

PROCEDURE FOR DECISION-MAKING CHART

A school site decision chart fashioned after the board-superintendent chart and others previously mentioned is also needed for the most desirable system of decision making at the school level. A school staff can generate all the basic items for the school decision chart, however, a simpler approach would be to use a sample chart and add, delete, or change items to suit the needs of that school.

If you are going to generate a decision chart, every member of the staff, either in a meeting or independently, should list topics they wish to have decided during the school year. These topics are then categorized by groups which tend to be staff relations, student items, academic programs, activities, behavior and discipline, supplies and textbooks, budget, facilities, special programs, and community relations. Once the topics are arranged by groups, they are placed on a decision chart for identification of levels of authority.

The levels of authority are similar to the other charts mentioned earlier in the book.

Level one: The teacher has complete authority to decide or act within the limits of the law, board policy, school policy, and bargaining contracts.

Level two: The teacher has complete authority to decide or act but must inform someone, usually at the school, such as the principal, the secretary, or another teacher.

Level three: The teacher has the authority to act only with the prior approval of either the principal or some other designated person.

Level four: The teacher may be consulted, but the decision or direction comes to the teacher from the principal or the central office.

The number of people, positions, or groups that might be identified as part of the decision-making process at an elementary or middle school is about 14 or 15.

Once the items to be put on the chart are resolved, the chart is sent to individual staff members to determine where they think the decision-making authority belongs for each item. After the staff returns the charts, the principal or someone compiles the results and records the total number of people responding to each level of authority.

SAMPLE DECISION-MAKING CHART

MD UNIFIED SCHOOL DISTRICT
DECISION CHART FOR TEACHERS
June, 1983

Teacher's Degrees of Authority

    I. I have complete authority to decide or act within the limits of the education code, board policy, policy as stated in the faculty handbook, contracts, and budget (COMPLETE AUTHORITY).

    II. I have complete authority to decide or act, but must inform_____of my action (ACT/INFORM).
           (position)

    III. I have authority to act only with prior approval of_____
           (position) (PRIOR APPROVAL).

    IV. I may be consulted, but decision or direction comes to me from the district office (DISTRICT DIRECTION).

Implementing the Degrees of Authority

    Listed below are the positions at an elementary school appearing in columns II and III.

    1. Principal
    2. Another teacher
    3. Grade Level Group
    4. Staff (Certificated, Administration, Classified)
    5. Secretary
    6. Custodian
    7. Faculty President
    8. Resource Teacher
    9. Psychologist
    10. Speech Teacher
    11. Nurse
    12. Librarian
    13. Tutor
    14. Site Council
    15. Parent Club

KEY:
X = Teacher or district in column I or IV
( ) = Position identified in parenthesis in column II, III
* = Item from superintendent or principals' decision chart
Numbers = where teachers thought the decision should be

I COMPLETE AUTHORITY
II ACT/INFORM I
II PRIOR APPROVAL
IV DISTRICT DIRECTION

I	II	III	IV	
			18 X	1. Decide what time school should start and dismiss.
2	3	10 (1)	3	2. Develop yard duty schedule.
11 X	3	4		3. Decide to exchange recess duty with another teacher by mutual agreement.
7	6 (1, 7)	2	3	4. Add items to staff meeting agenda.
4	5	6 (1)	3	*5. Take students on a field trip.
1	6	7 (1)	4	6. Have secretary duplicate materials.
1	5	8 (1)	4	7. Request that another teacher cover your class.
18 X				8. Call a substitute for your class.
16 X	2			9. Leave campus during your lunch hour.
	2	5 (1)	11	10. Assign a student to another classroom.
2	8	1	7 X	11. Decide if there should be collection of monies—pictures, milk, Parent Club, Outdoor Education—in the classroom.
6	3		9 X	12. Distribute materials to students from outside agencies.
5 X	5	1	7	13. Drive student home after school hours.
4	9 (1, 15)	1	4	14. Communicate directly with Parent Club on concerns vital to teachers.
	3		15 X	15. Select school photographer.
16 X		2		16. Conference with parents outside the contract day.

I	II	III	IV	
1		1	16 X	17. Obtain a free period for elementary period.
	4	11	3 X	*18. Decide when to have minimum days.
1	1	2	14 X	19. Select grade assignments within our school.
1		3	14 X	20. Decide transfer policy—who should have to move.
	2	2 X	14	21. Select resource people most appropriate for this school.
4	5	4	5 X	22. Decide that students from your class will not participate in special education.
	1	2	15 X	*23. Abandon report cards in favor of parent conferences, or some other reporting system.
3	1	3	11 X	24. Decide use of released time.
5	4	1 (4)	8	25. Decide type of staff development.
17 X			1	26. Assess the appropriate level of instruction for specific students.
15 X	1		2	27. Determine the academic expectations for specific students.
4			14 X	28. Set appropriate dates for giving CTBS tests.
17 X			1	29. Prescribe a program to fit student needs.
17 X	1			30. Decide which techniques to use to motivate students to learn.
17 X	1			31. Decide which teaching process to use to reinforce learning.
17 X	1			32. Decide which teaching process to use to promote retention of learning.
17 X	1			33. Decide which technique to use to teach transfer and application of knowledge.
17 X	1			34. Decide the rate and degree of learning that should be attempted for each student.

I	II	III	IV	
18 X				35. Decide that specific students should be provided additional review in another series before advancing to a higher level of difficulty in your reading series.
18 X				36. Establish size and composition of classroom reading groups.
18 X				37. Determine the early or late reading assignments for your classroom.
12 X	5	1		38. Direct small groups to work in the learning centers.
9	7 (1, 3)	1	1	39. Decide to regroup students across class assignments for specific subject domains.
9 X	7	2		40. Direct small groups of students to do research in the library.
4	10	4 (12)		41. Decide to use the library for class group activity three times a week.
2	1	6 (1)	9	42. Decide on retention of students without parents' permission.
14 X	4			43. Recommend retention for a student.
14 X	2	1	1	44. Determine schedule within the classroom
1		1	16 X	*45. Decide on a principal or a superintendent.
			18 X	*46. Help decide appropriate number of administrators for district.
17 X	1			47. Decide and implement classroom environment.
6 X	4	5	3	48. Decide open house and back-to-school night format.
7	10 (15)		1	49. Change room parents.
17 X	1			50. Use parent aides in your classroom.
	1	5	12 X	51. Exchange teaching assignments of two appropriately credentialed teachers.
3	7	7 (1)	1	52. Participate with students in environmental education program.

I	II	III	IV	
1	5	2	10 X	53. Decide on busing and individual cars for field trips.
4 X	9	2	3	54. Recommend student placement and grouping for next year's class.
14 X	2	1	1	55. Send newsletters home regarding class activities.
17 X	1			56. Send weekly progress reports home for specific students.
2	11	3 (1)	2	57. Send a student home to get his books, homework, instrument, etc.
6 X	9	2	1	58. Decide that your class will present a program for a Parent Club meeting.
	3	1 (1, 3)	14	59. Select new teacher required for vacancy at local school.
3	8	6 (3)	1	60. Decide that all classes at your grade level will present a program for Parent Club meeting will present a program for Parent Club meeting.
5	6	5 (3)	2	61. Decide that all classes at your grade level will have a community potluck dinner.
5	10	2 (3)	1	62. Schedule the time allotment for sharing textbooks within grade level.
3	7	4 (1)	4	63. Arrange with another teacher to have older students assist younger students in the classroom during the instructional day.
	6	2 (1)	10	64. Change regularly scheduled lunch hour for your class.
17 X	1			65. Decide which activities students will participate in during rainy day lunch periods.
7 X	3	4	4	66. Use the computer service for teacher-made tests in your classroom.
12 X	3	2	1	67. Have a special "dress up" day for your class.
2	2	3	11 X	*68. Have a fund-raiser for your classroom.

I	II	III	IV	
5	5	5 (1)	3	*69. Request funds from students to implement an extended curricular activity—cooking, tasting experience, art program.
12 X	5	1		70. Conduct a "clean campus" program with your class.
5	10 (1)	1	2	71. Set up sports activity involving another class, classes, or grade level during instructional time.
1	2	11 (1)	4	72. Arrange activity with another school— sports activity, spelling contest, or field trip.
7 X	2	3	6	73. Decide and implement curriculum content and time allotment.
1	3	7 (1)	7	74. Decide not to follow the curricular guidelines as established by your school.
2	2	6 (1)	8	75. Apply for pilot programs.
1		6 (4)	11	*76. Devise supplemental report cards for the school.
5		2	11 (3)	77. Determine method of student evaluation for supplemental report cards.
11 X			7	78. Implement additional student testing and measuring.
4		13 (3)	1	79. Determine which grade levels will participate in CTBS testing beyond district requirements.
7	2	3 (1)	6	*80. Have parent sign release for student to receive psychological services.
8	9 (8, 9)	1		81. Recommend that student should be screened for special education.
8 X	8	1	1	82. Report concern about student's home environment—cleanliness, abuse, or non-supervision.
2	11	3 (13)	2	83. Change time when students from your class would receive tutoring services with the resource teacher.

I	II	III	IV		
3	11	2 (8)	2	84.	Change time when students from your class would receive tutoring services with the resource teacher.
3	10	2 (1)	1	85.	Excuse students from your class from instrumental music.
5	4 (1)	5	4	86.	Decide which students should or should not be removed from the classroom for assemblies.
7	1	5 (1, 3)	5	87.	Establish a workable lunchroom discipline policy.
14 X	2		2	88.	Establish a workable classroom discipline policy.
15 X	3			89.	Give a referral slip to students not assigned to your class.
14 X		2	2	90.	Implement all rules and regulations for all students.
14 X	2		2	91.	Suspend student from class.
9	8 (2)		1	92.	Assign a student from another class after-school detention in your classroom.
8	3	3 (1)	4	93.	Collect reimbursement from student for lost or damaged school books.
5	1	4 (1)	8	94.	Borrow non-consumable materials from another school.
		8	10 (1)	95.	Loan materials to another school.
3 X	6	8	1	96.	Have students pick up supplies from room.
6	1	5 (1, 3)	7	97.	Ascertain supply needs for the year.
4	3	10 (1)	1	98.	Purchase special items for your classroom and submit bill for reimbursement.
3	2	8 (1)	5	99.	Contract for a film through an outside agency.
3	3 (5)	7	5	100.	Take school material, equipment home to prepare lesson plans.

I	II	III	IV		
2	1	1	14 X	*101.	Decide which textbooks should be placed on the state matrix.
3	1	5	9 X	*102.	Decide which textbooks will be recommended from the matrix for use in the district.
5	2	5	6 X	103.	Select from recommended list those textbooks most appropriate for local school programs.
10 X		5	3	104.	Select textbooks or material most appropriate to student level.
1			17 X	*105.	Determine budget cuts — reducing number of aides.
2		4 (1)	12	106.	Apply for outside funding for a special local project.
1		(1, 3)	17	107.	Decide how money is to be distributed and transferred among non-personnel budget categories locally.
1		2 (1, 3)	15	108.	Set bell schedule.
1	6	3 (1)	8	109.	Call maintenance about non-functioning air conditioner.
1	3 (1)	8	6	110.	Use our facilities to meet with teachers from other schools to discuss curriculum.
12 X	2	3	1	111.	Have students exit through pod rather than classroom doors.
5	7	4 (1)	2	112.	Request that custodian set up chairs for an evening program your class is presenting.
4	2	3 (1)	9	113.	Collect reimbursement from students for damage to school equipment, furniture, buildings.
1		(1, 4)	17	*114.	Decide color scheme of school paint.
5	5	5 (2)	3	115.	Change regularly scheduled PE times.

. . .

COMMENTS

Opinions vary widely over most of the items as to where the level of authority belongs; few items show consensus when this chart is first used. This points out the need to have such a decision-making process within the school to develop greater clarification and understanding among the staff. Frustrations occur when staff does not understand clearly who has the authority to make a decision about an activity. Such frustrations are a basis for potential irritation and conflict, particularly on important matters in which both the teacher and the principal feel that it is within their territorial prerogative to make the decision. It is better to discuss and resolve these matters in an unemotional study session where consensus can be reached.

Once a master chart is compiled, one copy is posted in the staff room, another is given to each teacher, and one is sent to the central office. Usually the chart is redone every two or three years unless a significant change of staff occurs within the school.

By having these levels of authority resolved, energy and time of staff is freed for concentration on student learning achievement.

Chapter 16
High School-Junior High Decision Making

Effective decision-making processes are essential in a complex system such as a high school with almost 2,000 students and over 100 employees. Even in smaller high schools of students or less ambiguities regarding decision-making authority continually occur. Who decides is often as crucial as what is decided. For these reasons I feel it is necessary to identify decision-making authority in the high school.

Identifying and resolving decision-making authority at the high school level is not easy, but it can and should be done. Such a process is not easy because it involves numerous groups—parents, students, teachers, counselors, administrators, and various committees. A high school also has curriculum committees, booster clubs for music and athletics, and other groups. The school often has a faculty senate, departments for the various subject areas, and a site council comprised of representatives from the community, parents, students, staff of teachers and non-teachers. The students also have a student council with various committees.

A high school is affected by innumerable pressures: decisions made by the board, the superintendent, the assistant superintendents, and the directors; stipulations of negotiated contracts which delineate hours, wages, conditions of work; plus state and federal legislation.

Teachers, non-teaching staff, counselors, counseling teams, the principal, and vice-principals should all be involved in the decision-making process. Not delineating, clarifying, and understanding the levels of decision-making authority can lead to misunderstandings, conflict, and frustration. Therefore, I recommend that a well-defined system of decision making be implemented at each high school and junior high.

I have included the junior high in this chapter because it tends to be organized more for subject matter departments, much like the high school. I included the middle school in the elementary school chapter because most middle schools tend to be organized with an emphasis on the individual student, with a minimum of subject departments. Including the middle school with the elementary chapter and the junior high with the high school chapter will give the staff in those schools ideas and examples for designing their decision-making processes, and will not necessitate a repetitious third chapter for the middle or junior high school.

STUDENT INVOLVEMENT

Increasing evidence shows that the meaningful involvement of students in school government enhances the probability that the school will become more effective.

American high schools typically have not involved students in the legitimate influence and control over their school life. The major educational decisions are made by professionals. Young people are expected to obey such adult decisions and to believe their best interests are being served. In more and more schools across the country, students are expressing their indignation at this situation.

I believe students should be involved in establishing rules and regulations for student conduct at their school. If the concept of democracy is to be taught concomitantly to students attending American schools, these schools should exemplify democratic practices and allow students the opportunity to actively participate in the operation of their school.

Student involvement can include any method by which the students are actively included in the planning, development, implementation, or evaluation of decisions which directly affect their lives as students in the high school or junior high. These can be individual or group decisions.

It may be easier for administrators to make all the decisions. However, it is that kind of unilateral action which seemingly has caused much dissatisfaction among student and teacher groups throughout the country during recent years. Unilateral decision making has con-

tributed to the emergence of strong teacher unions and student dem-
onstrations in the past.

Administrators should not make the mistake of giving a false
impression that students and staff are being involved. Nothing is more
devastating to group involvement than its members believing what
they say or do will not make a difference because the decision has
already been made.

Research shows that increased participation in decisions affecting
the members of an organization tends to increase learning, improve
morale, decrease absenteeism, curb vandalism, and slow down
employee turnover.

Assuming it is important to involve students in school decision
making, what are some of the reported practices and suggested
methods of involvement? Students definitely want to participate
in decisions made about the day-to-day operation of the school. Students need to be meaningfully involved in decisions about policies
concerning smoking regulations, curriculum change, grading practices, dress and grooming, scheduling, student behavior, assembly programs, study halls, hall passes, open vs. closed campuses, budget, and
student rights.

Students have been meaningfully involved in many districts in curriculum writing teams, evaluation of films and instructional materials,
and compilation of research data. In an important effort to expand
their curriculum, high school students also become involved with
community needs through volunteer work—tutoring, intercity project
work, recreation assistance, helping the disabled and aged, supporting a school levy, or influencing community policy by serving on
some city commissions and advisory boards.

A high school educator should take an honest, in-depth look at the
present form of student government by answering the following
questions:

● Is it a vehicle for giving all students a voice in the development of
school policy?

● Is its membership open to all students or are some excluded
because of poor grades, unpopularity or inarticulateness. In other
words, does it include students from every segment of the student
population?

● Does it deal with meaningful issues that concern most of the
students in school, or is it merely another exercise in the theory of
democratic process?

• Do students view it as being a "farce" or as a viable mechanism for student involvement?

• If it were suddenly disbanded, would its absence be felt by the students and staff? Would they care?

• Does it deal with total school concerns, or is it the tool for the "pet" projects of a select few?

I am convinced that meaningful student involvement in decision making is important at junior high and high school levels.

DECISION-MAKING CHART

PROCEDURES

The procedure for high school and junior high decision charts is much like those mentioned previously in this book for board-superintendent, superintendent-principal, and principal-teacher at elementary and middle schools.

You can start by asking all staff members to submit what they think are the kinds of decisions that have to be decided at this high school, and by devising a decision chart by categories. Next, send the sample decision chart to each individual staff member and student representative for identification of where they think the level of decision should be for each particular item. After receiving input, compile the results, select a representative group from the staff and student body, and decide where each item's level of authority should be.

The decision chart at a high school should be redone every three years. The final decision chart should be given to every staff person in the school, the representatives on the student council, the school site council, the district office, and the school board. In addition, several copies should be readily available in staff lounges and student body centers. Any other committees or groups involved with the high school should also have access to the chart. Chances are that the master chart at the high school will be referred to more frequently than other decision charts that have been developed in the school district.

What follows is an example of a decision chart that was used at one of our high schools.

SAMPLE CHART
NORTHGATE HIGH SCHOOL
DECISION-MAKING PROCESS
MAY, 1983

We are trying to identify decision makers in this school. This is not easy, so the form we are asking you to use is somewhat complex.

The information we gather from parents, students, teachers, counselors, and administrators will be used for further discussion which we hope will lead to a clearer understanding of who should make which decisions.

For example, if we find that the teachers feel they should design a bell schedule when in fact the curriculum committee is making that decision, referring to a formal agreement previously made on who decides will be helpful.

The following is a brief description of the various categories of decision makers.

Thank you for going through this process.

Jack M.

GROUPS, COMMITTEES AND INDIVIDUALS

ON-SITE ADMINISTRATIVE STAFF: Usually refers to the principal or sometimes a vice-principal.

COUNSELOR OR COUNSELOR TEAM: The counselors at Northgate High School meet regularly to make decisions. Often a counselor has to make an on-the-spot decision.

TEACHER: This includes special education teachers.

CURRICULUM COMMITTEE: The chairpeople of each department meet every two weeks to discuss schoolwide curriculum matters.

STAFF SENATE: All of the employees in the school, except administrators, elect representatives to an executive council. Usually, but not always, their concerns are related to working conditions.

DEPARTMENTS: The school is divided into areas such as math, industrial education, science, etc. These departments meet regularly.

SITE COUNCIL: Elected representatives from community, parents, students, staff (teachers and non-teachers).

STUDENTS: Students meet in various committees such as student body senate, student curriculum committee and so on. They also hold schoolwide elections.

DISTRICT OFFICE: Through policies set by the board, the superintendent, assistant superintendents, and directors there are many decisions that affect the school.

CONTRACT OR LAW: The teacher and the non-certificated employee associations or unions negotiate contracts that focus on hours, wages, and conditions. The state and federal government have a wide variety of laws that directly affect decisions at a school.

HIGH SCHOOL DECISION-MAKING QUESTIONNAIRE

Please check your position role:
Teacher _____ Parent _____ Student _____ Administrator _____
Counselor _____ Non-Certificated _____ Department Chair _____

After reading each statement, mark the level of decision-making involvement you feel is appropriate to each group or area. Use the following symbols to indicate levels of involvement:

0 NO INVOLVEMENT (be sure to write in 0)
1 BE INFORMED
2 STUDY, DISCUSS AND MAKE A RECOMMENDATION TO THE ADMIN.
3 MAKE FINAL DECISION

GROUP OR AREA CODE:

T = TEACHER	SC = SITE COUNCIL
ADM = SITE ADMINISTRATORS	D = DEPARTMENTS
C = COUNSELORS	S = STUDENTS
CC = CURRICULUM COMMITTEE	DO = DISTRICT OFFICE
SS = STAFF SENATE	CL = CONTRACT OR LAW

GROUP OR AREA AREA TO DECIDE	T	ADM	C	CC	SS	SC	D	S	DO	CL
1. Design a bell schedule.	1	3	1	2	1	0	2	1	0	0
2. Select teachers.	1	3	1	1	1	1	2	1	1	0
3. Evaluate teachers.	2	3	0	0	0	0	2	0	1	0

(etc.)

4. Develop master schedule.
5. Make room assignment.
6. Allocate instructional budget.
7. Determine class size.
8. Accept new students in classes that are out of balance or that exceed maximum.
9. Develop inservice.
10. Suspend student from school.
11. Suspend student from class.
12. Determine grading policy.
13. Evaluate substitutes.
14. Supervise students during non-class time.
15. Approve field trips for large groups.
16. Determine what system to use for scheduling students—walk-through or machine load.
17. Decide when to dismiss a class.
18. Decide to temporarily change classrooms.
19. Design staff meeting agenda.
20. Communicate directly with Parent Club on concerns vital to teachers.
21. Decide when to have minimum days.
22. Decide the rate and degree of learning that should be attempted for each student.
23. Decide open house and back-to-school

GROUP OR AREA										
AREA TO DECIDE	T	ADM	C	CC	SS	SC	D	S	DO	CL

24. Decide whether parent aides are
    used in classroom.
25. Decide how to spend student body
    funds.
26. Decide to transfer students in or
    out of class.
27. Decide what information to be sent
    home with students.
28. Send a student home to get his
    books, homework, and
    instruments.
29. Decide to have a special activity
    that could disrupt other classes.
30. Develop school goals and
    objectives.
31. Decide to take school material and
    equipment home to prepare
    lesson plans.
32. Set dates for extra-curricular
    activities.
33. Arrange activity with another
    school-sports activity, math con-
    test, and field trips.
34. Decide not to follow the curricular
    guidelines as established by
    departments.
35. Decide to apply for outside funding
    for a special project.
36. Decide to call district maintenance
    about non-functioning school
    equipment.
37. Request that custodian set up chairs
    or move furniture for a special
    class event.
38. Collect reimbursement from stu-
    dents for damage to school
    equipment furniture, and
    buildings.

GROUP OR AREA AREA TO DECIDE	T ADM C CC SS SC D S DO CL

39. Allocate M.G.M. funds.
40. Choose club and class advisors.
41. Enforce Title IX.
42. Establish general needs statement for school.
43. Make final decision on debated grade for student.
44. Determine basic academic competencies.
45. Drop student from class permanently.
46. Develop school improvement plan.
47. Allocate special project funds such as ISMS.
48. Evaluate over-all instructional program.

. . .

COMMENTS

The complexity of operating a high school and the occurrence of many diverse activities will necessitate referral to the chart to locate the immediate level of authority. Staff should have considerable flexibility and resources in order to solve problems that arise in the learning process.

These last 13 chapters—"Excellence in Administration"—should provide a wealth of ideas and examples for practicing administrators.

Part III
Excellence in Programs

Chapter 17
Marketing Techniques for Schools

The public has a right to know, factually and without propaganda, what is happening within its agencies. Schools have a legal obligation to let their consumers know toward what goals and in what manner the educational programs in their schools are progressing. Consequently, I feel that open communication is absolutely basic for school districts. Schools must effectively practice a marketing philosophy that is responsive to their consumers—parents, students, and citizens of the school district.

Over the course of my career in education I have found it interesting to observe and study the area of communication with the public. Communication in school districts began under the theory of public information. With increasing sophistication, communications became public relations. Within the last decade, that sophistication has grown to the extent that a more correct term for the practice of public relations in non-profit organizations such as schools would be "marketing."

Since my first superintendency, more than two decades ago, I have always made certain that, no matter how small the school district, at least a part-time employee was in charge of public information. I used almost every proven technique known at that time to fulfill the public's right to know what was happening in their schools.

COMMUNICATIONS POLICY

One of the first steps to be taken by a school district is the adoption of a communication policy which commits the district to open, on-going communications with all of the district's publics—students, staff, media, parents and the non-parent community (including non-parent citizens, local organizations, and public agencies). What follows below is a sample of a communications policy and communications procedure.

SAMPLE

MD SCHOOL DISTRICT
COMMUNICATIONS POLICY

The MD School District Board of Education is committed to establishing and maintaining open communications with its various publics: the community at large, district employees, students, and parents.

It is further committed to encouraging feedback from the above mentioned publics on all aspects of educational issues and positions.

COMMUNICATIONS PROCEDURES

As a public agency committed to the establishment and maintenance of open communications, the MD School District recognizes as routine the following procedures designed to keep all interested parties informed about district issues, board and administrative actions, educational programs and procedures.

GENERAL COMMUNITY

A complete agenda will be made available to the media on the Friday prior to regularly scheduled board of education meetings.

Packets of background information about agenda items will be made available to media representatives at regularly scheduled board meetings.

Persons attending board meetings will be allowed to speak if they have made a written request to the board chairperson.

Board members and administrators will make a concerted effort to cooperate with media representatives in their efforts to obtain factual information, recognizing the problems of media deadlines and the reporters' needs for authoritative informational sources.

All administrators will have the responsibility to provide accurate information about their area of supervision, either personally or through an officially designated spokesperson.

A prepared news release, including biographical information and job description, will be made available to media representatives at the time of administrative appointments. Efforts will be made to provide recent photographs and to arrange a press conference as soon as possible following appointments. Consideration will be given to deadlines and scheduling.

The school district will officially respond to published or broadcasted concerns, questions or criticism only to correct factual or statistical inaccuracies or misrepresentations; or to provide specifically requested information.

STAFF

Regular efforts will be made to apprise staff members of all actions, decisions, and recommendations of the administration and the board of education.

Opportunities shall be provided for continuous exchange of current information between administrators at the district office and at all levels in the field.

Local school administrators will encourage and assist staff, parents, students, and public to become knowledgeable about board and administrative decisions, the rationale supporting those decisions, and the impact of those decisions on groups and individuals affected by them.

Field administrators will make a continuing and conscious effort to keep district administrators aware of staff, student, and community attitudes, opinions and needs.

Regular administrative meetings shall be held to provide opportunities for interchange between administrators on predetermined subjects.

Field administrators will be encouraged to suggest topics deemed by them to be in need of exploration or restatement either in an administrative bulletin, at meetings of the administrative council, or at meetings of level administrators.

PARENT GROUPS

Each school administrator will establish a comprehensive program for communication with the school parent population.

Each school administrator will strive to create an atmosphere encouraging parent feedback and participation in local school activities and programs.

STUDENTS

Each school administrator will use all available, effective means of communication to keep the school population informed about policies and procedures which affect them as students.

Administrators shall in turn encourage reaction from the student population.

ASSESSING OPINION

In addition to disseminating information and encouraging feedback from all publics, district and site administrators will periodically poll specified samples of parents and students concerning priorities, goals, and major issues.

. . .

In addition to the procedures to carry out the board policy, a communications plan should be written for the district. A sample plan follows:

MD SCHOOL DISTRICT COMMUNICATIONS PLAN

THE CHARGE

The MD School District Board of Education has adopted a communication policy which commits the district to open, ongoing communications with all of the district's publics—students, staff, media, parents, and the non-parent community (including non-parent citizens, local organizations, and public agencies). This MD Communications Plan has been devised to implement that policy.

SOME COMMUNICATIONS FUNDAMENTALS

One of the fundamentals of the plan is the established fact that credibility is strongest at the individual school level. Studies indicate that the primary source of parent information about schools is the students—not so much what they say as how they feel about school. The second most common source is other people—other parents, school employees in all positions from principals to aides. Third is the mass media, and last is district publications.

Non-parents receive their information about schools predominantly from the media. Invariably they have a negative attitude, if that is their only source. Other people—parents and employees—represent the second most common source of information for non-parents. Students and community organizations are the third and fourth most common sources respectively.

Another basic fact is that direct communication—meaning directly from a source to a recipient or from an inquirer to a source—is more effective than indirect communication: the greater the number of intermediaries, the weaker the signal.

Indirect communications do have a real value, however, which must not be overlooked. For example, although the "Outlook" is written by the superintendent specifically for management personnel, its messages are to be passed on by the administrator to staff, students and parents, as appropriate.

The schools are the link between the various publics and levels of organization; therefore, they are the focal point of the MD communications.

THE PLAN

The plan provides for a two-way flow of information between:
- The various publics and their schools.
- The schools and the district offices.
- The district office and the board of education.
- The district offices and districtwide publics.
- The schools by areas and levels.

School Responsibilities

Each school must establish, maintain, and periodically evaluate its communications with staff, students, parents, and non-parent community. Although the methods will vary from school to school and from level to level, all publics must be included.

Communication between the schools is carried out through level and area meetings. It is enhanced by principals participating as representatives of each level on the negotiating team, at cabinet sessions, and at board meetings.

District Responsibilities

The district office is responsible for establishing and maintaining channels for both regular and spontaneous dissemination of information to and feedback from district publics.

The district office is further responsible for furnishing whatever assistance it can to the schools as they devise and carry out their two-way site communications plans.

The district office shall also provide:
- Information about pertinent legislative, board, and administrative decisions and events.

- Answers to requests for specific information as quickly as possible.
- Mailing assistance in the form of student and parent address labels; instructions for use of U.S. Postal Service and daily district mail deliveries.
- Artist, writing, and production consultation for newsletter and handbook production.
- Inservice training for the handling all types of communication techniques.
- Advice concerning local media contacts.
- Up-dated district communications tools—telephone extension lists, distribution lists, maps, organization charts, directories.
- Printing and word processing services for schools and special programs.
- Audio visual presentations concerning district programs; speakers on all aspects of education.

The effectiveness of both district-wide communications efforts and services to schools must be evaluated periodically.

Individual Responsibilities

Every MD employee, volunteer, parent, and student is a potential spokesperson for some aspect of our educational system.

Each program, school and division administrator assumes the responsibility for relaying information to his publics and for receiving and relaying or responding to input as appropriate.

Since support staff members regularly come in contact with parents and other members of the community as well as each other and students, they must be included in communications efforts.

All personnel should be alert to information which is appropriate for districtwide or communitywide dissemination, and forward it to the marketing office. Forms will be provided to facilitate the report process.

Each school, program, and department should identify one person, perhaps the secretary, to serve as a resource person for communications activities.

Beyond the Plan

Some spontaneous or special contacts are not represented but should be recognized as important and used for maximum effectiveness. Consider, for example, the communications value of visits to schools or departments by members of the board of education, district-level administrators, media representatives, parents, and non-parent citizens. Consider as well the impact of a quick, courteous answer either in person or by a pleasant voice on the telephone.

Communications happen whether we plan them or not. If a plan is to be successful, however, everyone must make a conscious effort to serve as an effective communicator.

IMPLEMENTING THE PLAN

Since one of the fundamentals of the plan is the established fact that credibility is strongest at the individual school level, it follows that frequent letters from the principal to parents and citizens in the attendance area are a highly effective way of transmitting information regarding the educational program. Two letters from the GG elementary school principal follow as a typical way to keep parents informed about programs at the school.

SAMPLES

GG ELEMENTARY SCHOOL
200 Harry Drive
PH, CALIF. 94523

March 28, 1980
TO: Parents
FROM: LM, Principal

Every parent wants to know how his school is "doing." Is it good, medium, or poor? How does it compare to other schools? Does it create an atmosphere of trust and confidence? I have some information of this type, so I am taking the time and expense to mail two letters to each family.

Earlier this year, 25 percent of our parents received a "climate survey" to respond to. A "climate survey" is a fancy name for asking people what they think of something, in this case, the general school atmosphere. Here are some of the results. Letter grades are used because most people understand As, Bs, Cs, and Ds.

	PARENT OPINION	TEACHER OPINION
Is there trust and respect between students and teachers?	B	A
Do the teachers seem cheerful, and are students happy to be in class?	A	A
Are parents "listened to" by the school?	A	A
Is there an effort to improve the student's adjustment to school?	B	B-
Do teachers work together cooperatively?	A	A
Do the school teachers and administrators go "back to school" to improve their professional abilities?	B	B
Does the school emphasize the "basic skills" as well as the "arts"?	B-	A
Is each child expected to work near the top of his individual abilities, and do students know how they are doing in school?	B	B
Is learning carried on in appropriate groups, and do students needing special help get it?	B	B
Are there enrichment activities for students needing such activities?	C-	B
Are students encouraged to follow rules without excessive "put downs"?	B-	B
Do the students and staff understand and respect the school rules?	B	A
Are students and staff members rewarded when they do a good job?	B	B-
Do the school personnel attempt to solve problems instead of ignoring them?	B-	B-
Are the school goals periodically reviewed with an eye toward improvement?	B	B-
Can the school work constructively with conflict situations when necessary?	B-	A
Are school personnel available for conferences, and will they discuss issues and problems?	B-	A-
I can influence the teachers thinking when it is necessary, and teachers are interested in parents' opinions.	B-	A-

	PARENT OPINION	TEACHER OPINION
There are enough teachers and supplies provided to do a good job.	B	B
The school plant is well maintained with enough space for different types of classes.	B	B

What do the results mean? I am struck by the similarity of all the opinions of the parents and teachers. There is very little disagreement in any area.

Our school received very high marks for (1) having a cheerful and constructive atmosphere, (2) paying attention to parents' opinions, (3) for teacher cooperation, (4) for solving conflict situations, and (5) for communicating with parents.

The only area receiving a C mark was "offering enrichment classes." This would indicate improvement is needed at our school.

There are many areas that can be improved, and my next letter will outline some of these areas and what the school staff hopes to accomplish. (Thank you for reading this!)

Sincerely yours,
LM
Principal

GG ELEMENTARY SCHOOL
200 Harry Dr.
PH, Calif. 94523

April 27, 1980

Dear Parents,

This is the second of to letters being mailed to each parent. In the first letter the results of the school "climate survey" were reviewed. The results were given in letter grades. In this letter I hope to inform you about the training our staff is receiving to improve their job skills and new programs which help us deal more effectively with children.

Our staff has already begun advanced training in the area of "basic competencies." Mrs. Baca, Mr. More, and I attended a three-day workshop which laid the groundwork for using a guide which outlines the teaching of basic skills from grades one through eight. Each teacher will know how their grade-level material fits into the total picture of basic competencies.

Another activity our teachers will be involved in is observing other teachers at work. These observations are intended to help them pick up good ideas and new teaching strategies, and to see exactly what is being taught at other grade levels. Few teachers ever have the chance to see other teachers at work, and it is a very educating experience. Observing aides being used in other schools certainly helped us get off to a good start with our aide program.

All of our staff members will be attending a workshop addressing the subject of "Working with Student Learning Problems." This is not meant to imply a serious handicap, but rather problems most "normal" students have while they go through school. Few students excel in all subjects, and it is common for most students to be frustrated or puzzled with subjects from time to time. Most students can also be more efficient in their learning habits. The workshop will concentrate on interpreting reading errors, helping students work independently, using spelling tests as diagnostic tools, and improving ways of working with parents.

Our school has been on the "SIP" (School Improvement Program) since January, and this has brought several significant improvements to our school program. The aides in each primary room enable the teacher to be more flexible in giving much more attention to all students. So many programs emphasize giving help to the slow or gifted student that we try to use the aides so all students get more attention. The SIP program has also brought enrichment to our school in the study of the good points of different cultural backgrounds and classes in parenting for those parents who are interested.

Our school staff has been very open to programs of self-improvement. It is easier to just do the same old thing than to try to upgrade our job skills. Our staff deserves credit for the hard work put in to qualify and develop a program for the SIP funds and for the other state funds for the conferences and visitations. All of the monies have come from sources other than what is normally provided for your children's basic education by the school district.

I have attended three conferences designed to help me be a better principal. These have been valuable for me; I have learned new skills in the counseling area which weren't even talked about when I went to school. Times do change! Another realization I have had, from talking to administrators from other parts of the state, is that we have a highly successful and unique program at GG School.

> Sincerely yours,
> LM
> Principal

P.S. Thanks for the good turnout at Open House. About 90 percent of our parents were able to make it.

KEYS TO EFFECTIVE COMMUNICATION

Keeping in mind that the schools should be the focal point of the district communication program, and that they are the link between the various publics and the levels of organization, it is my belief that each school must establish, maintain and periodically evaluate its communications with staff, students, parents and non-parent community. Although these methods will vary from school to school and from level to level, all publics must be included. An example of a selective dissemination list follows.

Define the publics you want to reach with information. There is no such thing as "general public." Below are some examples of publics.

> Parents, staff, students, neighbors, local businesses, community organizations, civic leaders, legislators, board of education members, senior citizens, other schools, district administrators, other school districts, county officials, law enforcement agencies, special interest groups, retired district employees, representatives of industry, social service agencies, alumni, employee organizations, and other groups.

Decide the most effective method to reach each of the identified publics:

> Personal note, telephone call, school newsletter, door-to-door flyer, bumper stickers, county schools bulletin, lawn signs, announcements at meetings, organizational newsletters, note home with students, class announcements, student newspaper, parent newsletter, special meeting/party/gathering, sound truck, sign board, brochure, bill board, sandwich boards, picket signs, demonstration, survey, handbooks, media.

Plot your information campaign. No two will be the same, but as you repeat techniques, they become easier, and you can take on more.

- Establish priorities for the dissemination techniques.
- Plot them on a time chart or calendar.
- Assign tasks.
- Do them!
- Evaluate the efforts on paper for next time.
- Refer to your evaluation before you begin to plan your next effort.

Keep in mind that:

It is best to delegate to one person the responsibility for coordination. Effectiveness of the total effort will suffer if everyone proceeds without reference to the whole program.

Personal contact is more effective than the written word. The further one goes from eye contact, the less effective the communication effort becomes.

There is no shortcut to success. Communication is a never-ending, individualized effort. What succeeds today may fail tomorrow.

Objective evaluation is essential. Appraisal by the project participants is insufficient. You may think that you are doing a great job—and may well be—but the techniques may not work for that audience or for that message.

The media are businesses. They sell advertisements to make announcements and to carry messages. Electronic media do have to carry public service announcements, but newspapers do not, though they sometimes do for good will.

It is the media's job to carry news. Create news and you will get coverage. If you want puffery, go the personal contact route. If you want "publicity", buy an ad. Honestly analyze your own motivation to ensure success.

Not everyone is going to be interested in all projects— nor should everyone be.

Activities should not be scheduled in competition with known events. There is only so much that people can do and only so much information they can absorb and that the media can carry. Christmas, for example, is a time to avoid.

It is better to emphasize large scale events than to spread workers thin over long periods of time with little happenings in which it is hard to create interest. It is also easier to get support for quality rather than quantity.

The community can help. Businesses benefit from sponsorships and your activity benefits from more readable flyers or signs. Such sponsorships are "win-win" situations. Make the most of them.

ISSUING ANNUAL REPORTS

One way to reach various publics is to use an annual report. Using the local newspaper to publish an annual report is effective. Buy ad space or inserts, then tell your story in a professional layout. In the long run, this is an inexpensive way to reach a large number of people. This approach worked for us in a community in which the newspaper was read by the majority of citizens who lived there. Each year the public knew all the pertinent facts about their schools. By using a two-color insert in the newspaper, we could subsequently place the inserts in businesses, offices, and other well traveled public places. In addition, they were used throughout the school district during the year.

POLLS

A review of public information, public relations, and marketing is not complete without commenting on polls and polling techniques. Most of us are familiar with the Gallup Poll of the public's attitudes toward public schools conducted annually by George Gallup for the Phi Delta Kappa magazine. Such national polls are helpful in providing all of us with information regarding the public's opinion about schools. However, we should understand that the nature of polling is usually based on superficial images and perceptions on the part of the public.

I have found over the years that while many people feel education has problems, they think that their local school or district is doing well. The national and local polls were not telling us the same message. Therefore, I think it is important for a local school district to conduct its own poll on a school-by-school basis because people generally have a very high opinion of their local school. That kind of

information is imperative to have on hand since critics do emerge
from time to time. Having data on hand also maintains a certain
positive spirit and stability in the local school and the district. If the
local school develops problems, the public opinion poll will so indicate. This can be a constructive indication of possible improvements
according to the perception of the consumers—the parents and the
students.

LOCAL POLLS

What follows are some sample questions and responses from a
parent survey. This will give you an idea of the kind of questions you
can ask, and exactly what kinds of answers were received in the
district that conducted the poll. Although this example shows districtwide results, you should break them down for each school
attendance area as I did.

PARENT SURVEY
DISTRICTWIDE RESULTS

	Percent Yes	Percent No
1. Do you feel that the school is placing the proper emphasis on the basic skill subjects, such as reading, math, English language?	78%	22%
2. Do you feel that your student has an opportunity to participate in a sufficient variety of educational experiences, such as media center activities, field trips, and creative and cultural arts?	83	17
3. Do you feel student discipline is properly handled at the school? If not, what do you recommend? (Please comment below)	77	23
4. Do you feel that your student's instructional program meets his needs?	77	23
5. In general, do you feel your student likes school?	94	6
6. Do you feel the school provides a satisfactory lunch program?	75	25
7. Do you feel the school is spending its money in a reasonable way?	81	19
8. Do you feel you are being adequately informed about your student's learning progress?	78	22
9. Do you feel the school has adequate building facilities?	67	33

10. Do you feel the school facilities are reasonably
well maintained? 97 3
11. Are you made to feel welcome at the school? 96 4
12. Do you feel your child's teacher/s is responsive
to your concerns? 97 3
13. Do you feel your principal is responsive to your
concerns? 94 6
14. Do you feel the superintendent is providing
proper leadership for our schools? 80 20
15. Do you feel the school board is providing
proper direction for our schools? 78 22
16. Do you know that board meetings are open to
the public and you are invited to attend? 77 23
17. Do you feel the other employees at your
student's school, such as secretaries, aides, and
custodians, are effective in their contacts with
members of the community? 95 5

Comments:

This and other local opinion polls for schools have proven positive.
In this particular instance, the local newspaper editor printed the
following editorial just before a board election.

DISTRICT'S IMAGE ON PLUS SIDE

Results of a recent parent survey in the Union School
District would tend to negate the image of the district that
some critics of the district and some trustee candidates
tended to paint.

We're not suggesting that the district board and administration are above criticism. But the image of a district that
is not responsive to its constituents, of an administration
in which the public has lost faith, of an administration that
has lost communication with parents, of a district in which
instructional programs are not being met, of a board that
provides inadequate direction: This is an image that just
does not come across in the survey.

It would appear to be an image harbored by a minority
of the parents in the district. For the survey shows the
exact opposite to be the case: A solid majority of parents

are satisfied with the school district operation, instructional program and administration.

To be sure, no survey or poll can reflect a complete and totally accurate picture of the answers being sought. But they can provide a fairly reasonable trend in the thinking of a given group.

The school district mailed a 17 question survey to every 10th family on each school's roster. It was in fact a random sampling. Of the 768 survey sheets mailed, 430 or 56 percent of them were returned. In every one of the 17 areas, some of the respondents did not answer the question, indicating they did not have sufficient information to answer.

The lowest percentage of yes (or support) votes was 67 percent to the question: Do you feel the school has adequate building facilities?

All other questions received a 75 per cent or more yes response, a response that has to be considered one of satisfaction. That means that only 25 percent or less of the parents who responded were dissatisfied with the district. And that ratio is solid support, no matter which way you look at it.

In six areas, the affirmative response was higher than 90 percent. Those questions were:

—In general, do you feel your child likes school? Yes was 94 percent.

—Do you feel your principal is responsive to your concerns? Yes was 94 percent.

—Do you feel that the other employees at your child's school, such as secretaries, aides, and custodians, are effective in their contacts with members of the community? Yes was 95 percent.

—Are you made to feel welcome at the school? Yes was 96 percent.

—Do you feel the school facilities are reasonably well maintained? Yes was 97 percent.

—Do you feel your child's teacher is responsive to your concerns? Yes was 97 percent.

And in the areas of administrative leadership, 78 percent answered yes to the question: Do you feel the school board is providing proper direction for our schools? And 80 percent answered yes to the question: Do you feel the superintendent is providing proper leadership for our schools?

The overall image of the school district is on the plus side.

Because local polls are generally supportive—more so than national polls—they provide a basis for the newspaper and community to establish a positive climate for schools such as this newspaper editorial did.

CHECKLIST FOR SURVEY RESEARCH

Now that I have convinced you to conduct a local poll, I suggest the following steps for you to consider before you begin.

- HYPOTHESIZING—What do you want to study?
- DESIGNING—Procedures and methods.
- PLANNING—Materials and personnel required.
- FINANCING—Support for the study.
- SAMPLING—Who and how many?
- DRAFTING—Framing questions.
- CONSTRUCTING—First draft of questionnaire.
- PRE-TESTING—Validity of questions.
- TRAINING—Teaching interviewers.
- BRIEFING—Instructing interviewers.
- INTERVIEWING—Securing data.
- CONTROLLING—Seeing that interviews are completed.
- VERIFYING—Checking data accuracy.
- CODING—Preparing data for analysis.
- PROCESSING—Organizing data for analysis.
- ANALYZING—Interpreting the data.
- REPORTING—Sharing the results.

QUESTIONNAIRE DESIGN CONSIDERATIONS

- Questions seek information required
- Questions free from ambiguity
- Cover letter
- Layout of questionnaire and quality of paper
- Brevity
- Pre-testing complete
- Lowest common denominator

- Coding requirements
- Incentive to respond required
- Question types
    —open ended (free response)
    —dichotomous (yes/no)
    —multiple choice
    —ranking
    —scale

DEMOGRAPHIC CHARACTERISTICS
Home ownership, mobility, marital status, household composition, education, occupation, chief wage earner ethnic background, political affiliation, religion, income, race, sex, age, name, address, and phone number.

SURVEY TECHNIQUES
Mail
- Non-response may be high—possible bias
- Relatively economical
- Questionnaire design critical
- Eliminates interviewer bias
- Validity of response can be questionable

Telephone
- Some sample members may not have phone or listing
- Relatively economical for local studies
- Questions must be brief
- Quick
- Must have trained interviewers

Personal Interview
- Usually expensive
- Must have trained interviewers
- Allows for probing and explaining
- Good feedback opportunities
- Takes time
- Response bias
- Some information obtainable without asking questions

SPECIALIZED SAMPLING TECHNIQUES
Systematic Sampling—Sampling from a listing of the population at a specified interval.

Stratified Sampling—Allotting subsamples to stratified segments of the population.

Cluster Sampling—Segregating judgmental clusters of the population for sampling or cluster census.

Area Sampling—Cluster sample on a geographic basis.

Multistage Sampling—Cluster sampling in which subsamples are drawn from larger primary sampling units.

Judgmental Sampling—Selecting a sample from a population on the basis of personal judgment.

REQUIRED SAMPLE SIZE

Tolerated Error	Confidence Level	
	95%	99%
+ - 1%	9,604	16,587
+ - 2%	2,401	4,147
+ - 3%	1,067	1,843
+ - 4%	600	1,037
+ - 5%	384	663
+ - 6%	267	461
+ - 7%	196	339

Example: If a random sample of 600 persons were drawn, we could be 95 percent confident—95 times out of 100—that the proportion of responses from that sample would be within plus or minus 4 percent of the true parameter of the entire population.

COMMENTS

As I mentioned at the beginning of this chapter, communication with the public has developed into a sophisticated approach called marketing. Such an approach can be most helpful to anyone in school work or in another non-profit organization. Schools, particularly, have been experiencing increasing problems in the marketplace due to declining enrollments, decreasing finances, and volatile demands placed upon our services from a highly critical clientele.

One of the best books I have found on marketing is *Marketing for Non-Profit Organizations* written by Philip Kotler and published by Prentice-Hall.

Kotler defines marketing as "the analysis, planning, implementation and control of carefully formulated programs designed to bring about voluntary exchanges of values with target markets for the purpose of achieving organizational objectives. Marketing involves organizing and studying the target market's needs, designing appropriate products and services and using effective communication and distribution to inform, motivate and service the market."

In other words, for educators, it means that we are an organization that must be consumer oriented for our students and parents. We must have well formulated programs, and well established goals and performance objectives. We must analyze the satisfaction level of our consumers from time to time, and communicate, motivate, and satisfy them.

Marketing certainly has its critics just as public information and public relations have had critics. For years I have received criticism because I have had a staff person with responsibilities for public information or public relations. However, I have always maintained that the public has a right to know what is going on with their public institution. Through a marketing philosophy one can increase the satisfaction and understanding of the consumer.

A marketing approach addresses five characteristics: customer philosophy, integrated marketing organization, adequate marketing information, strategic orientation, and an operational efficiency. By considering these characteristics, one can create an organization that is highly responsive, adaptive, and entrepreneurial in a rapidly changing environment. Certainly, as our society changes in an accelerated manner—as Toffler states in *The Third Wave* and his previous book *Future Shock*—it is obvious that we must assume a marketing philosophy if we want our public schools to survive.

We must understand the needs of our consumers—students and parents. We must improve the efficiency of our services by developing and delivering better programs and by making sure that we are effectively communicating with our consumers.

Chapter 18
Advisory Councils

Schools need to establish a close affiliation with their communities and parents to understand the needs of their consumers, to communicate with the non-parent community, and to foster interest in the volunteer program. Advisory councils are one practical means by which each school can do this. Advisory councils at the school site help ensure that the education of children is a shared responsibility—a partnership with the federal, state, and local community. School leadership also requires a local partnership among board members staff, parents, students and community members. Partnerships focus the talents and energies of the total community on student needs. Such relationships include exchange of information, decision sharing, services for schools, advocacy, and collaboration for maximum student learning.

As society becomes more and more service oriented, the power of consumerism continues to gain. Parents have a continuing interest in alternative schools and voucher programs which could offer free choice of a school of their liking. More frequently than not that interest can be put into action in today's contemporary society. Parents who have deferred child bearing, particularly in higher socio-economic families, may have accumulated discretionary income, because both have probably been working for a number of years, and can choose those schools which they consider to be outstanding.

If the power of consumerism can force a big conglomerate like General Motors to suffer thousands of lost dollars in a recall to replace a 20-cent pin in the tranmission differential in certain new cars, you can be assured that the same spirit of consumerism will lead parents, whose children are their most precious things in life, to demand that schools do a superb job of educating them. They would rather scrimp, save, then pay for a good school before they would send their child to one they find unacceptable.

Schools cannot ignore the fact that approximately three out of four voters are without school-age-children. Unless educators extend themselves to foster community involvement, that portion of the population with no direct vested interest in the well-being of the local school system will vote against educational measures on election day.

Volunteerism not only adds to the quality of the education students receive, but it has the secondary effect of improving the citizens attitudes toward public education. Volunteers, whether they are parents, community members, or representatives of business, labor, and industry, develop insight into the complexities of schooling. This leads to a more enlightened community-school relationship.

ADVISORY COUNCIL POLICY

Parent involvement, then, should be the immediate priority of educational policy makers; a wider and more diverse community involvement, the ultimate goal.

I believe every school should have an advisory council in order to enhance its educational program. An advisory council at the school site can be formed under the formal sanctions of school board policy or informally and independently through the efforts of the principal.

For those who wish to follow a formal route and establish an advisory council at the school under school board policy, a sample policy follows.

SAMPLE

MD SCHOOL DISTRICT
ADVISORY COUNCIL POLICY

The MD School District is committed to an effort to ensure that the education of our children is a shared responsibility involving a partnership with federal, state, local and community effort through the Individual School Management System. School management requires a partnership among participants covering boards, administrators, teachers, parents, students, and community members to bring together the talents and energies of the total community to focus on student needs.

The Individual School Management System offers local schools an opportunity to plan programs which will prepare students from all socio-economic groups with skills and knowledge that will enable them to choose the direction they wish to follow, be it higher education or the world of work, while becoming a productive member of society.

The following procedures contain common guidelines to be followed by all schools in establishing a school site council under the requirements of the Individual School Management System or any federal and/or state funded grant.

ADVISORY COUNCIL PROCEDURES
SCHOOL SITE COUNCIL COMPOSITION

A school site council shall be composed of the principal and representatives of classroom teachers selected by classroom teachers at the school, other school personnel selected by other school personnel at the school, parents of pupils attending the school selected by such parents; and, in secondary schools, students selected by students attending the school.

At the elementary level the council shall be constituted to ensure parity between (a) the principal, classroom teachers, and other school personnel, and (b) parents or other community members selected by parents.

At the secondary level the council shall be constituted to ensure parity between (a) the principal, classroom teachers and other school personnel, and (b) equal numbers of the parents and students.

At both the elementary and secondary levels, classroom teachers shall comprise the majority of persons represented under subdivisions (a) of this section. To ensure broad representation, "other school personnel" shall be interpreted to include classified, other support personnel, and/or administrative personnel.

Existing schoolwide advisory groups or school support groups may be utilized as the school site council if such groups conform to the provisions of this section.

The number of representatives on each site council is to be determined at the local level and may be 10 to 24 in membership. A composition pattern must follow the requirements as explained above. Members should serve two-year terms with half of groups A and B above being replaced each year.

Also, a secondary level school site council may include a community non-parent as a non-voting member. At least one parent should represent special education. Secondary schools should balance parent membership among feeder schools. Student members should represent as many segments of the student body as possible. In general there should be an effort to include students and parents on the council that represent all educational and socio-economic aspects of the school community.

School site councils are encouraged to include in their meetings other interested and helpful persons who serve in a consultancy role. An elementary school with seventh or eighth grades may include a student representative in such a role on its school site council.

SELECTION PROCESS

Consideration should be given to a variety of selection and replacement processes, and the final decision should be based on what is best for the school. Care should be taken to assure that persons or groups not usually or previously involved have an opportunity to participate in the selection process.

Possible Selection Processes

In each case, members are selected by their peers in one of following:

- Nomination and balloting within each required group.
- Appointment of the representative to the school site council by each required group.
- Nomination of candidates by existing school and community groups with final selection of representatives from each required group by their peers.
- Election or selection by peer group following volunteering for the position.
- If no members have been selected by a particular group in one through four above, the chairperson may on an interim basis, ask for volunteers and/or select members.

POSSIBLE REPLACEMENT PROCESSES

In each case the required composition of the school site council must be maintained. Replacement of individual members may be accomplished by any of the following, if such becomes necessary:

- Appointment by the chairperson
- Appointment by school site council recommendation
- Replacement by any method used for selection.

ROLES OF MEMBERSHIP

Each member is an equal voting participant. Each member may act as a liaison to his broad constituency, but does not represent any special interest group.

PURPOSE AND RESPONSIBILITIES OF THE SITE COUNCIL

Site councils are established by authority of the board of education as advisory to the principal and staff. Their purposes and responsibilities are to be resolved at one of their initial meetings as a result of a survey of parents in the school attendance area, and completion of the school site council decision chart.

INSERVICE NEEDS AMONG MEMBERS

The site council determines inservice needs based upon an assessment of the ability of council members to carry out their responsibilities. The council plans inservice activities. These may include budget processes, communication skills, trust building, shared decision-making techniques, conflict resolution, learning theory, time management, change process, advocacy, Delphi, brainstorming, prioritizing, concensus.

Inservice resources may include district staff, county office staff, universities, consortiums, outside consultants, organization staff. The council evaluates inservice based on achievement of goals.

PLANNING

The school site council collects information, understands meaning of goals, collectively determines goals, and involves other interested groups in the process.

ORGANIZING THE TASK

The school site council determines the organizational structure best suited to accomplish the task. Samples include standing or ad hoc committees, task force, committee of the whole.

IMPLEMENTATION AND OPERATIONAL EVALUATION PROCESS

The council will have ongoing responsibility to review with the principal, teachers, other school personnel, and pupils the implementation of the school improvement program and to assess periodically the effectiveness of the program. The council will also be responsible for annually reviewing and updating the school improvement plan and for establishing the annual school improvement budget. The following questions may be helpful in guiding the council's deliberations:

- Are the students the central focus of our deliberations?
- Do we have systematic procedures for problem solving and do we follow them when making decisions?
- Are we listening to each other?
- Do our procedures promote trust?
- Do we have full participation of our membership?
- Are we responsive to the whole community?
- Do our procedures result in broad school/community participation?
- Are we properly responding to the measured needs of the school?
- Are we seeing outcomes to the plans developed by the council?
- Do we usually resolve problems that we consider?

Based on the evaluation of this process, the council should be prepared to modify its procedures.

. . .

That policy and its procedures have served districts well. In one case, they guided a large school district with 44 school site councils. One elementary school used its school site council to coordinate the efforts of seven separate, legally constituted, federal project, advisory groups existing within that school. Its low socio-economic status qualified it for federal support for numerous programs. The school site council brought organization out of chaos and served as an umbrella for all seven multifaceted programs.

SURVEYS

I made mention of surveying the parents of the school attendance area to give direction to the council for planning purposes. One type of survey, a concise one, consisting of four questions, can be used.

- What is the school doing well that you would like us to continue?
- What should the school improve?
- What is the school doing that doesn't make that much difference?
- What is the school doing that you feel we could/should discontinue?

Usually that type of survey will generate more than enough ideas and responsibilities for the school site council to work on for a year or two.

If the school site council is trying to develop a true community school then one might use the following type of survey.

SAMPLE

HIDDEN VALLEY ELEMENTARY SCHOOL
500 Glacier Drive
Martinez, California 94553

May 5, 1981

Dear Neighbors and Parents,

The school site council of the Hidden Valley Elementary School is working toward the development of a broad "Community Education Program" in cooperation with the city of Martinez, Mt. Diablo School District and other community agencies.

This expanded program would provide a variety of services for all age groups.

In order to plan effectively, it is important that we identify the unmet recreational, educational, social and cultural enrichment needs of the Hidden Valley neighborhood. Accordingly, we are conducting a survey to enable residents to express their perception of unmet needs. The survey is being conducted by volunteers working with the Hidden Valley school site council.

A neighborhood school belongs to all of the people who live in the area.

We solicit your cooperation in answering these questions on the subject of your unmet needs.

We thank you for your time, your cooperation and your prompt reply.

Sincerely,
Joan T.
Principal

HIDDEN VALLEY SCHOOL SITE COUNCIL

Survey of Hidden Valley Neighborhood
Social, Recreational, and Cultural Needs

1. Do you feel that people in the Hidden Valley Neighborhood need more social, recreational, or cultural services? If yes, check all the services and facilities which you think are needed.

UNMET RECREATION NEEDS   UNMET SOCIAL NEEDS
Indoor gymnasium   Day care
Health clubs or physical   Counseling

education groups
Youth center
Special recreation for the handicapped
Hobby groups
After school activities for children
Drop-in center for teens
Senior citizen activities
Other _____

Legal Aid
Legal advocacy
Employment services

Consumer education
Information and referral

Crisis intervention
Drug/alcoholism treatment
Other _____

UNMET CULTURAL
ENRICHMENT NEEDS
Music
Painting
Drama
Crafts
Intergroup understanding activities
Other _____

UNMET FACILITY NEEDS
Multipurpose rooms
Meeting rooms
Gymnasium
Theater
Banquet facilities

Other _____

2. Which of the unmet needs you checked above do you feel are most important?

a. _____
b. _____
c. _____

3. What particular groups in the Hidden Valley Neighborhood are especially in need? (Check all that apply)

Senior citizens___Delinquents___Young adults___Youth
Culturally disadvantaged___Educationally disadvantaged___
Minority students___Minority groups___Medical:___alcoholics
Drug addicts___Formerly mentally ill___Offenders___
Past offenders___Single men___Transient and homeless___
Unemployed___School dropouts___Unwed mothers___
Single parents___

4. A multipurpose school community center can offer many types of services to individuals and families in the area as well as supply facilities for community organizations. Would you or members of your household approve or oppose construction and operation of such a center?

Strongly approve___Approve___Strongly oppose___Oppose___
Neutral___

If you approve or oppose construction of a multipurpose center, what are your major reasons for approving/disapproving?

5. If a school community center were established in the Hidden Valley neighborhood area, would you or members of your household use it?

6. Altogether, how many people live in your home (household) and how old are they?

___Total number of people (don't forget to count yourself)

___Number of persons 5 years or younger

___Number 6 to 14 years old

___Number 15 to 19 years old

___Number 20 to 34 years old

___Number 35 to 59 years old

___Number 60 years old or older

___Number attending private or parochial schools (list ages)

___Is this a single-parent household?

(Please make sure the number of people in all age groups adds to the total number of people in your household.)

7. Do you own or rent your home?

8. If adult education classes were offered at Hidden Valley, I would participate___in the day time___in the evening___not at all.

9. I would like classes to be offered in the following areas (please list).

PLEASE RETURN THIS QUESTIONNAIRE TO
HIDDEN VALLEY SCHOOL

. . .

DECISION-MAKING CHART

In addition to the survey, I mentioned that the site council should spend some time in the beginning resolving their decision making responsibilities. The following is an example of a chart that might be used.

SAMPLE

DECISION-MAKING RESPONSIBILITIES OF SCHOOL SITE COUNCIL

| ———————
School name	Not the Responsibility of the council	Direct Responsibility	Participate In	Must be Informed
Program				
Developing/modifying the School Improvement Plan				
Developing/modifying the site council bylaws				
Providing input as to instructional materials for School Improvement Program				
Reviewing the implementation of School Improvement Plan				
Budget				
Determining priorities for School Improvement Program Budget				
Allocating dollars to each category of School Improvement Program Budget				
Doing long range budget plan for School Improvement Program Budget				

Evaluation
    Interpreting test results

    Evaluating School Improvement Program

    Doing a self-evaluation as to role on the School Site Council

Other
    Informing the school community of School Site Council/School Improvement activities

    Providing procedures for the school community to communicate to School Site Council

Comments: Personnel issues are the responsibility of the principal. The following are some examples of personnel issues:

- Interviewing aides/volunteers for School Improvement Program
- Interviewing teachers
- Hiring aides for School Improvement Program
- Hiring teachers
- Evaluating aides in the School Improvement Program
- Evaluating teachers

. . .

PARENT ACTIVITIES

One of the main activities that the school site council would promote is the involvement of parents in the educational process at home by listening to their children read and by reading to them.

The following is a list of 14 other activities in five broad categories in which parents can be involved in the school instructional process.

ACTIVITIES EMPHASIZING READING

Ask parents to read to their child regularly or listen to the child read aloud.

Loan books, workbooks, etc. to keep at home for a short period of time as extra learning material.

Ask parents to take their child to the library.
LEARNING THROUGH DISCUSSION
Ask parents to get their child to talk about what he did that day in the classroom.

Give them an assignment that requires the children to ask their parents questions. e.g. let children write about their parents experiences.

Ask parents, one or both to watch a specific television program with their child and discuss the show afterwards.

INFORMAL LEARNING ACTIVITIES AT HOME
Suggest ways for parents to incorporate their child into their own activities, if possible, that would be educationally enriching.

Send home suggestions for game or group activities related to the child's homework that can be played by parent and child.

Suggest how parents might use the home environment (materials and activities of daily life to stimulate their child's interest in reading, math, etc.).

CONTACTS BETWEEN TEACHER AND PARENT
Establish a formal agreement by which the parents provide rewards and/or penalties based on the child's school performance or behavior.

Establish a formal agreement where the parent advises, supervises and assists the child in completing homework tasks.

DEVELOPING TEACHING AND EVALUATION
SKILLS IN PARENTS
Ask parents to come to observe the classroom (not to help) for part of a day.

Explain to parents certain techniques for teaching, for making learning materials or for planning lessons.

Give a questionnaire to parents so they can evaluate their child's progress or provide some other "feedback" to the teacher.

AIDE-ING PROGRAM

One of the best examples of how a school site council can encourage a close relationship between parents and teachers is found in the parent education program that the council called "Aide-ing in Education." It was a series of weekly seminars for parents conducted by the faculty of the school. The following program is an example of these parenting classes.

SAMPLE

AIDE-ING IN EDUCATION
What Parents and Teachers
Can Do Together!
A PARENT EDUCATION PROGRAM

(This program is arranged by the School Site
Council. Taught by the Hidden Valley Faculty)

HIDDEN VALLEY ELEMENTARY SCHOOL
PARENT EDUCATION SEMINARS

SERIES A

November 28,1980

"INCREASING STUDENTS' MOTIVATION TO LEARN"
(Discusses six principles of motivation and their use by
teachers in real classroom situations.)

December 5, 1980

"INCREASING PRODUCTIVE BEHAVIOR"
(Teaches the four basic principles of reinforcement theory
and their application to increase learning.)

December 12,1980

"MOTIVATION AND REINFORCEMENT
IN THE CLASSROOM"
(Two annotated lessons which demonstrate the use of mot-
ivation and reinforcement in the classroom.)

SERIES B

January 16, 1981

"HELPING IN READING"
(Demonstrates at several age levels, teachers applying motivation, reinforcement, practice and extending thinking
while helping students with reading.)

January 23, 1981

"HELPING IN MATH"
(Demonstrates at several age levels, teachers applying motivation, reinforcement, practice and extending thinking
while helping students with mathematics.)

January 30, 1981
> ## "IMPROVING PRACTICE"
> (Introduces three factors which must be taken into account before a student practices independently. Highlights four principles of efficient and effective practice.)

SERIES C

March 13, 1981
> ## "EXTENDING STUDENTS' THINKING"
> (Presents the six levels of thinking, and will demonstrate practical examples of classroom episodes showing their usefulness.)

March 20, 1981
> ## "READING A STORY TO EXTEND STUDENTS' THINKING"
> (Demonstrates how teachers use the six levels of thinking to extend students' thinking while listening to a story.)

March 27, 1981
> ## "RETENTION"
> (Demostrates ways to help students remember what they have learned.)

. . .

Imagine the potential respect and close relationship that school was building between parents and teachers. Imagine the satisfaction a teacher would feel doing one of these seminars.

Chapter 19
Community Schools

Create a center for both students and adults and keep that center open into the evening hours and on weekends, then bring together all the agencies in the community that can serve young and old alike. You have created a community school, one that goes beyond the education of students from kindergarten through grade 12.

The community schools that we developed in the Escondido and Mt. Diablo School Districts were part of a well planned, well organized total management system within which a local school site was given the flexibility to fulfill the educational goals of the school district. That management system has six basic components which have been discussed in the chapters in Part II, but which need to be repeated in the context of community schools.

- Planning.
- Organization of a school, or district for effective day-to-day operations.
- An accountability or evaluation component to determine how well we were doing the things we said we would do in the planning component.
- Staff development.
- A climate at the school which fosters a total learning environment in both the affective and the cognitive domains.
- Decision making.

In order to offer a total program to both the students and the adults
of a school attendance area, it is necessary to bring in several groups
to serve their varying needs. Community, social, health, and welfare
agencies, as well as recreational groups, must be identified and their
programs made available through the local school. Summer and year-
round adult school programs are part of the plan. The school must
have a citizens' advisory council comprised of between 15 and 24
people as discussed in Chapter 18.

An essential procedure in the first part of implementation is a needs
assessment to determine the total educational and social needs of
both the student and adult populations of the school area. A program
can be developed not only to take care of the educational needs of
youth and adults, but also to make available the necessary health,
recreational, social, and welfare programs.

The community school concept is well suited to areas that are low
socio-economic, transient, high mobility, and predominantly one-
parent families and apartments. It works especially well in neighborhoods with incipient deterioration, high vandalism, prevalent apathy,
and many rehabilitative needs.

Such a program entails bringing the total resources of city, county,
state, federal, and local school governments to bear on the many
obvious problems. It requires child care centers for the younger
children of the family, recreational programs before and after school
as well as on weekends, and adult school programs— during the
daytime as well as evenings and on weekends—with a major emphasis toward senior citizens. In other words, the school must become a
total service, recreational, and educational center for all ages within
the community.

The community school concept can also work well in affluent
neighborhoods. However, the program takes a different direction; it
offers recreational and cultural supplements to the basic educational
program. The following excerpt is from a report of one of our more
affluent community schools.

> Our fall session offered 36 classes; 450 adults and child-
> ren enrolled. We were delighted to have such a good
> turnout for our first session. However, our winter session,
> now in progress, was an even nicer surprise. We currently
> have a record enrollment of 483 people and are still sign-
> ing up the late comers. We hope to end up with more than
> 500 participants, involved in 39 courses.

In the community school, after school and weekend programs are designed for families—encouraging older and younger people to take part in activities together. Babysitting services are provided to free older members to engage in family activities in such centers as wood-shop, cooking, or crafts.

Experience has shown that vandalism decreases in a well executed community school program because people are present and actively engaged in programs. This discourages intruders or vandals from desecrating the facilities. Community residents begin to take greater pride in and depend more upon the local school center, and then make an extra effort to protect it and see that it is kept up.

Financing for the community education program comes from combined city, county, state, federal, and local school district resources. Outside funding and in-kind services help keep programs going, but money from adult school, summer school, and local average daily attendance should be made directly available to the local school site. Such site must also be given the authority to determine financial priorities for conducting the community school program.

Ultimately, where community school programs have been in operation for a number of years and the voting citizens have seen the benefits and have participated in the activities, more tax proposals have passed and even greater local support has been made available for the financial maintenance of the varied programs.

Some caveats should be mentioned concerning the community school concept. Coordination must be continually maintained to keep harmony among the various agencies and groups involved. Classrooms and school facilities get extra wear from constant use. Teachers and other school personnel do not have exclusive use of the facilities. Equipment and materials are sometimes rearranged without proper time—due to intensified usage—for setting up and taking down. Nevertheless, the benefits in activities and services to the people of the local school community make these problems seem minor.

The community school concept can best be told through a newspaper story written about the first program initiated in the Mt. Diablo School District at Cambridge Elementary School, led by a community-oriented principal. Our community schools have been modeled after the Mott Foundation Progam of Flint, Michigan.

CAMBRIDGE: BIRTH OF A COMMUNITY
By Kim Favors
Times Staff Writer

Florence Willis, who is 69 and lives alone in a senior
citizens' apartment building, used to dread the daily rau-
cus gathering of neighborhood youths behind her patio.

"They pestered us to death, and they cursed us," she
says.

All that changed last year—through the Cambridge
Neighborhood Center.

Now, "The kids are great. They come to visit, bring us
water, and clean our patios."

"Many of us felt trapped in our neighborhoods because
of rising housing costs," believes Bill Rodenkirchen, a
truck driver who lives in the Cambridge area, identified as
a lower income section of Concord.

"But now we're making our community a place we can
be proud of. Once again we're becoming a true neighborhood."

Bob Mercer, 18, has had a few "run-ins" with Concord
Police, and during the teachers' strike in the Mt. Diablo
district last September, was expelled from school.

Now he's the center's "right-hand man," bouncer for
the teen council, and entrepreneur of a new silk-screening
business.

The Cambridge Neighborhood Center, when its doors
first opened 14 months ago, was simply an unfurnished
portable trailer nestled next to classrooms at Cambridge
Elementary School, 1135 Lacey Lane.

Today the trailer is only sparsely furnished, but through
the efforts of enthusiastic citizens and local agencies it has
become a center for the health, educational, recreational
and cultural needs of some 500 families.

Any day or night of the week young and old may gather
in the trailer and adjacent classrooms to solve neighbor-

hood problems, take classes, dance, garden, receive family counseling, fight city hall, see films, and plan trips together.

Bill Rodenkirchen is chairman of the Action Council, a joint citizens/civic officials group that determines center policies and activities.

He believes the center may bring together an apathetic community.

"We're not trying to promote volunteers in the school nor classes nor recreation nor social services," he said, "even though our program either does or will include all of these.

"What we're really trying to do is make the Cambridge School and its center the focus of our neighborhood—the place where people can come and not only enjoy themselves but better themselves and their community in the process."

Last year, Rodenkirchen recalled, area residents became angered by the frequent and noisy parties two young men held in their rented home.

"The neighbors grew quite upset," he said, "so we held a meeting at the center between the neighbors, the renters, and their landlord."

The two men agreed to better control their parties and the landlord promised he would evict his tenants if there were additional complaints.

"Things quieted down, and unfortunately the two moved, but I think that because of this, all of the people in the area realized a sense of belonging, and became somewhat dependent upon one another, as neighbors would," Rodenkirchen said.

Another neighborhood problem the center tackled its first year was the relationship between area teens and the elderly residents of the nearby Rosemont Apartments.

"A year ago all I heard about were the terrible things that were happening in the park near the elementary school and the apartments," said Davie Wagstaff, the center's director.

"Senior citizens were afraid to use the park because of the teen-agers. It was a bad scene."

With the assistance of Bob Mercer, Wagstaff organized the teen council, whose 50 members promptly began planning fund-raising activities and trips.

"Then we discussed the fact that the teens had planned all these things for themselves, but what were they going to do for someone else." Wagstaff said.

Under Wagstaff's guidance they began delivering the salt-free drinking water many of the elderly citizens need, and assisted residents with housekeeping chores.

Florence Willis recalled the gradual change in her neighbors' relationships with the youths.

"Those boys used to be just terrible. But since they've been working with Davie, they've changed. Now we welcome them into our homes," Willis said.

"It's good to see the old get with the young."

The Cambridge Neighborhood Center, which opened Nov. 22, 1976, is a joint-agency pilot community school project, the first of its kind in Contra Costa County.

The three most influential agencies in its development have been the Mt. Diablo Unified School District, the city of Concord, and Contra Costa County.

Schools cannot afford to be a part-time enterprise. Their facilities must be made available into the evening hours every day, seven days a week, 12 months a year. They can no longer work independently of the many unmet needs of their community members.

Chapter 20
Financial Resources

Since the 1970s, when the taxpayers' revolt started in California and spread throughout the nation, it has been extremely difficult for schools to function adequately without necessary financial resources. Yet the budget has to be balanced:

This chapter will address five major areas to consider in keeping the budget balanced.

- Procedures necessary to keep the budget balanced under normal conditions.
- Individual school budget—how to enhance the financial condition at the school site level.
- Foundations as a means of fund raising.
- Organizing tax elections.
- Other ways to generate financial resources.

BALANCING THE BUDGET

GENERAL GUIDELINES

The following basic guidelines for the budget process are recommended for most school districts.

- Establish objectives.
- Take stock.
- Clarify needs.
- Identify priorities.
- Specify alternative programs and services to meet the needs.

- Estimate the cost of the program.
- Evaluate current programs, services, and activities.
- Build preliminary program format.
- Identify and cost out needed central support services.
- Build preliminary expenditures budget.
- Review preliminary estimates of anticipated revenue.
- Set priority needs on a districtwide basis.
- Build and present proposed budget with superintendent's message.
- Present the superintendent's proposed budget to the board for review.
- Hold public hearings.
- Modify and adopt tentative budget with board action.
- Review tentative budget at building levels.
- Review tentative budget at districtwide meetings.
- Announce superintendent's recommendations to modify tentative budget.
- Hold more public hearings.
- Present the final budget to the board for adoption.
- Submit the budget to the funding body or voters.

SPECIFIC PROCEDURES

The following five-step question-and-answer procedure is an example of another aid to budget building for a group who manages educational resources.

EXISTING CONDITION

How adequate are the information and analytical tools that are being used by the district to define the problem?

What is the current financial status of the district?

- The problem is more severe when the district is in a deficit spending pattern.
- Problems escalate when financial projections are unclear due to federal or state decisions.
- The financial status of the district is dependent upon the state financial plan due to the revenue limit—high wealth (squeeze) vs. low wealth, and the formula for enrollment—growth vs. decline.
- Federal decisions—PL 874, school lunch program, categorical funds—may have an impact on the district.
- Some of the most common factors for budget planning are enrollment, class size, staffing ratios, support

services, utility costs, transportation needs, food service, administrative services, books and supplies, and special education.

- Some districts may emphasize such special interests as choral and instrumental music, athletics, gifted, vocational, alternative programs, small class size, and more available periods per day for additional classes.

Who has been involved in the identification of the problem?

- District personnel: assistant superintendent, business manager, superintendent, board of education.
- County office
- State department of education
- State Legislature
- Legislative analyst
- Governor
- Congress
- Vested interest groups such as State Association of School Boards, State Teachers Association, State Administrators Association, Parent-Teacher Association, League of Women Voters, Taxpayers groups, and city government groups.

DESIRED CONDITION

Does the district know where it wants or needs to be in the future in this area?

- A balanced budget with reserves
- Board policy on allocation system
- Educational policy
- Community mores and traditions
- A quality instructional program
- Improved student outcomes
- Smaller or larger class size
- A long-range financial plan
- Negotiation peace with mutually acceptable contracts

Who must support a solution to the district's problem in this area in order for it to work?

- Board of education
- Superintendent
- Management team
- Certificated staff
- Support staff

- District support groups
- Community power groups: ethnic, conservative, business, and professional
- City leaders
- Budget advisory group(s)

CRITERIA AND CONSTRAINTS

What legal constraints confront the district in resolving budget problems?

- Education Code
- Court mandates
- Labor contracts
- Percentage of budget for salaries
- Ratio of Administrators per 100 teachers
- Length of school day
- Class size for kindergarten through eighth grade
- Balanced budget requirement
- Dismissal notification dates
- Causes for dismissal
- Single session kindergarten
- State financial plan
- Federal decisions on categorical programs

What controllable, but limited, cost factors are available to the district in resolving budget problems?

- Class size (no limit 9-12)
- Periods per day
- Support services
- Administrative ratios
- Substitute costs
- Inservice needs
- Conferences
- Utilities
- Custodial service
- Maintenance service
- Transportation
- Food service
- School closure
- Recreation program

What political constraints must be considered by the district in resolving budget problems?

- Attitudes of individual board members
- Commitment of board members to special interest groups
- Recall elections
- Re-election of board members
- Anti- or pro-administration board
- Political history of the district
- Community power groups
- Socio-economic make-up of the district
- Budget advisory groups
- Law suits
- City government regulations
- State and national legislative actions

ALTERNATIVES

What alternative solutions are available to the district that fall within the parameters of their controllable cost constraints?

- Increase kindergarten-eighth grade class size to legal limits
- Increase class size grades 9-12
- Limit the number of periods per day
- Reduce staff
    —Custodial
    —Clerical
    —Teachers by program or enrollment loss
    —Administrative
    —Counselors
    —Maintenance
    —Bus drivers
- Reduce athletic programs
- Reduce extracurricular programs
- Reduce utility costs with federal grants and state loans
- Increase walking distances to schools or establish paid service
- Close schools
- Eliminate non-mandated programs
- Increase income through non-profit groups, fees, elections
- Reduce district reserves
- Initiate an early retirement program
- Develop non-traditional use of resources

What alternative problem-solving processes are available to the district which fall within the parameters of their political constraints?
- Internal methods
    —Zero-based or zero-time budgeting study
    —Development of legal "musts" for all district
        programs with corresponding "shoulds"
    —Priorities for instructional needs
    —Goals and objectives based budget
    —Staff involvement
- External methods
    —Budget advisory group
    —Community surveys
    —Site utilization study group
    —Legislative action to support more state or
        federal money
    —Priorities for instuctional needs
    —Greater utilization of human resources

RECOMMENDATIONS
What improvements, information, and analytical tools would help the district define the problem?

What alternatives should be recommended to the district?
- An informed community is a must
- School systems reflect community attitudes
- Enrollment forecasts are critical
    —Short range—year to year, and changes during the year
    —Long range—cohort survival, birth rate, house-to-house, and pre-school survey
- Housing patterns—single or multiple family
- Drastic action to bring financial program into line
- Long range revenue plan based on best current information
- Long range expenditure plan based on best budget estimates

What process do you recommend for resolving budget problems?
- The process depends on the district.
- The district may be able to encourage the involvement of staff and community to increase understanding and to develop strong support groups.

- Decisions must be made that will enable the district to balance income and expenditures.
- The process must lead to decisions that can be implemented and supported.
- Staff at all levels must be informed and must contribute to solutions.

COMMENTS

Eventual cost reductions will come in personnel since 80 to 85 percent of all district costs are personnel costs.

Establish an early warning system to avoid surprises. Start the budget process early and be certain that information is widely gathered and widely shared.

INDIVIDUAL SCHOOL BUDGETS

To ensure maximum economy and wise expenditures so that the district will derive the greatest return from the educational program, it is imperative that an individual school know what its budget is and that the school has flexibility to raise additional money. In the budgeting processes over which I supervised, I made certain that funds were allocated to the school either on a per- student or a per-staff member basis. A student formula was used for supplies and equipment, and staff development funds were allocated on a per-staff member basis.

Once funds were allocated to them, the schools had flexibility in moving funds from one budget category to another as long as they reported those changes to the business office. The business office was told not to question the judgment of the local principal concerning the expenditure and transfer of funds from one category to another. Once the funds were allocated to the school it was up to them to spend their money according to their total budget and their priorities.

A system using computer print-outs was developed so that every school, as well as the district office, knew what its expenditure was for each month within eight days after the closing of the month. This system provided a check and balance for avoiding over-expenditures. District office administrators and the superintendent reviewed the monthly reports of the schools and alerted the school to any dangerous trends.

Each school had vandalism accounts; they were given funds if they maintained a low vandalism record. This money could then be spent for school purposes. The wise principal made certain that the vandalism account was tied in with the student body account; thus the students profited from the reduction of vandalism. The students, who actually did not commit the vandalism, did a better job than the local police in finding leads to track down those who were doing the vandalizing. The financial incentive of increasing student body funds became a significant factor in reducing vandalism. The student body did not always spend the additional funds for social events; they occasionally dedicated funds for school improvement projects such as beautifying the campus with the purchase of a minipark or dedicating a wall mural to the school depicting its history.

In addition, we created absenteeism accounts as incentives to lessen student and staff absenteeism. In California, as in many states, significant income originates from average daily attendance income. As our student attendance increased, the school profited from funds made available to them for purposes of their choice.

As staff attendance improved, substitute teacher savings were returned to the school for expenditures for supplies, equipment, or staff development. A significant reduction of absenteeism of staff occurred when they knew additional funds were available for their direct needs. Peer pressure minimized the need for supervisors to follow up on any excessive absences.

Having local businesses adopt a school is another excellent way to obtain additional funds as well as donations of supplies, equipment, and personnel time for schools. Such a program also nurtures a positive attitude and support for schools by businesses.

There is no end to creative ideas for increasing the funds for individual schools.

FOUNDATIONS

A trend to create foundations to provide major fund raising for local school districts is emerging. An independently governed foundation can be helpful in seeking broad community support. Such a foundation may have greater credibility than the district in arguing for school district financial needs. The foundation can seek leadership skills of people from different professions to supplement those already found in the district. For legal reasons, it must have its own governance independent of the school district.

Foundations can encourage businesses to donate funds or to sponsor athletic activities or academic programs. Such an approach also benefits the donor who may acquire favorable publicity for his business. Non-monetary gifts—computers, musical instruments, vehicles, or labor and professional time— are also valuable to the school district.

The success of a foundation depends, in a large part, on communicating the educational needs of the school district to the business community.

Some guidelines to follow in fund raising are:

- Decide in advance if a fund-raising program is right for your district.
- Determine your realistic fund-raising potential.
- Decide in advance what your fund-raising strategy will be.
- Make the fund-raising effort a broadly based community action program.
- Establish a structure with board approved policies and procedures; and assign staff to operate the fund-raising program.
- Start fund-raising activities with a plan.
- Delegate responsibility to an individual who has had prior fund-raising experience.
- Do not expect immediate large scale success; fund-raising results take time and a lot of hard work.

TAX ELECTIONS

I dispel the tempest of ignorance which threatens calamity to the community and the nation.

I provide the laboratories, libraries, and classrooms wherein the scientists, the statesmen, ministers, and teachers of tomorrow may find their strength.

I build the bulwarks which tend to ford the tides of time.

I shape the key to intelligent public opinion which unlocks the doors to economic, political, and social stability.

I yield returns more priceless than gold, more lasting than steel, more potent than the pen or sword—the returns of intelligent, thinking minds.

I insure the rights of childhood.

I am the school tax.

Author Unknown

School districts usually have a limited campaign fund for an election; they have a difficult time raising the large sums of money which are needed for an effective media campaign. Television, radio, and newspaper ads are expensive and are sent out to everyone in the community, not just registered voters. Such ads tend to incite unnecessary negative votes.

Despite all the difficulties, districts I have worked for over the years have been able to develop successful campaign strategies. We set up a process for an election that involved hundreds of people, but it was all done on a personal contact basis—which I maintain is the best of all procedures if you want to win the election. Many an election has been won by an unknown candidate who got out, met people, and let them know that he was interested in their welfare and concerns. We raised the tax rate more than 50 percent in one election by using just such a method.

The board of education established the need for the tax election. We made sure the need was spelled out succinctly. The board identified citizen leaders in the school district to endorse the election; their endorsements were included in our election literature. The literature was given primarily to people on a person-to-person basis rather through media advertisements.

We met with the registrar of voters to review a list of things we could and could not do during the election. We purchased both a complete list of registered voters, and a list of those, by precinct, who voted in the last election. We were able to influence the placement of two polling sites which were advantageous to us. For example, we were able to have one poll changed from an isolated trailer park inhabited by non-parents to a garage that was closer to homes with children. This change was legal—the registrar of voters had to locate polling places within an area containing a certain number of voters, and also had to make the polls conveniently accessible.

The election was organized by precinct and school attendance area. Each of the secondary schools and its feeder elementary schools were responsible for specific voting precincts.

The following chart shows the organizational plan for this procedure.

"YES" VOTE QUOTAS
FOR MARCH 17, 1975 ELECTION

SCHOOL	EMPLOYEE ENDORSMT QUOTA	"YES" VOTES AS OF PRECINCTS	TOTAL REGISTRD VOTERS BY PRECINCTS		YES VOTES NEEDED based on last election		YES VOTES AS OF
CENTRAL	560	6,7,8	1054	(6)	400	(6)	
			865	(7)	300	(7)	
			800	(8)	300	(8)	
CONWAY	320	13,15	1337	(13)	550	(13)	
			1157	(15)	500	(15)	
DEL DIOS	450	3	1342		500		
FELICITA	350	4	1595		600		
GLEN VIEW	330	16	1103		550		
GRANT	470	9,11	937	(9)	400	(9)	
			1229	(11)	500	(11)	
JUNIPER	340	1,5	1137	(1)	550	(1)	
			1025	(5)	500	(5)	
LINCOLN	570	14	1028		300		
MILLER	270	2	1501		600		
OAK HILL	310	10	1395		600		
ORANGE GLEN	380	17	1077		550		
ROSE	370	12	1096		600		
MAINTEN-ANCE	370						
DISTRICT OFFICE	510						
TOTAL	5,590		19,678		8,300		

As you can see in the illustration, we identified the number of "yes" votes we would need to win the election based on the total registered voters by precinct. We assumed that the additional voters who registered through our efforts would be "yes" votes.

Each school was given a required number of votes for each employee to obtain. Charts were established showing the school, their endorsement quota, how many "yes" votes they had acquired as of a certain date, the precincts for which they were responsible, the total number of registered voters that were in that area by precinct, and the number of "yes" votes needed based on the previous election results. The "yes" votes were tallied at frequent intervals to indicate how well we were doing in various precincts.

Campaign headquarters were established in the home of one of the citizens in the community. The home was centrally located and had a large recreation room with an outside entry which could be used without disturbing the couple living there. The room accomodated our computers, telephones, and display charts. Our computers contained the names of every registered voter and his background information. As we gathered "yes" votes from each of the registered voters, we kept track of the voter's school attendance area, precinct, and the volunteer worker who obtained the endorsement vote. As a result, we had an efficient accountability system.

The key to the process was each campaign worker's contact with a registered voter. We used a coding of five symbols to keep track of our potential votes. A"+" symbol was used for a definite yes vote; a "–" symbol for a definite no vote; a "O" symbol if we did not know; a "+" symbol inside an "O" for a maybe yes vote; and a "–" symbol inside an "O" for a maybe no vote.

We used this coding system to tally our "yes" votes, and to indicate our marginal—"maybe yes" and "no opinion"—votes for personal contact. Because we had identified more than enough votes to win the election if we concentrated on only the three categories of potential "yes" votes, we ignored the "no" and "maybe no" votes.

We defined the role of all campaign workers—board members, employees, chairpersons, and precinct workers. We had a chairperson and workers for each of the following areas: telephones, endorsements, transportation, babysitting, campaign finance, clerical, and election day. On election day we had people assigned to every precinct to make a 4 and a 6 p.m. report as to who had voted up to that time; we could then mobilize our telephone, transportation, and babysitting workers toward getting our "yes" votes to the polls before the eight o'clock closing.

With the efficient capabilities of the computer, and with good organizational efforts, I feel that the person-to-person strategy is the best one to use for a successful election. We felt every conceivable "yes" vote was identified and encouraged to vote. This campaign strategy works; we know it helped us to pass a difficult tax election which increased the tax rate 50 percent.

> Once upon a midnight dreary,
> While I pondered, weak and weary,
> Heard a voice outside my door,
> "School's a problem"....... Nothing more.
> Drew myself up toward the sound,
> A wee, sad imp was all I found.
> "Rooms in which to learn,
> Funds on which the schools can go.
> Without these I simply cannot grow."
> "Grow," I said, with mock despair,
> "You are strong, and bright and fair."
> "Yes," said he, "but my future world's
> Not one of simple play,
> What I am to be, in years to come,
> Is what the voters — vote — today."
>
> Author unknown

OTHER WAYS TO GENERATE FINANCIAL RESOURCES

To keep the budget balanced in recent years, it has been necessary to generate financial resources by reducing the budget. This has been an onerous task and one that has often resulted in trauma for employees and citizens alike. I have experienced some tumultuous board meetings at which vehement objections were raised against the reductions the board of education had to make in order to balance the budget. I have had to enlist police protection at some board meetings at which more than 800 people demonstrated and argued against such program reductions as closing schools or laying off personnel.

The following list includes 55 factors to consider in planning and reducing a budget.

- Attrition.
- Reassignment.
- Early retirement.
- Hiring freeze.
- Step and level classification freeze.
- Reduction of salaries.

- Reduction of hours worked.
- Reduction of number of days worked.
- Utilization of job sharing.
- Reduction of fringe benefits.
- Reduction of staff at all categories—teachers, administrators, service personnel, and support staff.
- Utilization of contracts for temporary employees and services.
- Acquisition of funds from other sources—federal programs and private grants.
- Reduction of pupil services to a legal minimum — nurses, social workers, psychologists, counselors, physicians, and dentists.
- Reduction of contracted consulting services.
- Reduction or elimination of extracurricular activities— drama, band, choir, athletics, and clubs.
- Establishment of extracurricular programs as self-supporting activities.
- Placement of extracurricular activities after school.
- Establishment of field trips as self-supporting activities.
- Establishment of outdoor education as a self-supporting activity.
- Elimination of elective class offerings which have low enrollment.
- Increase in class size.
- Reduction or elimination of non-mandated special programs.
- Establishment of driver training as a self-supporting activity.
- Placement of driver training during after school hours.
- Establishment of minimum class size, especially for high school electives.
- Development of intradistrict cooperative arrangements for providing services and programs instead of having each campus function autonomously.
- Development of interdistrict cooperative arrangements for providing services and programs—purchasing, food service, transportation, instruction, and personnel.
- Reduction of adult education offerings.

- Shift in summer "make-up" classes for those failing competency tests for graduation to the adult program or junior college.
- Reduction of summer offerings.
- Reduction of internal delivery of supplies and courier service by less frequent scheduling.
- Reduction of printing and photocopying costs by using spirit duplicators and carbon paper.
- Shift in hard money funding to soft money funding when possible.
- Reduction of the number of meetings called which reduces time spent and travel costs.
- Deletion of services that should, or could, be provided from other sources.
- Full indirect costs charged against categorical programs.
- Utilization of reserves.
- Reduction equipment purchases.
- Reduction of contracted services.
- Reduction of maintenance service.
- Reduction of food service to legal minimum.
- Charging of the use of facilities by those not eligible under the Civic Center Act.
- Application for legal reimbursement of mandated costs.
- Reduction of the purchase of books and supplies of all kinds.
- Reduction of library services.
- Reduction of student transportation.
- Reduction of staff conference attendance.
- Reduction of staff travel.
- Reduction in use of utilities.
- Reduction of equipment repair.
- Promotion of all income possible from the rental or leasing of facilities.
- Sale of all unnecessary real property, including land and equipment.
- Closure of all unnecessary school sites.
- When funding is gone, turn the operation over to the state which has legal responsibility for education.

CHANGING STATE LAWS

The following suggestions are for potential legal changes.

- Suspend or revoke minimum school year requirement.
- Suspend or revoke law requiring a school month of 20 days consisting of four weeks of five days (including holidays). Some states are using a four day school week.
- Suspend or revoke class size and pupil/teacher ratio requirement for elementary level.
- Suspend or revoke community service use law or authorize charging fees.
- Suspend or revoke laws requiring mental health, sight, hearing and dental checks.
- Suspend or revoke code regulations requiring maintenance of effort for state categorical aid.
- Suspend or revoke law requring adult education for citizenship training.
- Suspend or revoke law requiring volunteers not be used to replace classified personnel.
- Suspend or revoke guidance and counseling requirement for continuation high schools.
- Soften class maximum pupil/teacher ratio requirements for special education.
- Authorize increase in fees for child development.
- Suspend or revoke the requirement that kindergarten must be maintained.
- Suspend or revoke current laws of reduction of certificated staff.

INTERAGENCY COOPERATION

The following suggestions are for interagency cooperation.

- Schools and park districts:
    - —Joint school park development
- Schools and transportation:
    - —Joint powers agreement for all transportation by one district
    - —One district does all maintenance
    - —Reduce district bus runs by increasing pub lic service

- Shared facilities:
    - —Excess classrooms rented out to day care or pre-schools
    - —Police use facilities during peak tourist days, then help schools with patrols and special events
    - —Use state recreation bond money to build for use by both students and public
    - —Food preparation for other districts
- Joint business services:
    - —Data processing
    - —Business office functions
    - —Printing
    - —Insurance pooling
    - —Purchasing
- Library cooperation:
    - —City-school library
- Old schools:
    - —Lease to doctors
    - —Lease to lawyers
    - —Lease to handicapped for therapy

SCHOOL CLOSURE

One of the major areas to generate funds to balance the budget is the closure of schools. I have served in a district that declined from 50,000 to 35,000 students in five years. We closed 14 schools during that time, including two high schools. In addition, we laid off more than 400 personnel; made transportation a pay-as-you-go system; had students pay to participate in athletics; made several programs self-supporting; and froze all salaries at their current level for a one year period.

My position with the board and community was to close schools and consolidate attendance areas as our enrollment declined significantly. The money saved from the operation of the unneeded schools and the money gained from selling them could then be used to maintain and improve the educational program. Business and industry certainly would have done the same. Though closing schools seems unwise politically, we were able to operate programs in the remaining schools with their enrollment at a reasonable capacity level, and have funds for instructional programs and staff salaries.

The closing of an elementary school in the late 1970s could generate at least $100,000 in operational savings; a middle school or junior high could generate at least $150,000; and a high school could generate more than $750,000. In addition, as we leased or sold these schools, the amount of money increased.

Within a couple of years after the inconvenience of relocation, students, staff, and parents had adjusted well to the new school.

We set up two major groups to study the school closing situation: a citizens group of 25 leaders representative of their community; and a special staff group to gather data for a recommendation of school closures. The citizens group had access to staff data as well as other sources. Both groups studied the entire school district of 58 schools to reach a decision which would promote the most efficient and effective school district possible.

We developed a study matrix listing every school to be analyzed against 16 criteria ranging from obsolesence of facility, maintenance cost, transportation cost, environmental impact, to many academic quality factors. We conducted a series of different patterns in the analysis including whether we could achieve an efficient feeder pattern from elementary schools into junior highs and from junior highs into high schools.

The final decision by the board provided the school district with the best attendance pattern in years; and utimately provided a more articulated curricular program with closer planning among a high school and its feeder schools.

One of the most critical factors in school closures is to arrive at an acceptable solution for using the closed school. A vacant school is a constant reminder to the community of poor planning. Just as vital in the school closure process is the logistics of consolidating people, supplies, equipment, and programs between the closed school and the receiving school. A comprehensive, detailed, plan must be prepared, understood, and accepted by the involved parties. High school closures are especially sensitive.

MAJOR BUDGET REDUCTIONS

On two occasions I used adaptations of zero-based and zero-time budgeting methods to reduce expenditures: once when I became superintendent of a large district and found that I needed to reduce the budget by a million dollars in order to keep the district solvent to meet payroll obligations; and the other, after Proposition 13 in California, when I had to reduce $16 million of an $80 million budget.

In the first instance, I requested various segments of the community, employees, and student groups to indicate, through a survey, their priorities for 38 educational programs that the board of education and I had identified for potential reduction or elimination. We also provided opportunities for write-ins for other programs not among the 38 on our list.

I identified eight groups among the respondents to our budget reduction survey: employee job-alike groups, individual employees, employee unions, student groups, individual students, community organizations, individual citizens, and anonymous responses.

The survey listed the potential program reduction, the current program, the students affected, employee reduction, the implications of the program reduction to the curriculum, and the actual dollar figure if the program was eliminated.

The survey was sent to the various groups and individuals mentioned above, and also published in the newspaper to allow citizens the opportunity to send in their responses.

The process worked well even though we were under time pressures to study the budget. I had just become the superintendent and had found the district insolvent; I had to make reductions in that school year as well as in the next year.

In the second instance of budget reduction, which came after Proposition 13, I had to reduce the budget by $16 million. The board of education appointed a citizens committee of 25 leaders representing various segments of the community. The committee's charge was to independently develop budget reductions. Information, but no advice, was given by two assistant superintendents plus others who were brought in from time to time from other staff areas.

In the meantime, I worked with the staff to generate our recommendations to the board. The following steps were used.

- I convened all management personnel to tell them of the gravity of the budget situation and the process we were using to involve all staff.
- I asked all school personnel to make budget reduction recommendations on two different color forms— the white form was for reductions directly affecting them; the blue form was for reductions affecting others.
- The white and blue completed forms were submitted to the district office by a certain date.

- The district office eliminated those which served no advisory purpose because of multiple legal and contractual constraints.
- All major management groups responded on computer cards with an A to E ranking for each item on the recommended survey.
- The cards were processed on the computer.
- The superintendent's cabinet analyzed the rankings of the various management groups.
- The superintendent's cabinet, by a consensus method, made specific budget reduction recommendations to the board with supporting fiscal implications for each item.

The management groups were the elementary, middle school-junior high, high school, special education, and district office administrators. Originally, every staff person, teacher, and custodian were involved in filling out the white and blue forms that identified programs to be reduced. Management set priorities from that list. The employee union was represented on the citizens committee.

Both the recommendations of the citizens committee and of the staff were presented to the board of education at the same meeting. The two recommendations were remarkably similar.

COMMENTS

The process of budgeting and of obtaining financial resources is a vital part of the administration of a school district. I think it is essential for financial resources to be available at the school level and for the decision-making process to be primarily at that level. We must remember that the schools are owned by the citizens, and therefore, a consumerism and marketing philosophy must be followed that will involve as many people as possible all the time but especially during critical budget decisions.

Budgeting is not a pleasant task. However, the participants should feel that the process was as fair as it could be under the circumstances.

Chapter 21
Instruction for Effective Learning Programs

In the quest for excellence in learning we are forever endeavoring to find the optimally effective school. At the heart of that school is effective instruction. In the late 1960s and early 1970s some educators and community members were dismayed by research reports apparently showing that schools had little if any effect on the achievement of students. Such critics of education as Coleman and Jencks said that student achievement and other educational outcomes were predetermined by the family socio-economic status or were greatly influenced by pure luck. I believe that schools do make a difference and suggest that indicators exist which can show us what effective schools look like.

INDICATORS OF EFFECTIVE SCHOOLS

SLEZAK'S FIVE INDICATORS

As mentioned in Chapter 7, I have used five indicators to monitor our progress toward effective schools and toward improvement of our learning programs. Achievement scores in some of the basic skills such as reading, math, and writing are one indicator of effective programs. In one elementary school, through a systematic effort, we were able to raise the percentile rankings in the basic skill areas as much as 40 percentile points in three years. In one of California's largest school districts, we raised the achievement scores six and seven percentile points for the entire district over a four year period. Our math, reading, and writing scores were first and second among the 10 largest districts in the state.

		1975-76	1979-80
Grade 3	Reading	77	83
Grade 6	Reading	72	79
	Writing	74	77
	Math	76	80
Grade 12	Reading	76	80
	Writing	72	78
	Math	85	87

We also monitored whether learning climate, a second indicator, was improving. We measured learning climate by determining the satisfaction level of students, parents, and staff. The degree of satisfaction directly influences productivity of learning. A third indicator is the reduction of vandalism which is indicative of attitude and respect for the place of learning. The fourth and fifth indicators are the absenteeism of students and of staff. If we are going to achieve maximum learning effectiveness people must be present to spend time on task.

EDMOND'S FIVE INDICATORS

Ron Edmonds and his colleagues at Harvard University identified five factors that were characteristic of effective schools.

BUILDING LEADERSHIP

The principal displayed strong professional behavior, understood the contribution of teachers to the school's goals, regularly visited and observed classrooms, and made useful suggestions to improve instruction.

INSTRUCTIONAL LEADERSHIP

The adults in the building—parents, teachers, administrators, support staff—were consistent in statements about the school's instructional goals. They not only understood but abided by these aims. Consistency among statements was more important than the particular goals named.

THE LEARNING CLIMATE AND FACILITY

Effective schools were clean, attractive, organized, and physically secure. They had adequate instructional space. Newness and fanciness were not determining factors.

IMPLIED TEACHER EXPECTATIONS

Observers looked only at what teachers did, and not at what they thought or felt. Students were asked if they thought their teacher expected anyone in the class to fall below an acceptable level of achievement. In effective schools the students answered no. Teachers who expected achievement got it.

MONITORING SYSTEM

Effective schools had a system for monitoring and assessing pupil performance which was derived from their instructional objectives. The faculty did not continue practices that did not work. If achievement data or other feedback indicated a need for change, they were willing.

In Edmond's words, "to reach a set of fairly firm conclusions about the institutional and organizational characteristics that distinguish the effective schools from the ineffective schools, we conclude that it is not the family background that determines pupil performance, it is the school response to the family background that determines pupil performance." Schools which provide effective instructional programs do exist and their success is based on institutional characteristics which can be clearly described.

CAWELTI'S SEVEN INDICATORS

Gordon Cawelti, the executive director of the Association of Supervision and Curriculum Development, named seven factors that contribute to high scholastic achievement.

- Leadership by the principal.
- Favorable climate for learning.
- High expectations of students.
- Frequent monitoring of student progress.
- Adequate time on task for corrective instruction.
- Scrutinization of classroom management.
- Learning elements such as rewards at appropriate success levels.

The message of the literature is clear. Schools are not helpless in the face of the forces that influence a student before he gets to school.

Schools can, and do make a difference in the achievement of students. Schools produce results by creating a set of norms that expect and support achievement.

THE EFFECTIVE PRINCIPAL

CHARACTERISTICS
In all effective schools, the school principal is the key person.

The literature indicates that effective principals are outgoing, skillful with people, and communicate well. They have initiative, an awareness of their goals, and an inner security. As pro-active people, they are not afraid to stretch the rules; they understand the compromises that must be made to get things done. The effective principal develops an emotional climate for growth through such actions as being visible, smiling, speaking to teachers and students, and talking about the curriculum activities of the day. He stimulates teachers by creating and communicating a vision. The effective principal tends to be at the fifth level of Maslow's hierachy—self-actualization.

ADMINISTRATIVE APPROACH
The one person in the school who has the most influence in establishing an environment that produces achievement is the principal. Establishing that environment is no small task, nor can it be reduced to a simple formula. The principal who makes a difference brings to the job more than technical expertise. He dedicates mind, heart, and will to the achievement of one over riding goal—the success of every student. It is this desire to see students succeed that compels the principal to set high standards, to communicate those standards to teachers and students, and to make sure students are rewarded for achievement or reminded of the standards if they fail. The effective principal sees to it that the expectations for student success permeate the entire school.

THE EFFECTIVE TEACHER

CHARACTERISTICS
In an individual classroom, the teacher is the key person in developing an effective learning program. An effective teacher:
- Demonstrates enthusiasm for teaching and for the topics being taught.

- Provides opportunities for successful experiences for students.
- Demonstrates patience, empathy, and understanding.
- Identifies learning styles, rates of learning, and capabilities of students.
- Demonstrates an understanding of the processes involved in selection of learning content and method of presentation.
- Determines objectives and goals appropriate to each student or each group's identified needs.
- Specifies teaching procedures.
- Identifies assessment processes.
- Maintains student involvement in learning tasks.
- Uses activities which call for pupil planning, observing, describing, experimenting, and writing.
- Organizes and uses a range of appropriate instructional materials and equipment.
- Uses a variety of cognitive levels in questioning strategies.
- Gives directions clearly and completely the first time.
- Manages disruptive behavior constructively.
- Helps students recognize their progress and achievement.
- Uses a variety of evaluation methods which provide students with specific feedback.
- Teaches to an objective—one at a time.
- Monitors student progress and makes appropriate teaching adjustments.
- Uses the principles of learning (some of which are listed below) to facilitate the learning process of students.
  - —Anticipatory set
  - —Active participation
  - —Motivation
  - —Retention
  - —Reinforcement

TEACHING APPROACH

Good instruction requires constant diagnosis of students' learning needs. Effective teachers prescribe learning activities which meet those needs, and evaluate students' performance as they complete those activities. This approach to teaching contains five basic elements.

CONTENT ANALYSIS, TASK ANALYSIS

Content analysis involves determining a series of learnings for a subject area that builds upon one another from simple to complex. This makes it possible to determine which learnings precede and follow each other to form a sequential order. The teacher analyzes content to find a sequence of learnings describing what students need to learn in a subject area but not how to teach those skills. This sequence of tasks for a specific skill is referred to as a "task analysis".

DIAGNOSIS

The next step is to assess the student's entering skills in relationship to the task analysis so appropriate instruction can be planned. This process is called diagnosis. In diagnosis, the teacher determines which skill areas need instruction. The key skills that the student should master at each instructional level are the terminal objectives. Evaluation of the student's level of performance for each terminal objective completes a diagnosis.

PRESCRIPTION

After the diagnosis is completed and the teacher has determined which skill areas need instruction, a behavioral objective is written for each skill area. A taxonomy of cognitive skills is used to help the teacher identify those which are needed to meet the objectives.

INSTRUCTION

Specific teaching strategies and activities to help the learner master the objective are determined by the teacher. The time needed to complete the teaching-learning act, as well as the amount of practice and review needed, will vary with each learner. The teacher manipulates the variables of learning theory-transfer, retention, motivation, and reinforcement—in order to increase the probability that learning will occur. The teacher can apply these variables through a variety of teaching techniques—modeling, inquiry, group discussion, demonstration, role playing, and lecture.

LESSON ANALYSIS

After the learner has mastered the series of instructional objectives related to a specific skill area, he is given an opportunity to perform the terminal objective for that task at his level. If the learner demonstrates mastery of the skill area, the teacher refers back to the original diagnosis and begins work in another skill area. If the learner cannot perform the terminal objective, the teacher goes back to the task analysis to try to locate the difficulty.

OBSERVATION CRITERIA

As we consider essential elements of the instruction and diagnosis of the learning act, we need to identify what to look for during a lesson observation. Some things to consider are:

- What was the objective?
- Was it appropriate?
- Did the students appear to be correctly diagnosed?
- Did students have the necessary entry skills to reach the objective?
- Did the teacher "set" the students for the lesson objective?
- Were previously learned skills reviewed?
- Were students motivated before and/or during the lesson?
- Was reinforcement appropriately used?
- Was the lesson sequenced?
    - —Easy to difficult
    - —Narrow to global
    - —General to specific
- Were the students attending to the learning?
- Was there a clarity of meaning in instruction?
- Were directions clearly given?
- Was there active participation of the learner?
- Was there evidence of teacher monitoring during the lesson for comprehension?
- Were students given an opportunity to practice or apply skills taught in the lesson?
- Were techniques for retention used?
- Was transfer of learning built into the lesson?
- Did use of materials and activities facilitate the lesson?
- Did the teaching style fit the lesson?
- Were provisions made for evaluating the students prior to the end of the lesson?
- Were students given knowledge of results?
- If necessary, were provisions made for reteaching or extension?
- Were students held accountable for their learning?
- Was the objective achieved?

THE EFFECTIVE HIGH SCHOOL

We need to consider redesigning general education in our high schools. I would like to base these comments on work which has been done by Gordon Cawelti. During the past two decades, the curriculum in American high schools has been subject to a proliferation of elective course offerings. We now find ourselves preoccupied with the competency-based education movement and with the need to concentrate on what common learning should be provided to prepare all students for life in a democratic society in the 21st century. It is imperative that the high school curriculum retain an extensive offering of elective courses to capitalize on student interest, but these must be extensions of a general education curriculum.

Our schools have had and do have primary responsibility to transmit our political and cultural heritage, but in our effort to meet individual student needs, to innovate, and to be accountable, we have seriously neglected that responsibility. We should make no mistake about it, Russia transmits its culture, as does Cuba, China, and the free nations such as England, Japan, and Canada.

In response to perceived needs of individual students, high schools in recent years have developed instructional programs relating to drug abuse, sex education, moral education, values, use of leisure time, parenting skills, nutrition, and death. In response to the pressing problems of society, high schools have been asked to implement programs relating to energy, population, global affairs, the environment, law, career education, and ethnic studies. Seldom does anyone ask what is to be excluded if one of these new curricular programs is introduced, or where it should be placed in the total pattern of instruction. Nor have many people raised the question as to whether schools can engender any enduring effects on students in either knowledge or attitude in these areas.

As a result, we have created an overloaded, patchwork curriculum which lacks coherence and which detracts from the purpose of providing a general education for American youth. It is increasingly clear that we must synthesize this patchwork curriculum into a more coherent pattern of learning experiences which focus upon the needs of both the individual and of society.

These facts suggest the need for more interdisciplinary courses out of which advanced, elective courses must continue. Since schools clearly do not have time for students to have individual courses in art, music, theatre, literature and the like, a unified humanities course showing the interrelationship of all these subjects would be much more feasible. Similarly, a unified course in health could replace courses in nutrition, physical fitness, use of leisure time, sex and drug education.

CAWELTI'S MODEL

Cawelti's model for a high school curriculum outlines six major areas.

LEARNING SKILLS

This area includes mathematics, remedial and speed reading, composition, speaking and listening, problem solving, critical thinking, locational skills, computer literacy, and intellectual curiosity.

The high school must continue to teach these skills until minimal levels of competency are achieved; some students will require considerably more time for mastery than others; others will require basic English instruction before moving on to higher order learning skills.

EMOTIONAL-PHYSICAL HEALTH

This area includes physical education, nutrition, lifetime sports, drug abuse, use of leisure time, coping, stress management, parenting, health, human growth and development. An integrated program in this area can be developed by teachers of science, physical education, home economics, and counselors. The courses should be taught in an interdisciplinary manner employing the contributions of community professionals.

CAREER-VOCATIONAL

This area includes industrial arts, career education, vocational courses, distributive education, apprentice training, marketable skills, and work ethics. This area provides substantial opportunity for experiential learning, and for active involvement of the business and professional community.

CULTURAL STUDIES

This area includes art, music, drama, aesthetic education, literature, history, multicultural education, and ethnic studies. A unified humanities course is recommended.

SCIENCE-TECHNOLOGY

This area includes biology, physics, chemistry, earth science, physiology, and environmental education. This area would focus on acquiring knowledge in the natural sciences for application to daily life and to technological problems such a pollution and energy.

CITIZENSHIP-SOCIETAL STUDIES

This area includes economics, social sciences, and citizenship. Topics of concern include poverty, urban life, the economy, global studies, war, population control, and energy sources. The closest existing course would be a "Problems of Democracy" course similar to that recommended by Conant in 1959 except that it would be team taught. It would draw upon community resources and encourage student participation in data collection and analysis.

CLASS SIZE

As I have studied research concerning class size over the last few decades, I have noticed little difference in the learning program and the average achievement of pupils in classes between 20 and 40. Within the mid-range of 25 to 35 pupils, class size seems to have little, if any, decisive impact on the academic achievement of most pupils in most subjects above the primary grades.

We persist in grouping students in the 25 to 35 range though it seems to be the worse possible grouping for maximizing learning. Such a range does not allow for adequate discussion; the optimum size for discussion is 8 to 12. The lecture method alone can work effectively with more than 100 students.

Class size is dependent on the learning task. Teachers need small groupings of pupils for remedial work, counseling, and discussion. Other than for these purposes research indicates that class size will have little effect on student achievement unless the number is below 20 and the teaching approach is adapted to the smaller number.

EDUCATION FOR THE FUTURE

Because we live in a changing world, we have to continually change our instruction to be effective. Educational programs for the decades of the '80s and '90s will have to:

- Accept the learner's needs and purposes and develop experiences and programs around his potential.
- Facilitate self-actualization and strive to develop in all persons a sense of personal adequacy.
- Foster acquisition of basic skills—academic, personal, interpersonal, communicative, and economic proficiency necessary for living in a multicultural society.

- Personalize educational decisions and practices.
- Recognize the primacy of human feelings; use the personal values and perceptions of students as integral factors in instruction.
- Develop a learning climate which is perceived by students as challenging, understanding, supportive, exciting, and free from threat.
- Develop in learners genuine concern and respect for the worth of others in conflict resolution.

THE PEOPLE PROBLEM

We have the know-how and the technology to solve many of the age old problems of society. If we do not feed, clothe, and house the entire world it is no longer because we do not know how, it is because we cannot get ourselves to work together to reach that goal.

However, we find ourselves faced with a new problem—the people problem. Science and industry have made our society interdependent. Each of us is totally dependent on other people for even the simplest things in life. Thousands of people whom we have never seen are needed to provide so simple a requirement as a quart of milk.

Moreover, we have created a world in which the power of each individual for good or evil has been enormously increased. The more interdependent a society, the greater the possibility that an individual can disrupt the system. It is this utter interdependence that has made it possible for terrorists to threaten multitudes. A few people in the right place at the right time can create international havoc by holding a few hostages, or by killing a John Kennedy or a Martin Luther King.

This interdependence has made human problems the most pressing ones we face. We have left the era of physical sciences and entered the era of the social sciences. To live successfully in an increasing interdependent world requires, at the very least, intelligent citizens who understand themselves and the dynamics of human interaction; who can be counted on to contribute when needed; who are concerned for other people; and who can behave as responsible, problem-solving human beings.

Education in the past could be limited to providing youth with basic skills. That is no longer sufficient preparation for living in the world into which we are moving. The future, already upon us, demands education that prepares young people to understand both themselves and human interaction. Our society can tolerate a bad reader; a bigot is a danger to everyone. We have done a great deal about reading, very little about bigotry.

A glance around supports the truth that our greatest problems are human ones—over population, pollution, ecology, energy, poverty, war, peace, civil rights, starvation, physical and mental health, and terrorism. Even use of the nuclear bomb is a human rather than a technical problem. It is not the bombs we need fear, but the persons who might use them. The social sciences—psychology, sociology, anthropology, and political science, which were specifically developed to deal with human problems, are each more than a hundred years old. Yet in most places they have not been admitted to the curricula of our public schools. Occasionally they are elective courses for high school seniors and then only as a reward for good grades in traditional courses.

SELF-CONCEPT

Research has shown us that self-concept is a vital factor in a person's success or failure in school, on the job, or in social interaction. It is also a vital factor in determining psychological health or adjustment. Healthy people see themselves in positive ways as liked, wanted, acceptable, able persons of dignity and integrity. The opposites of such self perceptions are characteristic of delinquents, criminals, and the mentally ill.

Students behave according to their self-concept. They learn best when they see themselves in positive ways: students who see themselves as capable will achieve; students who do not will find ingenious ways to avoid involvement.

VALUES

Values provide the criteria by which we make our choices. People seek what they value and avoid what they do not. Students who value what they are being taught are eager learners. Schools that ignore the values of students, ignore important determinants in learning and in personal growth.

Since people behave according to their values, value exploration should be an important objective in the curriculum. This does not mean that schools should decide what values a student should hold. Values are personal and private; they are derived from experience, exploration, and discovery. Schools, on one hand, must demonstrate positive values in every aspect of their organization and practice; and, on the other, must, throughout the system, encourage and facilitate student exploration of values.

Controlling behavior is only dealing with symptoms; changes in behavior occur at the deeper level of feelings, attitudes, and beliefs. Encouraging changes at this deeper level can obviate the need for behavior control. The behavior of a white child picking on a black one can be controlled by a teacher's use of methods of behavior modification so that the white child learns not to pick on the black one-at least in teacher's class or when that teacher is in the neighborhood. If the same child, however, can be helped to see the black classmate as "a kid just like me—"someone with similar problems, someone who likes many of the same things, then the aggressive behavior may disappear of itself. Not just temporarily when the teacher is around, but for all time.

PERSONAL MEANING

Learning has two parts: exposure to new information or experience; and the personal discovery of meaning. Most educators know how to deal with the first part. They are experts at giving people information. They have been doing it for years; it is a thing they do best. Helping students discover the personal meaning of information is a different matter and the source of most of our failures. The drop out, for example, is not a drop out because educators did not tell him information; they did that over and over. The student dropped out because he never discovered the personal meaning of what they had to offer. Learning from one's own perceptual orientation is the personal discovery of meaning. Information will affect a person's behavior only if it has personal meaning to that individual. Learning is a deeply human, personal, affective experience.

PERSONAL NEED

People learn best when they have a need to know. They work hard for things they need; they ignore or avoid what seems irrelevant or destructive to their personal fulfillment.

CHALLENGE OR THREAT

The discovery of personal meaning is deeply affected by student experience of challenge or threat. People are challenged by goals interest them and which they believe they can achieve. People are threatened by events with which they feel inadequate to cope. It follows then that schools must find ways of challenging students without threatening them.

FEELING OF BELONGING

Learning is also deeply influenced by student feelings of belonging or of being cared for. For most people the experience of belonging is accompanied by feelings of excitement, interest, and the desire to be involved. Feelings of alienation, on the other hand, are accompanied by a desire to avoid embarrassment or humiliation; and by feelings of dejection, apathy, disappointment, anger, or hostility.

COMMENTS

Effective instruction begins with an understanding of the human condition: what people are like; how they behave and learn; and what problems they face. Methods, techniques, and ways of organizing may come and go, but basic changes in thinking about people and learning can last for generations. We must make the *odyssey to excellence* now, laying the foundation for education in the decades of the future.